The New Competitive Advantage

The Renewal of American Industry

MICHAEL H. BEST

OXFORD
UNIVERSITY PRESS

Great Clarendon Street, Oxford OX2 6DP

Oxford University Press is a department of the University of Oxford.
It furthers the University's objective of excellence in research, scholarship, and education by publishing worldwide in

Oxford New York

Athens Auckland Bangkok Bogotá Buenos Aires Cape Town Chennai Dar es Salaam Delhi Florence Hong Kong Istanbul Karachi Kolkata Kuala Lumpur Madrid Melbourne Mexico City Mumbai Nairobi Paris São Paulo Shanghai Singapore Taipei Tokyo Toronto Warsaw

and associated companies in Berlin Ibadan

Oxford is a registered trade mark of Oxford University Press in the UK and certain other countries

Published in the United States
by Oxford University Press Inc., New York

First published 2001

British Library Cataloguing in Publication Data
Data available

Library of Congress Cataloguing in Publication Data

Best, Michael H.
The new competitive advantage: the renewal of American industry/Michael H. Best.
p. cm.
Includes bibliographical references and index.
1. Competition—United States. 2. Industrial management—United States.
3. Comparative organization. I. Title.
[HD41 .B382 2001] 338.6′048′0973–dc21 2001021559

ISBN 0–19–829744–0
ISBN 0–19–829745–9 (pbk.)

10 9 8 7 6 5 4 3 2 1

Typeset by Florence Production, Stoodleigh, Devon
Printed in Great Britain
on acid-free paper by
T.J. International Ltd., Padstow, Cornwall

ACKNOWLEDGEMENTS

Conversations about technological change are 'in the air' at the University of Massachusetts Lowell. Chancellor William Hogan and Vice-Chancellor Frederick Sperounis have led the way in advancing a model of how a technology-oriented university can play a leadership role in regional development. I am fortunate. Few economists have such opportunities for ongoing discussions with engineers, scientists, and entrepreneurs on links between innovation, technology, production, and the creation and diffusion of knowledge. These discussions form the background for the concern with regional economic growth at the heart of this book. But even in this congenial institutional environment, the influence of one individual stands out.

I have gained enormously over the years from conversations and shared endeavors with Professor Sukant Tripathy. Sukant was a gifted advanced materials scientist. I worked with Sukant on a wide range of issues. These included diversification of the jute industry of East Bengal; the search for 'clean energy' solutions that address simultaneously the challenges of the technological divide between rich and poor regions and global warming; the pursuit of analogies between self-assembly processes amongst molecules in laser impacted nanostructures and networked business enterprises; and the role of 'systems integration' as a source of competitive advantage in Silicon Valley and Boston's Route 128. Tragically, Sukant died in a swimming accident just after this manuscript was completed. The void is permanent in the lives of the many that he touched.

The United Nations Industrial Development Organization in Vienna is the other institution with which I have worked closely over many years. Frederic Richard, Cristian Gillen, and Giovanna Ceglie, in particular, have been allies in searching for new understandings of local capability development, technology management, and approaches to technology assistance.

Involvement in industrial competitiveness projects over nearly two decades has resulted in intellectual partnerships that have shaped the emerging methodology and content of the 'capabilities and innovation' perspective developed in this book. These include Robin Murray in North London and Cyprus; Tea Petrin and Ales Vahčič in Slovenia; Cristian Gillen and Robert Forrant in Jamaica and Honduras; Vlado Kreačič and David Ellerman in Moldova; Rajah Rasiah in Malaysia; Aidan Gough in Northern Ireland; and Robert Forrant and William Lazonick in Massachusetts. The methodology involves a constant back and forth between guiding concepts and primary research as change strategies and programs are designed, debated, and implemented. This has involved, as well, the study of hundreds of business enterprises, and numerous educational institutions, research centers, and industrial policy agencies in different parts of the world. The debts to individuals who have shared their time, experiences, and expertise in interviews can only be acknowledged collectively.

Many have participated directly in the preparation of this manuscript. Jane Humphries has commented on and listened to many of the ideas. Aidan Gough, too, of the Northern Ireland Economic Council has left a major imprint on the conceptual contours. Christos Pitelos suggested the title. John Bradley, Steve Landau, Eric Martin, Sir George Quigley, Arthur Francis, Alan McGarvey, Merritt Roe Smith, Gianni Lorenzoni, Ben Fine, Steven Sass, and Stan Engerman have offered helpful suggestions. David Musson gave wise advice on the introduction and first chapter. Urska Cvek and Marjan Trutschl provided technical assistance. Urska and Richard Sherburne helped with the graphics and Gregory DeLaurier, Ann Newton, Sarah Dobson, and Lynn Childress with editing. Fred Sperounis provided intellectual and institutional support.

Elizabeth Garnsey and Brian Loasby helped shape my ideas on Edith Penrose and the idea of the entrepreneurial firm. I benefited from discussions with Mark Harvey on Polanyi's concept of instituted processes. I have drawn from Bruce Tull's unpublished work on the 'precision corridor' of the Connecticut River Valley. I have gained from projects with colleagues in the University of Massachusetts Lowell community including Robert Forrant, Krishna Vedula, Steve McCarthy, Robert Wagner, Ken Gieser, Larry Gross, Chris Tilly, Phil Moss, Aldo Crugnola, Nick Schott, Sammy Shina, Fran Eagle, William Mass, and Michael Fiddy. William Lazonick and Mary O'Sullivan's dining room has been the site of countless conversations with friends from all corners of the globe in the 'Chandlerian school' of organizational capabilities. The Judge Institute of Management Studies, Cambridge University proved to be a stimulating environment to try out many of the themes while I was the Arthur Andersen Visiting Fellow in 1999.

I have learned from a group of students who have written dissertations under my direction on topics related to 'industrial districts' in different contexts. These include Rich Parkin, Bruce Tull, Marcela Miozza, Roman Habtu, José Tavara, Curtis Haynes, Maribel Aponte, Ron Caplan, and Alison Dean. Other former students who have influenced my thinking include David Lubin, Tony Guglielmi, Frank Johnson, Al Ruthazer, Frank Stathas, Peter Ungaro, and Jack Plaistek.

Finally, my son Lawrence has generously consented to interruptions in my soccer-training program to work on my book. But perhaps my potential as a goalie has not suffered greatly.

It goes without saying that responsibility for errors and omissions rests with the author alone.

M.H.B.

Cambridge, Massachusetts and Oxford
January 2001

CONTENTS

LIST OF FIGURES

LIST OF TABLES

LIST OF BOXES

PREFACE

What a difference a decade makes. In the early 1990s many books were being published on the loss of competitiveness of American industry. My book, *The New Competition*, published in 1990, described the loss of American industrial leadership in terms of the rise of both the Japanese model of business organization and networked groups of small firms represented by the 'third Italy'.[1] The former challenged American high-volume manufacturing industries such as cars and semiconductors and the latter were eroding market share in design-led 'fashion' industries such as apparel, shoes, and furniture. Both business models and associated production systems were able to achieve performance standards in cost, quality, flexibility, and/or design that could not be matched by American Big Business, which was organized according to different principles of production and organization. These models were the New Competition of the 1970s and 1980s that eroded the competitiveness of the American economy.

The State of Massachusetts was particularly hard hit. Between 1986 and 1992, employment in manufacturing dropped by one-third, from 675,000 to 450,000. The Massachusetts Miracle, the term used to describe the economic good times linked to the establishment of America's first high-tech district, was over. Companies like Digital Equipment Corporation, Wang Laboratories, Prime Computer, Data General, and Apollo laid off thousands of workers at a time. The new, high-tech industries such as the minicomputer were but recent examples of a long tradition in the region of declining industries—textiles, shoes, shipbuilding, furniture, and watchmaking. But the pace of the decline this time was much more rapid.

[1] Refers to the north central region of Italy that enjoys high per capita income but few large firms. The region retains competitive advantage in design-led and fashion industries.

Unexpectedly, however, Japanese industry lost its way in the 1990s and by the middle of the decade the productivity of American industry was growing at rates not witnessed for over two decades. Massachusetts, too, was undergoing an economic resurgence. While books and articles were still being written on the decline of Route 128,[2] occupancy rates in industrial office space were shooting back up as fast as they had declined. By the end of the decade, Massachusetts had the second highest per capita income in the United States. This time around, however, there have been few new Fortune 500 firms and the economic resurgence has been accompanied by little fanfare.

What happened? Why did the American economy regain industrial leadership across a range of industries? Why did regions like New England avoid long-term economic decline with the waning of 'mature' industries as experienced by, for example, the North of England? What explains the resurgence?

This book addresses these and related matters. My overall goal in writing the book is to present an analysis of regional growth dynamics in which technology is integral. The approach here has much in common with the emphasis on technological change in the 'neo-Schumpeterian' perspective and the cluster analysis of Michael Porter. But it does not fit easily in either. I have labeled it the 'capabilities and innovation perspective'.

Alternative economic perspectives are receiving increased attention because of the failure of the neoclassical theory of growth to offer insights into industrial change in rich and poor nations. Likewise, the 'new growth theory' offers a framework for examining the 'knowledge' economy but, like its neoclassical rival, it operates at too high a level of aggregation to control for business models and production capabilities including technology management. The business enterprise in both old and new growth theories is thus highly abstract and deterministic. The internal organization of the firm in neoclassical growth theory is determined by external parameters, over which it has no influence. Price and product design, for example, are imposed on firms by market forces. But without an account of business organization, growth theories are ill equipped to address experiences like the decline and rebirth of American industry or rapid growth in knowledge poor regions of the world. Policy, too, suffers as such economic theories address matters of public policy but are silent on matters of business policy.

[2] Route 128 is a highway that orbits Boston with a radius of approximately 10 miles which became home to an agglomeration of high-tech firms.

The capabilities and innovation perspective hopes to address these shortcomings. It is an economic analysis of industrial performance in which technology management is central. But it is also an extension of an economic development perspective that began with the publication in 1776 of Adam Smith's *An Inquiry into the Nature and Causes of the Wealth of Nations.* Smith's masterpiece contains a treatment of production and technological change as well as a theory of price and resource allocation. The neoclassical branch of economics is only an extension and reworking of the latter.[3] The study of production has languished in the economics curriculum.

The capabilities and innovation perspective extends Smith's principle of increasing specialization from individual skills to organizational capabilities as part of a dynamic process by which business enterprises individually and collectively develop capabilities and, in the same process, strategically reconstitute markets. All business enterprises seek to differentiate their product in the marketplace. Entrepreneurial firms, by definition, seek to develop distinctive capabilities by fostering an interactive dynamic between their own technological capabilities and market opportunities. For such firms, the ongoing process of production is simultaneously a process of capability development. Entrepreneurial firms produce things and capabilities. For these firms, capabilities are both inputs and outputs of production.

The market, too, is integral to the process of capability development. But the concept of the market is different in a process view of capability development than in the theory of efficient resource allocation. Instead of the market being a parameter, for the entrepreneurial firm the market is both a signaler of opportunities and an object of ongoing, strategic reconstitution. The process of shaping capabilities is simultaneously the process of reading and responding to market opportunities and of redefining the products that constitute the market.

An understanding of the dynamic between distinctive capability and market opportunity is critical to understanding both business perform-

[3] The claim that a free market system can produce an allocation of resources that satisfies independent optimality rules is a powerful idea. It connects the 'invisible hand' to a body of theory. A market system is self-regulating and, in theory, it can produce an optimal allocation of resources. But the elegance of the idea does require the assumption that all resources are commodities. The allocation generated by a price system will be one in which the prices received for resources allocated in any single endeavor will exceed or equal their value used anywhere else. The equation of price with marginal cost is generated automatically by price adjustments dictated by the laws of supply and demand. The theory assumes that inputs are both homogeneous and commodities. If a key resource is not a resource but a capability, claims about prices adjusting to generate levels of output that also represent allocative efficiency must be qualified.

ance and regional processes of growth and decline. Regions that enjoy a high per capita income are generally regions with a critical mass of business enterprises with the capacity to add value to the resources they use. The idea of regional specialization implies that firms do not compete alone in the global marketplace but as members of networked groups of firms sharing and building on distinctive regional capabilities. A region's capacity to initiate and sustain high value added production depends upon its capability to foster and reproduce entrepreneurial firms.

The point is that sustainable regional growth depends not upon the longevity of specific firms but upon a networked population of interacting, specialist business enterprises. Greater specialization within a region shifts the patterns of inter-firm relationships which rebound back on the specialization process within firms. Understanding these relationships is crucial to distinguishing dynamic from static clusters. The term 'cluster dynamics' signals interactive processes of capability development and specialization within and amongst firms within a region. I argue that a dynamic between internal organization and inter-firm relations underlies different models of innovation and patterns of regional competitive advantage.

'Competitive advantage' in the title of the book evokes the role of capabilities in establishing inter-regional and international leadership in performance characteristics by a region or nation's business enterprises. The title also evokes the approach of anchoring capabilities in principles of production and organization. Business enterprises operate within a regional production system which is constituted by principles of production and organization. The 'new' in *New Competitive Advantage* refers to innovative advances in capabilities that enable a region's business enterprises to set previously unattainable performance standards based on more advanced principles of production and organization. In *The New Competition* (Best 1990), the principles of *interchangeability* and *flow* were examined in different institutional contexts to explain changes in both regional and national industrial leadership. In this book, the principle of *systems integration* is added to explain the New Competition of the 1990s in the form of the resurgence of American industry. Silicon Valley and Boston's Route 128 are case studies.

Systems integration is a principle of both production and organization, and a method of analysis. As a principle of production and organization it goes some distance in explaining the new model of technology management that has emerged in America's high-tech regions.

But as a method of analysis, systems integration focuses attention on the holistic character of the processes that underlie capability development and govern productivity advances.

An important distinction must be drawn between technological capability and technology management capability. While entrepreneurial firms develop unique technological capabilities, sustained growth depends upon developing the capability to manage technological change on an ongoing basis, something that I call technology management capability.

Technology management, too, works at both the enterprise and industrial policy levels. The term signifies an integral link between technology capability and business organization. Technology management is a capability to foster ongoing technological development. To telescope a major policy theme, national or regional technology management is to the theory of the developmental state what demand management is to Keynesian economics or money supply management is to monetarism. Sustained growth is about, in part, anticipating long-term technological trajectories whether a region is a leader or follower in technological innovation. Technological changes are continuously creating new challenges and opportunities for application to new product development and industrial diversification. I argue that the success of regions in responding to these challenges and opportunities depends critically upon its skill formation processes.

Developing and sustaining both a firm and a region's technological capabilities is not simply a technological exercise. Capabilities are social achievements that take time and organization to develop.[4] Technology management, at both the enterprise and regional level demands coordinated development of business model, production capabilities, and skill formation. At the enterprise level a firm cannot integrate technological advances into a production facility that lacks flexibility or with a workforce that lacks the requisite technical and organizational skills.

Analogous mutual adjustment processes among business model, production capabilities, and skill formation underlie sustained techno-

[4] The term 'competitive advantage' complements 'comparative advantage', an enduring principle of economics. However, the term 'comparative advantage' has been associated with the misleading presupposition that specialization is a function of relative endowment of the 'factors of production' (land, labor, and capital). The factors of production, in turn, are assumed to be commodities and independently productive. From the capability perspective, productivity cannot be reduced to individual factors of production for purposes of explaining growth or competitiveness. The 'factors of production' are embedded in capabilities, which, in turn, shape productivity. The term 'competitive advantage' is used here to emphasize the organizational dimension of specialization. The principle of specialization is simply too important to be identified with the 'factors of production' of textbook economics (see Ch. 3).

logical change at the regional level. For example, the process of new firm creation enhances the process of technological diversification. Similarly, inter-firm networks nurture regional technological specialization. To extend the underlying process of technology capability development from growing firms to growing regions requires a skill formation process that matches manpower needs with labor force skills.

Technological transitions have always been part of the capitalist development process. But to the extent that enterprises and regions develop technology management capabilities, the pace of innovation will quicken and generate tendencies to greater concentrations of high value added industrial production with associated implications for regional competitive advantage and inter-regional inequalities. At the same time, however, the idea of technology management suggests that the technological future is not determined independently of organizational capabilities, corporate governance, and public choice.

These issues are important not only for academics in refining theories and understanding, but also for firms assessing their capabilities and business opportunities, and for economic and industrial policy-makers evaluating growth challenges and opportunities in their locality or regional economy. Failure to develop technology policies can be as deleterious to regional growth as it is to company success. Economic decline can erode a region's heritage of technological capabilities just as diminished sales can drive down a company's capital base. Regions with limited capabilities will sell commodities in the international marketplace but will suffer low levels of productivity and value added.[5] The policy challenge is to combine a region's technological heritage with new technologies to periodically reinvent a region's competitive advantage. This theme of technological continuity and change as being critical to sustained growth recurs throughout the book.

Thinking of economic development in terms of the development of capabilities rather than the accumulation of capital demands new measures of economic success. It is inadequate to explain productivity and competitive advantage in terms of measured inputs of factors of production, ignoring the mediating role of capabilities. Critically, it focuses attention on the role of design in economics. There are two ways to make more with less: improve resource allocation and redesign the

[5] The case for free trade is unambiguous in the efficient resource allocation perspective. For the capability and innovation perspective it depends upon a region's organizational capabilities to use trade and foreign investment to tap into the world's pool of technological capabilities in ways that advance local production capabilities. Otherwise regions can become trapped in low value added activities and productivity growth will be limited.

process. The first is the heartland of neoclassical economics. The second is central to the capability and innovation perspective. For example, I will argue below that the resurgence of the American economy has more to do with the decentralization and diffusion of design capabilities than with improvements in resource allocation.

A comment about the book's sub-title is in order. While the central concern is an explanation of the turnaround in American industry in the 1990s, the perspective developed is both narrower and more general. It is narrower in that the approach is regional and my focus is primarily on two, albeit leading, regions within the United States. But it is also more general. I have included chapters on Malaysia and Northern Ireland to illustrate this theme.

I have had the good fortune to be involved at close hand in industrial restructuring projects and the development of economic policy in several quite distinct contexts—notably Massachusetts, Northern Ireland, Malaysia, London, Slovenia, Cyprus, Jamaica, Honduras, and Moldova. With colleagues, I have studied in detail the evidence of the Massachusetts economy over time. It was the hub of America's industrial revolution in the early 1800s and more recently the site of America's first high-tech industrial district. It is my conviction that any theory or economic perspective that seeks to explain business performance and economic growth should work in different places and historical contexts such as these.

The book is intended as a contribution to these various lines of enquiry and concerns. I hope it will be of value to different groups: to students of business and economics; to economic policymakers and industrial strategists challenged with developing economic policy in a competitive and uncertain world; to managers and business planners making a range of decisions about their company's investment strategies and capability development programs; and to citizens concerned with issues of sustainable growth and economic equality. An understanding of growth dynamics is important to making informed choices at enterprise, governmental, and educational levels.

While the capability and innovation perspective draws upon a long heritage in economic thought beginning with Adam Smith's fundamental principle of increasing specialization it introduces new terms and reinterprets old terms. For ready reference, I have supplied a glossary of terms used in the text.

For Lawrence

and in memory of

Sukant Tripathy

CHAPTER

1

Introduction

GROWTH ANOMALIES

Growth has a powerful impact on economic well-being. An annual productivity growth rate of 3 percent, for example, doubles income each generation while a rate of 1 percent takes nearly eighty years. While growth, like new patterns of trade, generates winners and losers, it has a salutary effect on politics: sustainable growth generates fiscal resources for income-equalizing institutions and public investments such as education, healthcare, and transportation. But setbacks in growth can engender processes of decline that are resistant to reversal. Thus, policies that impact positively or negatively on growth can have powerful short- and long-term effects on a region's well-being.

The problem is this. Growth is a poorly understood process or set of processes and real world growth experiences are continuously throwing up surprises. The terms 'miracle', 'puzzle', and 'paradox' are used to described the unexpected and unexplained. Examples of terms that suggest a lack of explanation include the following.

1. The 'New Economy' to explain a return to growth in 1990s America in spite of low savings. The term 'new' suggests something fundamental has changed in how the economy operates. Information technology is often cited.
2. The productivity 'paradox' of 1970s and 1980s America in which 'computers showed up everywhere except in the productivity statistics'. In fact, economic growth dropped from annual rates of 3 percent during the two decades preceding 1973 to only 1 percent during the ensuing two decades exactly the period during which information technology penetrated into economic life.

3. The Massachusetts 'miracle' of rapid growth beginning in the 1970s followed by an equally unexpected severe downturn that destroyed one-third of manufacturing jobs.

4. The East Asian 'miracle' describing rapid and sustained near double-digit growth rates for two to three decades.

The capabilities and innovation perspective I present here is a conceptual framework designed to advance an understanding of regional growth. A distinctive feature of this perspective is the central role played by technology in understanding both growth experiences and levels of productivity. As we shall see in the next section, technology is not absent in conventional growth perspectives, but it is backstage. Recent contributions have converted the business enterprise from a 'shadowy figure' in economic analysis into a pivotal player in the dramas of growth. Michael Porter's cluster analysis, in particular, has brought both business organization and the region back into focus. The starting point for a review of the role of technology in growth perspectives is Robert Solow's model of long-term steady state growth for which the Nobel Prize was awarded in 1987.

COMPETING PERSPECTIVES

Old Growth Theory: Diminishing Returns

Solow's theory of economic growth was developed in the 1950s. The model predicted that while growth would slow in the long run, the instability of the 1930s was an aberration.[1] To explain the long-term stability of capitalist growth, Solow converted the Ricardian assumption of diminishing returns from land to capital.

The variables in Solow's model are capital and labor, the 'factors of production' in neoclassical growth theory. The model predicts declining growth rates in the capital rich countries because of diminishing returns as more capital is added to a limited supply of labor. The existence of diminishing returns to capital means that permanent increases in the proportion of investment to national income will only result in a short-term gain in output, not a sustainable increase in the growth rate.

[1] Solow's model countered the implication of the Harrod–Domar growth models that the economy was on a knife-edge between accelerating growth and spiraling recession.

Consequently, for Solow's diminishing returns growth model, the long-term sustainable rate of growth is determined by the growth of the labor supply. Two predictions follow; neither has proven consistent with real world economies. The first is that growth rates will decline in capital rich countries because of diminishing returns. In fact, no such trend is discernable. The second is that capital poor countries will absorb capital from capital rich countries because of higher rates of return and thereby grow faster. While some poor countries have grown fast, most have not, and therefore the predicted convergence of growth between rich and poor countries has not occurred.

While technology is not a variable in Solow's growth model, it figures prominently in his empirical studies of growth. But it comes in through the back door. In a series of studies the growth of output experienced in the United States substantially exceeded what could be attributed to growth in inputs of capital and labor alone (Schmookler 1952; Fabricant 1954; Kendrick 1956; Abramovitz 1956). Solow's own study decomposed annual changes in aggregate output per hour of labor input for the United States between 1909 and 1949 into two components: increases in capital per labor hour and a residual not explainable by the first. The accumulation of capital could account for only 12.5 percent of the increase in output per labor hour; the rest was attributed to the residual factor which Solow termed 'technical progress'.

Thus, technology is important, indeed dominant, within the causes of growth but *exogenous* to the model of growth. Solow opined that technology probably increased at a relatively constant rate over the long term.[2] Since a role for technology is not defined, the contribution of technology is represented by a scalar that simply multiplies any increase in growth generated by the labor input up to the measured level of the real world.

[2] In Solow's growth model technology is not measured directly, but as the 'residual' output effects that are not directly accounted for by increases in capital (K) and labor (L). 'It is possible to argue that about one-eighth of the total increase is traceable to increased K/L and the remaining 7/8ths to technical change' (Solow 1957: 316). Solow defines 'technology' and 'technical change' as 'a short hand expression for *any kind of shift* in the production function' (312). For Solow the pace of technological change is 'essentially constant in time' (316). Edward Denison decomposed Solow's residual into an array of components including government regulation, gender mix in the labor force, and education (1979). Dale Jorgenson and associates have refined input measures over the ensuing decades to build an econometric model which attributes fully 83% of growth to endogenous changes in capital and labor, with the remaining 17% accounted for by technological change and fertility rates (1996). Thus, the sources of growth in Jorgenson's model do a volte-face to Solow's original estimations: 12.5% of growth for Solow could be attributed to capital accumulation (he did not consider human capital). Jorgenson's model assumes a perfectly competitive, constant-returns-to-scale neoclassical production function that employs constant-quality indexes of both labor and capital input and investment goods output.

The lack of an explanation of technical change has not inhibited its citation as the primary cause of growth in the real world. Paul Krugman asks how did today's advanced countries achieve sustained growth for over 150 years? He answers 'Technological advances have led to a continual increase in total factor productivity—a continual rise in national income for each unit of input' (1994: 67–8). He refers to Robert Solow's estimate that 'technological progress has accounted for 80 percent of the long-term rise in U.S. per capita income' (67). Following tradition, he does not explain technology or the forces that drive it.

Krugman uses the same model to explain the East Asia 'miracle'. He writes that the rapid growth in 1970s and 1980s East Asia, except for Japan, was not based on technological progress or increases in total factor productivity but only on increases in inputs of capital and labor, a growth trajectory subject to sharp diminishing returns. The conceptual distinction he makes is interesting and certainly plausible. But the theory of growth to which he appeals lacks the conceptual categories in production and organizational capabilities to substantiate or refute the claim. Did the levels of technology in East Asia not change appreciably over two to three decades of rapid growth? All the theory and its applications tell us is the extent to which measures of capital and labor do or do not account for growth. It is either silent or eclectic on the content of the 'residual'.

Technology is like the rabbit in the magician's hat. Technology disappears in the model as diminishing returns to capital predict a growth slowdown; technology appears in descriptions of the real world to 'explain' growth experiences.

New Growth Theory: The Role of Ideas[3]

The lack of consistency between conventional growth theory and evidence led to the emergence of a rival 'new growth theory' with the publication of an article by Paul Romer in 1986. New growth theory breaks with the assumption of diminishing returns by making productivity increase *endogenous* to the production function. Productivity might increase from increasing returns to scale, whether directly within the production function or through the application of *produced* R&D or through the *production* of human capital. It follows that techno-

[3] This section draws heavily from Scherer (1999).

logical change in the form of the creation of knowledge is not exogenous to the production process.

The public good dimension of ideas plays a central role in the new growth theory. A public good, as distinct from a private good, is one in which the consumption by one individual does not exclude its consumption by another. It can be 'consumed' over and over again without depletion or loss of benefit to previous consumers. Ideas are prime examples. The value of a cooking recipe to the original user does not diminish with its diffusion to new users.

Ideas, such as improved recipes, have a second quality. The application of a new idea can increase output without an increase in physical inputs of capital and labor, thus countering diminishing returns. A new production process idea such as mass production can increase output without increasing inputs of 'factors of production'. Diffusion of the new idea, because of its public good character, can lead to higher output without reducing output in the initial users.

The new growth theory implies that knowledge rich countries will grow faster than knowledge poor countries because of the combination of specific designs embodied in unique products and generic knowledge underlying the creation of specific designs. The knowledge embedded in specific designs can be excluded from rivals by patents; the knowledge pool that underlies specific design activities is in the public domain in the form of published articles and patent applications. Knowledge rich countries have an advantage in tapping the dynamic between specific design knowledge and the pool of generic knowledge. Therefore R&D has a bigger payoff in knowledge rich countries.

The debate between the 'growth accounting' school and the new growth theorists has centered on the issue of growth convergence or divergence between rich and poor countries. The Solow model predicts convergence; the new growth theory predicts divergence. The debate does not offer insights into why some poor countries have grown fast or why American industry has undergone periods of competitive decline and resurgence. This is because, in part, both old and new growth theories are relentlessly macro and therefore highly aggregated.[4]

Nevertheless, the introduction of ideas into an understanding of economic development is a major step towards freeing neoclassical growth theory from the presupposition that growth *is* capital

[4] Ironically, given its highly aggregative character, the microeconomic foundation of neoclassical growth theory is one of methodological individualism. Thus, everything economic is explained in terms of individual maximizing behavior.

accumulation. We turn now to perspectives that operate at lower levels of aggregation.

Schumpeterian Innovation

Joseph Schumpeter put the entrepreneur at the center of the growth process. The Schumpeterian perspective breaks with the microeconomic foundations of neoclassical economics and the highly aggregated growth models. Firms compete by new products, processes, technologies, materials, or forms of organization. In this, the Schumpeterian perspective treats as variables what the neoclassical perspective holds constant.[5]

R&D, technology, and innovation are placed at the center of the Schumpeterian growth process. Empirical research starts with the public good nature of R&D and seeks to measure the social rate of return for R&D investment (Schmookler 1966; Mansfield 1980; Scherer 1982). The social rate of return to investment in R&D is found to be 50 percent. Since much cannot be appropriated by the investors, perfectly competitive markets will under allocate resources to R&D and innovation will suffer. Therefore, imperfect competition and/or government regulation can enhance growth by enabling R&D.

Thus, the public good aspect of R&D raises one aspect of the growth process which can be influenced by policy. Without subsidization, R&D will be underfunded and growth will be lower. The problem is deeper, however, as it suggests that monopolistic competition in product markets may enhance growth. Monopolization means higher profit margins which can fund R&D. Furthermore, monopolized markets make it easier for investors to appropriate a higher portion of the returns to R&D thereby encouraging greater investment in R&D.

Schumpeter referred to perfect competition as the 'bacilli of depression' because it cut margins, diminished innovation, stifled technological change, and threatened industrial decline. Edith Penrose referred to perfect competition as the god and the devil: it is the god because rivalry counters monopolistic lethargy, but it is the devil because competition squeezes the margins required for R&D investments and growth.

[5] In fairness, the challenge that Schumpeter addressed was to explain economic progress. The challenge that motivated neoclassical economists was to describe the constitution of an efficient allocation of resources. The neoclassical theory of growth was built on a conceptual framework to explain both.

The neo-Schumpeterian perspective has a long heritage in economics going back to Adam Smith's wealth creation process. For it was Smith who introduced technical change into production. Continuing this tradition has meant, in the case of Schumpeterian economics, breaking with the foundations of the neoclassical theory such as the production function, perfect competition, and the 'economic man'.[6] These foundations have served the resource allocation side of Smith but undermined the wealth creation side.

PORTER'S CLUSTER

Michael Porter's purpose is to develop a conceptual framework to guide business strategy and public policy. Porter focuses attention on units of analysis which come between conventional macroeconomics and microeconomics, the economy and the individual. Aggregates such as the economy 'must by necessity focus on very broad and general determinants that are not sufficiently complete and operational to guide company or public policy. It cannot address the central issue for our purposes here, which is why and how meaningful and commercially valuable skills and technology are created' (1990: 9).

The central organizing concept for Porter is the *home base*. In Porter's words: 'Competitive advantage is created and sustained through a highly localized process' (1990: 19). Paradoxically, Porter notes, even with increased globalization 'the home nation takes on growing significance because it is the source of the skills and technology that underpin competitive advantage' (19). The home base 'is where a firm's strategy is set and the core product and process technology (broadly defined) are created and maintained' (19). '[The] . . . process of creating skills and the important influences on the rate of improvement and innovation are intensely local' (158). Localization is reinforced by external economies which 'do not cross national boundaries easily' (144).

'The basic unit of analysis for understanding competition is the *industry*' (1990: 33, emphasis added). To understand competitiveness and productivity, for Porter, the unit of analysis cannot be the 'economy as a whole but . . . specific industries and industry segments' (9). But

[6] Schumpeter was not fully appreciated by leading neoclassical economists. In the words of Robert Solow: 'Schumpeter is a sort of patron saint in this field. I might be alone in thinking that he should be treated as a patron saint: paraded around one day each year and more or less ignored the rest of the time' (Solow 1994: 52, cited in Scherer 1999: 28).

while the basic unit of analysis is the industry, success is explained in terms of clusters: 'Nations succeed not in isolated industries . . . but in *clusters* of industries connected through vertical and horizontal relationships' (73, Porter's emphasis).

For Porter, firms are not the source of competitiveness. Instead, firms derive their competitive advantage from their home base environment.[7] The environment, in turn, is shaped by four 'determinants of national advantage': factor conditions; home demand conditions; related and supporting industries; and firm strategy, structure, and rivalry. The four elements form a mutually reinforcing system, the Porter 'diamond'.

Competitive advantage based on only one or two determinants is possible but not sustainable. 'Advantages throughout the "diamond" are necessary for achieving and sustaining competitive success in the knowledge-intensive industries that form the backbone of advanced economies' (1990: 73).

In the decade of the 1990s, Porter's diamond and cluster analysis was widely adopted as a conceptual framework for shaping regional and national industrial strategies. By introducing concepts such as business strategy, value chain, home base, and cluster to economic analysis, Porter has enriched policy discourse.[8] His competitive advantage framework brings into view a richer understanding of the sources of industrial development and a menu of industrial policy options that are obscured, or denied, by the market failure framework. By focusing on skills, business development, and clusters, Porter offers policy options beyond the pursuit of the perfect competition ideal, tax incentives, subsidies, and physical infrastructure.

Porter's home base concept is useful for describing existing, high productivity clusters. They involve sophisticated local customers, a range of complementary and supporting industries, advanced and specialized skills, and strong domestic rivalry. But multinational companies and inward investment have played a key role in, for example, Singapore and Ireland's exporting industries, in contradiction to Porter's home base thesis. These high growth cases seem to have been the beneficiaries of technology transfer and innovations created elsewhere. Does this mean elements of the cluster are not required

[7] 'Something about these locations provides a fertile environment for firms in these particular industries. While my discussion is framed in terms of nations, the geographical concentration of industries within nations will be important to explain. Government policy at the state and local level has an important role to play in shaping national advantage' (1990: 29).

[8] Porter's business strategy paradigm is an example of 'structuration' in that structure and agency are intertwined in the constitution of the object of study and explanation (see Giddens 1976 for a theoretical treatment of structuration).

locally to achieve high growth? Relaxing the conditions required to describe a cluster results in a proliferation of clusters and the concept loses meaning.[9] Tightening the conditions undermines the power of the concept to explain high growth rate cases in countries which lack already existing home bases.

To preview my book, the capabilities and innovation perspective extends Porter in several ways. It

(1) anchors entrepreneurial firms in a capability development and market opportunity dynamic;
(2) anchors regional growth in the capability development processes of entrepreneurial firms;
(3) distinguishes technology from technology management and applies both to understandings of growth and competitive advantage;
(4) integrates production into business organization and builds a conceptual framework for understanding production in terms of principles;
(5) characterizes mutual adjustment processes within and amongst firms to stretch the concept of cluster to one of cluster dynamics;
(6) accounts for a set of internal/external dynamics which link internal organization of business enterprise to the forms of inter-firm relationships;
(7) develops a policy perspective that accounts for mutual complementarity amongst production capability, business organization, and skill formation.

THE PRODUCTIVITY TRIAD

Technology is acknowledged as critical to high income and rapid growth. Where does technology management capability come from?

The capability and innovation perspective focuses attention on three interactive domains that shape a region's capability development processes: business model, production system, and skill formation. Capabilities mediate between the resources of a region and their productivity. They constitute a Productivity Triad. The Productivity Triad provides a framework for analysing or x-raying an economy to identify its challenges and opportunities. In this respect it is a tool

[9] For example, twenty-two clusters are identified in Portugal (Porter 1998).

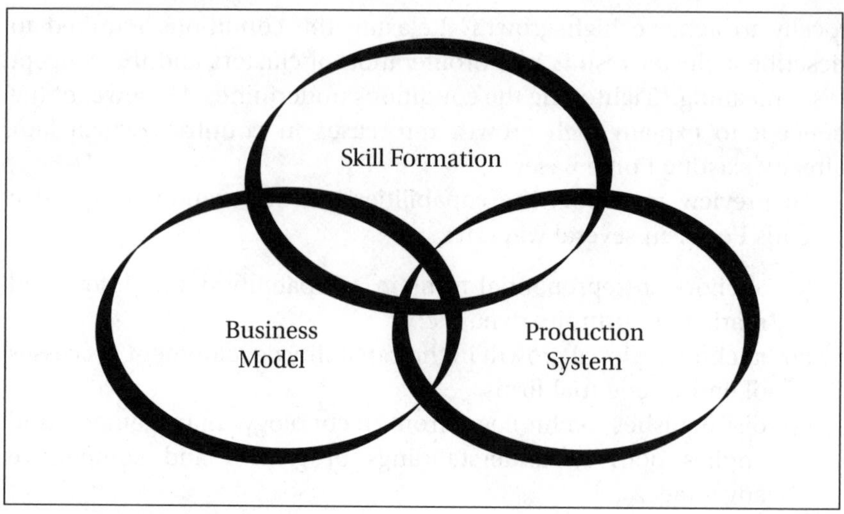

Fig. 1.1. Productivity Triad

similar to Porter's Diamond.[10] In the chapters ahead each of the domains of the Productivity Triad will be examined. Nevertheless, the overlapping of the three domains as shown in Figure 1.1 visually expresses their interconnectedness.[11] Here each domain will be briefly introduced.

[10] The elements of Porter's Diamond are firm strategy, structure, and rivalry; demand conditions; factor conditions; and related and supporting industries. The concept of the entrepreneurial firm of the capabilities and innovation perspective imposes a dynamic between technology capability and market opportunity as the driver of change. For Porter, rivalry amongst leading firms is the driver and the firm and market conditions are independent determinants of competitive advantage. Ironically, the internal organization of the firm does not feature in Porter's Diamond. For the capabilities and innovation perspective, capability specialization within the entrepreneurial firm is an element in the internal/external dynamic that fosters regional technological specialization and competitive advantage. These ideas are developed in Ch. 3.

[11] Interconnectedness complicates analysis and exposition. The method of analysis deployed in this book is to examine enterprise and regional capabilities from three conceptual viewpoints. We look consecutively from a viewpoint that highlights the production system, from a second viewpoint that focuses on business organization, and a third viewpoint that targets skill formation processes. The challenge is to develop conceptual viewpoints that capture both the defining features of each domain and the interconnections that shape and reshape them. Triple vision may be an aid!

Business Model

In the domain of the business model we are looking at enterprise organization for processes of capability development. The starting point is the technology capability and market opportunity dynamic that defines the entrepreneurial firm. The goal of most firms is to establish distinctive or unique capabilities to gain a competitive advantage in the marketplace. Entrepreneurial firms are a class of enterprises that develop ongoing processes of capability development as part of a technology capability and market opportunity dynamic.

The internal dynamic of the entrepreneurial firm can be housed within a range of different models of business organization. In *The New Competition,* I examined models as distinctive as the Springfield Armory, Big Business, the *Kaisha,* and industrial districts in the form of networked groups of specialist enterprises as represented by the 'third Italy'. In the chapters ahead a number of models including a new open systems business model are explored. Each business model is associated with different technology management capabilities, models of innovation, production systems, and skill formation processes.

Processes of capability development go beyond the boundaries of entrepreneurial firms to that of clusters of enterprises. Crucially, in 'open system' networks, entrepreneurial firms focus on core capabilities and use networks for complementary capabilities. This involves horizontal or multi-enterprise integration as distinct from vertical integration. A new dynamic between internal organization and inter-firm competition is established. In pursuit of its goals, the entrepreneurial firm propagates new productive opportunities, which are pursued internally or pushed outside, producing opportunities for new enterprises, spin-offs or existing enterprises with the requisite capabilities (a process of 'techno-diversification').

The rebounding pressures of product-led competition in the market on the internal organization of the firm reinforce the drive to develop unique products and production capabilities. The leaders of today pursue product-led strategies and operate high-performance work systems. To compete on the basis of rapid introduction of new products they integrate design and manufacturing processes.

Open systems also mean that a technical change at one link in the network of enterprises will create new pressures and opportunities for specialists in each of the complementary capabilities. In this way design changes and technology advances are leveraged regionally. The decentralization and diffusion of design within a region foster a transition to product-led competition both within the region and between the region and other regions. Regions that make the transition to product-led competition can enjoy a competitive advantage over regions in which the dominant mode of competition is price.

Entrepreneurial firms foster a third capability development process which is leveraged by cluster dynamics. Driven by technology capability and market opportunity dynamic, entrepreneurial firms are forever advancing their own capabilities. In the process the region's technological capability seabed is revitalized by the ongoing activities of its inhabitants. It is a virtuous circle. Regional technological capabilities spawn entrepreneurial firms, which upgrade regional technological capabilities, which spawn more entrepreneurial firms.

Thus, a region's technological capabilities are an outcome of a cumulative history of technological advances embedded in entrepreneurial firms. But the historical process is also collective. Just as individual entrepreneurial firms develop unique technological capabilities, a virtual, collective entrepreneurial firm extends a region's unique technological capabilities. The regional process of technology capability advance will likely involve a succession of firms, with new firms building on advances made by previous innovators. Regional specialization, in the form of industrial districts or clusters, is the outcome of the technology/market dynamic played out at the level of the collective entrepreneurial firm. By examining the dynamics of a region's business model, we are at same time examining the region's technological heritage. This is shaped cumulatively and collectively over time by the ongoing sequences of capability and market dynamics.

Production Capabilities

Production capabilities are an expression of an underlying but unifying principle of production and organization. Competitive strategy and production systems are bound together. Any effort by business managers to advance performance outcomes that does not put in place the requisite production capabilities will not be able to compete against firms that have done so. Competing on the basis of rapid new product development, without having a production system in which manufacturing and design are integrated will only produce frustration. Competitors that have integrated design and manufacturing will be equipped to smoothly introduce new technologies in support of new product concepts on a regular basis.

Firms that establish a new product development capability in sync with ongoing production operations establish a platform for competing on the basis of short cycle times in the design to manufacturing process. The regional diffusion of an organizational change methodology aimed at rapid new product development capability can multiply the number of entrepreneurial firms.

Technology management rather than simply the periodic introduction of a new technology is the key to driving an ongoing new product development capability. It is a variant of driving the technology capability and market opportunity dynamic. In the hierarchical, functionally departmentalized business model, technology management was limited to the confines of R&D laboratories. New technologies would be introduced into production at irregular intervals but with considerable resistance and severe 'teething' difficulties during which quality and output suffered. Changes were highly disruptive to production performance and were to be avoided. The business model was well suited for a world of long production runs, predictable product life cycles, and limited technological change. Technology management was an obstacle to be avoided. Some firms, in R&D intensive sectors, pursued the technology/market dynamic of the entrepreneurial firm. They, too, however, separated technology management from production. The lack of technology management capability meant that new technologies would often mean investment in new-dedicated facilities.

Regions develop production systems that combine context-independent principles of production and organization with region-specific technological capabilities. Principles such as interchangeability, flow, and systems integration have general applicability. But the application of flow in the American mid-west, for example, underlies a regional competitive advantage in the mass production of high-volume, consumer products. New England, in contrast, is virtually void of mass production enterprises and specializes in low-volume, complex product systems utilizing, in many cases, technologies with a long heritage in the region.

Skill Formation

The growth process in knowledge-intensive industries is limited by the supply of engineering and scientific personnel required to staff rapidly growing firms. In fact, innovation and skill formation are opposite sides of the same technology development coin. Regional growth will be choked if the requisite numbers and types of graduate engineers are not produced by the education system; three conditions must be met for success. The first involves characterization of the demand for specific technological skills. The second involves investment in technical education. The third involves skill formation in the workplace. As we shall see, a region that can institute skill formation processes in anticipation of technology transitions can build competitive advantage.

To summarize, the concept of Productivity Triad captures the systemic character of change at enterprise and regional levels. The three domains of production system, business model, and skill formation are not separable and additive components but interconnected subsystems. Each domain captures a different dimension of capability. The business model domain of the Productivity Triad captures the technological uniqueness of enterprise and regional development. This is the domain of the entrepreneurial firm and the technology capability and market opportunity dynamic that defines it. Every firm strives to develop a distinctive capability that cannot easily be imitated. But every firm also operates within a regionally based production system. The production system is constituted by production capabilities anchored in enduring principles of production and organization. More advanced production systems offer enabling conditions for entrepreneurial firms that, in turn, advance a region's technological capabilities. The history of the evolution of production capabilities in the world's most advanced regions offers a roadmap to industrial development.

A region that successfully negotiates a transition to more advanced production systems creates an organizational infrastructure for entrepreneurial firms to drive technological change and productivity growth. The problem is that making the transition involves complementary organizational change in all three domains. The interconnectedness of production, business, and skill has critically important implications for governmental policymaking. When firms and regions become stuck in low productivity triads, the government may be the only institution that can coordinate organizational change in all three domains of the Productivity Triad.

The examples of capability development in Chapters 2 through 5 of this book refer to cases that established new bases for regional competitive advantage including Route 128 and Silicon Valley. But the perspective is more general. The concepts and methods that can explain the sources of high productivity and sustained growth in the most technologically advanced companies and regions are tools for analyzing capability development processes in lower productivity enterprises and regions. It has been said that human anatomy contains a key to understanding the anatomy of the ape. Analogously, understanding the most advanced capabilities offers clues to clarifying the challenges to and opportunities for capabilities development in enterprises and regions stuck in lower productivity systems.

CHAPTER OUTLINE

In Chapter 2 the evolution of technology management is explored within a historically derived production system framework. Five production systems are distinguished in terms of a unifying and enduring principle of production. A case study exemplar is elaborated for each to illustrate the links between production capabilities, skills, and performance standards. While technology management has only been integrated into production systems as an ongoing process in recent times, the origins of technology management as a lever for advancing industrial performance are traced back to the emergence of the world's first precision machine tool industry.

In Chapter 3 the entrepreneurial firm is introduced as the agent of change in a theory of regional specialization and growth. The conceptual genealogy of the 'entrepreneurial firm' began with Adam Smith's principle of increasing specialization, was extended to the region by Alfred Marshall and to the business enterprise by Edith Penrose. Building on Penrose, the entrepreneurial firm is defined in terms of a dynamic between technology capability and market opportunity.

The internal dynamic of the entrepreneurial firm is seen as the driver of a set of regional growth or 'cluster' dynamics based on processes of technological differentiation and integration across networked groups of specialist business enterprises. A model of inter-firm or cluster growth dynamics is presented which links technological specialization with new firm creation; technological diversification with inter-firm networking; and technological innovation with industrial diversity. These processes underlie unique patterns of regional specialization.

In Chapter 4 three models of innovation are elaborated. The first is an American Big Business model in which innovation is concentrated in R&D labs and isolated from production. The second is a Japanese inspired model of incremental innovation that integrates applied research and production. The third is an 'open systems', regional innovation model that mutually integrates applied, developmental, and basic research with production. The concept of regional innovation capability is an extension of the entrepreneurial firm in two ways. First, the technology capability and market opportunity dynamic is extended from the firm to an analogous, if virtual, 'collective entrepreneurial firm' operating at the regional level. Second, technology management is merged with innovation capabilities by integrating basic research into the production system.

Silicon Valley is used as an example in Chapters 2 through 4 to illustrate the theme that America has developed a new model of technology management and is comprehensively reorganizing the business system around the new model. The new model is associated with *systems integration* capabilities that have established a higher level of performance standards for industrial leadership. Firms, or networked groups of firms, have demonstrated a *regional capability* to innovate and rapidly reinvent products. The new model of technology management emerged in response to, and is an extension of, the product-led competition that had previously driven the high growth experiences of, for example, Japan in flexible, mass production (lean) manufacturing and the 'third Italy' in design-intensive, fashion industries, and agile manufacturing. The new competitive advantage derives from the application, diffusion, and deepening of the principle of systems integration. The deepening refers to the integration of basic research, much of which is located in universities and government-funded laboratories, with technological, developmental, and applied research, most of which is located in entrepreneurial firms.

A central theme in Chapter 4 is that the conversion of technological advance into regional growth entails instituting an entrepreneurial firm and regional education dynamic. In fact, industrial innovation and skill formation are parts of a single process. The education system supplies the technical labor force to enact the regional innovation and growth dynamics. In addition, the technology diffusion process that underpins industrial growth is made possible by engineering methodologies that enable a scaling up of an advanced and technically specialized labor force. This dynamic between advances in technology by entrepreneurial firms and refinement of corresponding engineering methodologies by regional technical colleges and universities is often overlooked. Isolated entrepreneurial firms do emerge outside of the skill formation system of a region but rapidly growing regions depend upon an interactive dynamic that fosters technological development within firms and supplies them with the skilled individuals to operationalize research plans. Manpower development planning is about advancing the supply of technically skilled labor in sync with the growth rate of technologically advancing firms within a region.

Chapters 5 to 7 are applications of the capabilities and innovation perspective to different regions. Chapter 5 is a study of Route 128, the high-tech region surrounding Boston. Massachusetts in the 1950s was suffering from the loss of its traditional industries, textiles and shoes, and its industrial future looked bleak. But by the early 1980s the 'Massachusetts miracle' heralded the emergence of America's first high-tech industrial district. The 'miracle' turned to dust with the abrupt loss of one-third of the state's manufacturing jobs between 1986 and 1992. It appeared that the forces of decline were deeply entrenched. Few predicted the industrial resurgence that followed.

Fewer still expected the extraordinary techno-diversity that has accompanied the resurgence. The resurgence of Route 128 has not been in the high-volume, consumer electronics industry in which East Asian nations have remained world leaders. Instead, the competitive advantage of Route 128 is in precision equipment, complex products and systems, and the development of new technologies. But the new applications stretch across numerous industrial categories and, in many cases, redraw old boundaries.

Systems integration is a common feature. A key implication of systems integration is the capability to redesign whole systems to fully exploit design advances in sub-systems. Route 128 has the regional capability to rapidly integrate and reintegrate activities and technologies required for rapid new product development in complex product systems. In this process, advances in capabilities anywhere in the regional system can be integrated into the regional system of capabilities. The regional competitive advantage is reinforced by a regional innovation system which converts ideas into products and, in the process, develops new technological and scientific knowledge and thereby new capabilities. Central to sustaining regional growth dynamics in the new business model is a process of new firm creation that parallels the processes of technology differentiation, integration, and reintegration.

Many have attributed the region's industrial success to innovations originating in the plethora of research universities and government funded laboratories. Important as these institutions are to innovation, centering attention on them risks a narrow concept of innovation which obscures regional innovation processes including the role of technology-driven firms and the heritage of technological capabilities and skills. The continuity of technological capability is central to the idea of the entrepreneurial firm, developed in Chapter 3. In the case of Massachusetts, continuity of technological capability also operates at the regional level and has been a critical element in sustaining competitive advantage as firms and even industries have come and gone. But along the way firms big and small have made contributions to advancing the region's unique technological capabilities.

Several generic post-war technologies are examined. Behind each lies an impressive skill base in technology-related disciplines and engineering methodologies, which facilitate industrial transitions, technology diffusion, and long-term growth. For example, turbine technology, central to the region's global leadership in jet engine production, has a genealogy that began with innovations in water turbine technology to power textile mills located in Lowell, Massachusetts in the mid-1800s. Techno-diversification is a consequence of a transition to a new, open systems business model, a model more appropriate to exploit the opportunities offered by systems integration at the technological level.

In Chapter 6 the capabilities and innovation perspective is applied to Malaysian electronics, a case of rapid growth for over three decades but with disappointing productivity gains. In fact, Malaysia has not one, but three electronics clusters. Each cluster has distinctive internal dynamics and is related to global production systems in distinctive ways. The most successful of the three regions in advancing local production capabilities has benefited from a regional developmental agency that coordinated the three elements of the Productivity Triad to create a world-class high-volume production system. However, the region is now at an impasse. All three domains must be reintegrated within production systems with more advanced technology management capabilities. Comparing the performance of the three regions offers policy lessons for 'governance of cluster dynamics'.

Chapter 7 turns to Northern Ireland.[12] The region has a long industrial history. But the region's industrial heritage has not combined technological continuity with change. While traditional industry has declined, the product mix and sectoral composition of industry have been resistant to change. In short, the region has not enjoyed the benefits of regional growth dynamics driven by entrepreneurial firms. The fault is not lack of industrial policy initiatives. Few regions have had more expansive industrial policies of the conventional, capital-subsidizing form. Nor have research centers and graduate programs

[12] The choice of regions is based on the author's familiarity with each.

been neglected. Nevertheless productivity levels are stubbornly low and both innovation and growth have been disappointing. To better understand why, the region's business model, production system, and skill formation processes are examined from the capabilities and innovation perspective.

Chapter 8 draws out the industrial policy challenges and opportunities from the capabilities and innovation perspective. Industrial policy is only as good as the economic perspective that informs it. The emphasis of the capabilities and innovation perspective is on capability development rather than capital accumulation as the force behind higher productivity levels. Once industrial policy is conceptualized as capability building a new policy terrain opens up. Getting the growth 'fundamentals' right focuses attention on fostering and integrating processes of new firm creation, open systems networking, production capability development, technology management, technological transition, and skill formation. A central claim is that technology management is a powerful tool for growth of firms, regions, and nations at every level of industrial development. Success, however, depends upon corresponding principles of production and organization being in place.

Since the publication of Rachel Carson's *The Silent Spring* in 1962, we have been warned that the failure to account for the environmental impact of products and processes could unleash powerful forces that put ecological life-support systems at risk. However, the pursuit of environment goals has often lost out in public debate. The argument in Chapter 9 is that the terms of the debate have been biased by the assumption of an environment or growth tradeoff: ecological preservation, the assumption holds, comes at the cost of slower economic growth. The theme of the chapter is that technology management can play a major role in fostering economic growth and a healthy environment. The capabilities and innovation perspective is shown to cast light on public policy and business strategy considerations hidden or ignored by the tradeoff assumption.

CHAPTER

2

Production Systems

THE IDEA OF TECHNOLOGY MANAGEMENT

Suddenly, and unexpectedly, in the early 1970s the annual rate of productivity increase in the American economy dropped from the 3 percent level that had persisted for much of the post-war period to 1 percent. The productivity slowdown persisted for nearly two decades. The slowdown was dubbed the 'productivity paradox' because it coincided with a period of rapid technological progress associated with the diffusion of the computer. Slow growth and the failure of firms investing in R&D to generate new product revenue streams led to the dismantling and/or downsizing of corporate laboratories. Noting the cutbacks in both corporate and federal funding of long-range fundamental research led many to argue that America was failing to maintain the research foundation that has supported its competitive advantage in new technologies and high-tech industries. Predictions of a hollowing out of American industry were commonplace.

Instead, the 1990s witnessed a resurgence of industrial growth and productivity. Why the productivity slowdown and why the resurgence? Is technology the explanation? If so, what are the links between technology and growth? Why, for example, the resurgence in growth following the downsizing of both corporate R&D laboratories and post–Cold War cutbacks in federal funding of R&D?

Both formal economic theory and textbook economics have little to offer on the subject of technology (Lipsey 1993; Nelson 1998). Technology is not ignored, particularly in growth theory, but as a concept, technology lacks substantive meaning. Why, when everyone agrees that technology must be important in understanding productivity and growth, does it appear as such a shadowy figure in economic theory and textbooks?

The reason, in part, is that technology by implicit assumption is applied science. Technology is a shadow to science, the main character. Technological change is assumed to be a consequence of advances in scientific research. As a dependent variable, technological change has no explanatory power.[1]

The beauty of the assumption is its simplicity for policy prescription: funding science leads to technological breakthroughs, innovation, new products, and growth. It also simplifies growth theory. The assumption of a linear sequence from science to technology to production bypasses the complex set of analytical and empirical relationships between science and technology, the role of business organization in mediating technological advance and product development, and links between applied, developmental, and basic technological research. But embracing the 'science-push' assumption comes at a cost: the presumed relationship not only obscures the real world relationships but misrepresents them.

The science-push image of technology, fortunately, has a rival. The alternative is an image of science and technology as two largely independent, if parallel, activities. A host of empirical studies conclude that technological advance builds on past technology and science builds on past science.[2] This is not surprising if David Billington's aphorism is considered: 'Engineering or technology is the making of things that did not previously exist, whereas science is the discovering of things that have long existed' (1983: 9).

The rival image creates space for developing an economic concept of technology that cannot be mapped from advances in scientific research. To date, the focus of most technology and growth research in the United States has presupposed the technology-as-shadow image and associ-

[1] A related explanation of why technology has not been integrated into economic theory is that concepts, such as technology, that are required for a dynamic theory of the firm undermine the assumptions required for allocative efficiency theorems of neoclassical economics (Best 1990: ch. 4). Nelson argues that the research agenda of both neoclassical and the new growth theory 'hold the modeling as close as possible to the canons of general equilibrium theory' (1998: 499).

[2] Sherwin and Isenson's (1967) study of post–World War II technological inventions claims that only 0.3% can be traced to scientific discoveries. See also Layton (1971), Mulkay (1979), Kline (1985, 1991), and N. Rosenberg (1992).

ated linear sequence beginning with scientific R&D driving innovation and productivity gains (Nelson 1998). This is understandable; the United States has unique scientific R&D capabilities. But if the rival image of technology is closer to the mark, it calls for a better understanding of the relations among technological research, production capabilities (such as new product development), and business and industrial organization. This is the domain of technology management.

For technology latecomer nations, technology management and technology policy are central concerns. Technology latecomers can potentially achieve faster growth rates than the technology trailblazers by tapping the world's pool of proven technologies. But, perhaps surprisingly, the domain of technology management is also important to understanding the resurgence of American industry.

Five heuristic case studies are presented to explore the idea of technology management from a production perspective. The cases highlight the production-embedded character of technology management. The method of analysis is to explore technology management from the context of major innovations in production principles and associated organizational capabilities. It develops and anchors the technology capability side of the technology/market dynamic that drives the entrepreneurial firm (see Chapter 3).

An implication is that technology management can be a lever of growth for firms and regions if the requisite principles of production, models of business organization, and skills are in place. Otherwise, no amount of investment in R&D or technology transfer or commitment to technology policy will impact on growth.

The challenge of technology management in leading industrial regions today is to develop the organizational capability to combine and recombine new and existing technologies with production in the pursuit of rapid new product and new industry development. The challenge to firms in technology follower regions is to develop technology management capabilities that build on and enhance their competitive advantage. This does not mean a one-off introduction of a new technology or 'turnkey' plants but the development of technology management capabilities.

But introducing technology management into economic analysis presents a challenge as well. We must embed it in an analysis of production. The five production system models developed in this chapter are summarized in Table 2.1. The rationale underlying the table is as follows. Each production system is defined in terms of one of three principles of production: interchangeability, flow, or systems integration (column 4).[3] The original application (column 2) of each principle in history enabled a new competitive advantage based on an order of magnitude increase in performance standards (column 3).

The historical example in column 2 is used to illustrate the principle. But the principle, once established, offers a vision to advance productivity by restructuring production independently of place and time. Each principle can be distinguished in terms of its application (column 5). The transition to higher production principles enables the firm to implement advanced production capabilities (column 6).

Technology management capability (column 7) is increasingly integrated into ongoing production operations as production systems advance (column 1). The final column links the production system to complementary forms of inter-firm or industrial organization.

The production system framework summarized in Table 2.1 illustrates a simple business policy idea: competitive strategy and production system are bound together. Any effort by business managers to advance performance outcomes that do not put in place the requisite production capabilities will not be able to compete against firms that have done so. Competing on the basis of rapid new product development, as we shall show, without having a production system in which manufacturing and design are integrated, will only produce frustration. Competitors that have integrated design and manufacturing will be equipped to introduce new technologies smoothly in support of new product concepts on a regular basis.

Replacing the implicit assumption that technology is applied science does not simplify either theory building or policymaking. It does, however, liberate our conception of economic growth processes to take into account technology, business organization, and skill formation. This will go some distance to replacing the 'paradoxes' and 'miracles' with explanations of rapid or otherwise unexplainable growth experiences.

The story of technology management and industrial transitions begins in America. In 1800, America was an industrial hinterland without indigenous manufacturing capabilities. A half-century later the leading British engineers were heralding the 'American System of Manufacturing' as an advance over British arms production and machine

[3] For example, the principle of flow can be applied to single products, as in the case of Ford; extended to multiple products on the same assembly line, as in the case of the Toyota production system; or, extended to encompass new product development, as in the case of Canon. Each of these applications, shown in column 5, is expressed in an advance in production capabilities identified in column 6.

Table 2.1. Production system models

(1) Production systems	(2) Exemplar	(3) Performance breakthrough	(4) Production principle	(5) Application	(6) Production capability advance	(7) Technology management vehicle[a]	(8) Inter-firm organization
PS 1	Armory	standardization	interchangeability	product parts	product engineering	specialist machine	open networks
PS 2	Ford	cost (economies of time)	flow	single product	throughput efficiency (synchronization)	exogenous (R&D lab pipeline)	market or vertical integration
PS 3	Toyota	flexibility and quality (inventory turnover)	flow	multiple products	incremental innovation (cellular manufacture)	process innovation (shopfloor incremental) AR	closed network
PS 4	Canon	new product cycle time	flow	new products, technology adoption	new product development	applied R&D (design + manufacture) DR + AR	closed network
PS 5	Intel	new technology cycle time	systems integration	technology innovation (multiple technologies)	new technology development	technology integration teams (R&D + manufacture) BR + DR	open networks

[a] AR = applied research; BR = basic research; DR = developmental research; R&D = research and development

making. In five decades America made the transition from a nation of farmers to a metalworking power that set the world standard for production capability and, in many cases, manufacturing innovation capability. To understand the transformation it is necessary to look beyond the textile industry, in which America was largely imitative, to the machine tool industry. It was here that a new model of technology management was emerging that would engender entirely new production capabilities and establish a competitive advantage across a range of industries.

THE AMERICAN SYSTEM AND INTERCHANGEABILITY

Surprisingly, the timeless principles of mass production are not widely understood in many parts of the world either by academics or practitioners. The first principle, interchangeability of parts, was established nearly a century before mass production became a hallmark of industrialization. The American System of Manufacturing, as the British labeled it, was based on interchangeability. Developed at the Springfield Armory in Springfield, Massachusetts in the early 1800s, interchangeability revolutionized production (Hounshell 1984; Rosenberg 1976; M. Smith 1970; Tull 2000). The concept of interchangeability is as relevant today as ever. Before interchangeability each drawer in a desk was hand-sanded and hand-fit, each firing pin on a rifle was hand-filed. Without interchangeability armies would still need to include a regiment of hand-fitters to repair arms and furniture manufacturers a department of hand-sanders to individually fit pieces. The idea is simple, but it is rarely deployed in Third World factories today.[4]

Designing a production system around the principle of interchangeability was, at the same time, the origins of technology management. A range of specialist machines had to be designed and built to convert the principle into practice. Product engineering emerged as a set of standard procedures, an organizational capability, and an occupational category to specify, identify, design, make, set up, modify, adopt, refine, and operate efficiently the requisite machines. The rudiments of process engineering also appeared as methods were established to lay out, interface, standardize, measure, operate, and trouble-shoot machining activities along a production line. The elements of a production

[4] For a case study and application to Jamaica, see Best and Forrant (1994).

management system were taking shape. Technology management was no longer a one-off affair in which a machine with superior performance capacity was introduced; instead, it was becoming an ongoing organizational capability of industrial enterprises.

Product engineering means first, deconstructing a product into its constituent pieces. Second, reorganizing the flow of material according to the logical sequence of operational activities for manufacturing the piece. Third, analyzing each operation for simplification by identifying, modifying, and designing machinery. Fourth, networking with machine tool companies to make, modify, and maintain machines, tools, and streamline processes.

The stock of a gun at the Springfield Armory was subjected to a product engineering exercise. To eliminate hand-sanding, and the need for craft-skilled woodworkers, a bank of fourteen specialist lathes were designed, built, and integrated into a production line. The performance of each machining operation, tended by a machine operator, was measured by precision gauges and compared with formal specifications. Failure meant adjustments to the machine and/or operator tasks.

In early industrial New England, an inter-firm technology management dynamic was set in motion between specialist machine users and makers. Incremental and radical innovations in the machine tool industry were both induced by machine users and fed back to increase productivity in production.[5] The system was not centrally managed. It was self-organizing with powerful, timely, boosts from orders and services provided by the Springfield Armory.[6] But without the development of a set of (informal) management practices known as product engineering for guiding the design and development of machines, it likely would not have been self-sustaining.

Inadvertently, New England became the site of a regional technology management capability. The world's first precision machine tool industry, created in the wake of applying interchangeability, facilitated the integration and mutual development of production and technology. But it also diffused the new principle to the whole region and other parts of the country and, by so doing, created a vehicle for transferring technology across sectors (N. Rosenberg 1996).

[5] For examples of both types of innovation and references to original sources, see Best and Forrant (1996*a*) and Forrant (1994).

[6] The district model of industrial organization is associated with networking as distinct from pure market or hierarchy as a mode of coordination of economic activity (Becattini 1978; Best 1990; Brusco 1982; Marshall 1920; Piore and Sabel 1984). Networking suggests long-term, consultative relationships which facilitate investment in design and R&D.

While the makers and users of the specialist machines were independent firms, they were fueled by a regional innovation process which, in turn, was anchored in a community of workers and practical engineers skilled in the development, use, and improvement of the new technologies. Inspectors from the Armory traveled the region identifying improvements in machines and methods that were introduced into the Armory. The Armory's open-door policy, in turn, was abundantly used as a source of patterns and castings by machine shops. To facilitate the 'collective innovation' and diffusion processes, Colonel Roswell Lee and his attorneys fashioned a patent policy that limited the claims of inventors but engendered continuous improvement and regional innovation. After a series of patent battles, the courts decided in the 1820s that any new tools developed while producing contract arms were to be available for use by both the national armories and private contractors. As a consequence few inventions associated with the rise of interchangeable manufacturing were patented. In the words of Bruce Tull: 'the lack of patent protection, along with regular communication between armories, ensured rapid diffusion, adoption, and further incremental improvements of the newly emergent technologies' (2000: 88).

New skills also played a critical role. While the idea of product engineering was not always formalized into standard operating procedures, without the emergence of a set of tools and skills associated with blueprint reading, metallurgy, geometry, and trigonometry the machine-making sector would not have flourished. It did and with it the management of technology became an organizational capability. Often as not, technology management as a capability was embedded in the tacit knowledge and skills of workers who learned product engineering without ever knowing it was an organizational accomplishment that introduced a whole new world of production potential over its craft predecessor.

The latent production potential of the new system was revealed in the first year of the Civil War. In 1862 the Springfield Armory produced over 102,000 arms, nearly a tenfold increase from 1861 (Tull 2000: 201). In the process the Armory was a powerful agent of technology diffusion as the new production system was driven through a vast supplier network. Tull states:

> If there was still any question on how to produce precision components in the North, the Civil War was a period of massive diffusion of 'armory practice'. Hundreds of firms subcontracted to produce either complete arms or components, and the Armory continued its practice of openly sharing its machinery

patterns with virtually every contractor, subcontractor or machine builder in the northern states. (164)

The centrality of networking and technology diffusion to the growth process was also established in early industrial New England. The practice of technology management was not found in textbooks or management training courses; instead, it was embedded in the dynamic relationships between machine makers and users and in the skills of the labor force. The elements of product engineering, a machine tool sector, and a skilled labor force provided the method and means for the region to make the transition from an industry organized according to the principle of craft to one organized according to interchangeability.[7]

Application of the production principle of interchangeability led to the redefinition of a whole range of products and created new industrial sectors.[8] In its wake, New England enjoyed a rapid rate of industrial growth. It demonstrates that production organization can be the source of competitive advantage.

HENRY FORD AND SINGLE-PRODUCT FLOW

Henry Ford wrote: 'In mass production there are no fitters' (1926: 40). The implied emphasis on interchangeability does not describe what was novel about Ford's plants. Henry Ford's plants were organized according to the principle of flow. The point is captured by one of Ford's most successful students, Taiichi Ohno, creator of the Toyota just-in-time (JIT) system:

> By tracing the conception and evolution of work flow by Ford and his associates, I think their true intention was to extend a work [read 'material'] flow from the final assembly line to all other processes. . . . By setting up a flow connecting not only the final assembly line but all the processes, one reduces production lead time. Perhaps Ford envisioned such a situation when he used the word 'synchronization'. (1988: 100)

Ohno identifies the single term that captures the revolution at Ford Motor company even though it does not, I believe, appear in Ford's published writings. It was not interchangeability, as stated by Ford, the moving assembly line, or economies of size, but synchronization. It is

[7] The lack of a craft tradition meant less resistance to the new principle of production than in gun-making regions of England.

[8] See Best (1990: ch. 1).

captured in the words of Charles Sorensen, Ford's chief engineer: 'It was . . . complete *synchronization* that accounted for the difference between an ordinary assembly line and a mass production one' (1957).

Sorensen uses the term in a more expansive description of the Model T where all the 'links in the chain' were first connected at the Highland Park plant in August 1913:

> Each part was attached to the moving chassis in order, from axles at the beginning to bodies at the end of the line. Some parts took longer to attach than others; so, to keep an even pull on the towrope, there must be differently spaced intervals between the delivery of the parts along the line. This called for patient *timing* and rearrangement until the flow of parts and the speed and intervals along the assembly line meshed into a perfectly *synchronized* operation throughout all stages of production. (1957: 130–1, emphasis added)

Sorensen finishes the paragraph with the phrase: 'a new era in industrial history had begun'. Few would deny this conclusion. But, ironically, most explanations do not capture the fundamental challenge that ushered in the new vision of production and thereby the real difference between the old and the new approach to production as articulated by Sorensen.

The production organizing concept for Ford and his engineers was timing. The challenge was to regulate material flow so that just the right amount of each part would arrive at just the right time. In Ford's words: 'The traffic and production departments must work closely together to see that all the proper parts reach the branches at the *same time*—the shortage of a single kind of bolt would hold up the whole assembly at a branch' (1926: 117, emphasis added). Making one part too few slowed the flow; making one part too many produced waste in the form of inventory and Ford was vigilant against the 'danger of becoming overstocked' (117).

Sorensen referred to the process as 'progressive mechanical work' which reached its pinnacle with the introduction of the V-8 engine at the River Rouge plant in 1932:

> All materials entering the Ford plant went into operation and stayed there. They never came to rest until they had become part of a unit like an engine, an axle, or a body. Then they moved on to final assembly or into a freight car for branch assembly, and finally to the customer. It was a glorious period; a production man's dream come true. (1957: 231)

The vision of a flow line concentrated the attention of engineers on barriers to throughput. A barrier, or bottleneck, occurred wherever a machining operation could not process material at the same pace as the previous operation. The bottleneck machine was the activity that constrained not only the throughput at that machine but of the production system as a whole. Increasing the pace of work on any other machining activity could not increase output, only inventory.

Henry Ford's assembly lines can be seen in this light. It was not the speed of the line that was revolutionary in *concept*; it was the idea of synchronizing production activities so that bottlenecks did not constrain the whole production system. Unfortunately, all too often the basis of mass production was mistakenly defined in terms of economies of size when it was really synchronized production that drove the rate of throughput up and the per unit costs down.[9] Flow requires synchronization which, in turn, requires system integration.

Sorensen's assistant superintendent on the first assembly line was Clarence Avery. Avery spent a total of eight months working in every production department. In Sorensen's words: 'Beginning at the bottom in each department, he did all the physical work necessary to understand its operations, then moved on to the next' (1957: 130). Avery then moved into Sorensen's office and elaborated the whole system:

> With firsthand familiarity with each step in each parts department, Avery worked out the *timing* schedules necessary before installation of conveyor assembly systems to motors, fenders, magnetos, and transmissions. One by one these operations were *revamped* and continuously moving conveyers delivered the assembled parts to the final assembly floor. (130, emphasis added)

Linking up an assembly line was a final step and one that, by itself, had no direct impact on throughput time.[10] A conveyor line is a physical linkage system that integrates all of the requisite machining and other operations required to convert material into finished product. Before a conveyor can be connected operations must be 'revamped' one by one to equalize the cycle time for each constituent operation. A cycle time is the time it takes to complete a single operation, usually on a single piece-part. Ohno argues that Ford's engineers did not go the whole way: they did not equalize cycle times for *one-piece flow* (see next

[9] A prime example is Lenin's admiration of Henry Ford and Frederick Taylor which, based on the mistaken view that mass production was about economies of size, figured in the identification of modernism with giant factories throughout the Soviet Union and Eastern Europe (T. Hughes 1989; Robin Murray, unpublished paper, Sussex University).

[10] The rate of material flow was not determined by the pace of the conveyor line. Instead, the speed of the conveyor line was adjusted to the pace of material flow. The pace of material flow depends upon the slowest cycle time in the whole production process. Otherwise timing would be thrown off.

section). But they did balance material flow so that the right parts would arrive at the right place at the right time.[11]

The principle of flow yields a simple rule to concentrate the attention of engineers: equalize cycle times. Optimally, every operation on every part would match the standardized cycle time, the regulator of the pace of production flow. Failure to synchronize appears as inventory build-up in front of the slower operation. Any activity that takes more time does not meet the condition and requires engineering attention. The way to increase the flow of material is not to speed the pace of the conveyor belt but to identify the bottleneck, or slowest cycle time, and develop an action plan to eliminate it.

Ford's assembly line, from the perspective of flow, was primarily a signaling device or a visual information system for continuous advance in throughput performance. It established a standard cycle time. The engineering task was to revamp each operation into conformity with the standard cycle time.[12] Every time a bottleneck was removed, productivity and throughput advanced.

The visual signaling feature of inventory in the system was not obvious or perhaps even understood before it was implemented. Ford attacked inventory because it was waste and waste added to costs. But without a near-zero inventory system, the signaling function of the conveyor line would be knocked out. With the near-zero inventory system, the work assignments of engineers were signaled by material build up on the line. They were prioritized without central direction. Ford approved; this meant less indirect labor which, for Ford, was another form of waste.

Scheduling, too, was decentralized in Ford's system. The idea that Ford's system could indeed operate without chaos would have seemed, understandably, far-fetched. At an output rate of 8,000 cars per day, production of the Model A, with 6,000 distinct parts, involved 48 million parts in motion. A huge planning and scheduling department would seem to be necessary. But instead of chaos, Ford's plants were orderly. Schedules were met and order was achieved by the application of the synchronization rule: equalize cycle times. Once the system was in sync,

[11] Some of Ford's heavy machinery stamped in lot sizes of greater than one. This meant that inventory crept into the system as piece-parts were pulled into assembly one at a time. The output of all machines was regulated by the standard cycle time but cycle time was not equated for the fabrication of each piece-part. In this, Ford's plants were single-product but not single-piece flow. This point is elaborated in the next section.

[12] Equal cycle times does not mean each machine is operating at the same pace but that just the right amount of parts for each car are made in each time cycle.

increasing the speed of the line, the operational efficiency of individual machines, or the intensity of work could not produce more cars.

Production rates could be increased in two ways: reduce the cycle time of the slowest operation (successive elimination of bottlenecks) and driving down the standardized cycle time. To this day production managers would not believe that the Ford system would work if, in the meantime, the Japanese had not demonstrated it. This is why it is known by the Japanese term: *kanban*. A failure to understand Ford's assembly line as a visual scheduling device, backed by standardized cycle times, is what led American volume producers to build huge, centralized planning and scheduling departments. Their efforts have demonstrated that no amount of information technology can avoid bottlenecks in such systems.[13]

Like interchangeability, the principle of flow is simple but implementation demanded a revolution in the organization of production and the management of technology. Ford simplified the organizational challenge, including coordination, by constraining the production system to one product. The technological challenge was considerable. Equalizing cycle times for even a single product was a monumental achievement. Equalizing cycle time for more than one product was inconceivable without organizational innovations that go well beyond Ford's system. In fact, the conveyor line itself precludes multi-product flow (see next section).

Synchronization and the equal cycle time concept necessitate two technology management activities both for Ford and for today. First, adjustments are required in operational activities to meet the synchronization constraint. Ford could not simply purchase machines 'in the market' even if a market existed for high-volume machines. Achieving the narrow time and timing specifications required by the principle of flow involved Ford engineers in continuously 'revamping', searching for new technologies, adjusting, re-gearing, retooling, fitting new jigs and fixtures, and redesigning machines and plant layout. This was a never-ending process for Ford, as it is for practitioners of the management philosophy of continuous improvement today.

Second, the pursuit of new technologies is to reduce the standard cycle time. Ford attacked the standard cycle time by addressing generic

[13] Ironically, the Ford production system was self-regulating much like a perfectly competitive market system in economic theory. Instead of prices as the adjustment mechanism, surpluses and shortages of inventory set in motion corrective forces; instead of the 'invisible hand' the reaction agent was the engineer re-establishing equal cycle times.

technologies that impacted on all machines. One example is power. Before Ford, most manufacturing plants were powered by centralized power systems and machines were linked to the source of power by lines and shafts.[14] The synchronization rule would have no meaning in such a system. Ford innovated. He substituted wires.[15] And he built his own power system.

The River Rouge plant was fueled by powdered and gasified coal that powered steam turbines designed and built by Ford and his team. Immediately obvious was the impressive 90 percent efficiency rate in conversion of energy consumed to electricity and functional heat. The Rankine (Carnot efficiency) barrier restricted thermal efficiencies of purchased electricity from centralized power stations from surpassing 35 percent. Ford's generators included a number of innovations: they were a third less in size than turbines then available, the first to use all-mica insulation, and relied upon a 'radically' different system of ventilation.[16]

Why did Ford pursue innovation in electric power generation? Part of the answer is that the cost of power determined the location of plant (Ford 1926: 116). More important, implementation of the principle of flow depended upon and was intertwined with technological innovations in electric power. Flow applied to car production is impossible without the electric motor: the [unit drive] electric motor meant that plant layout and machine location could be freed from the dictates of a central power system and the associated shafts and belts. Power, for the first time, could be distributed to individual machines and machinery could be arranged on the factory floor according to the logic of product engineering and the material conversion process.

Ford's innovation in electricity supply enabled his engineers to organize the plant according to the logic of material flow; competitors departmentalized factories according to machining activity. For Ford, the independently powered machines went to the material; for his competitors, material went to the machine and the machine was located by the power system.

[14] See Devine (1983). I have drawn heavily on Devine's work in this section.

[15] Belts and shafts cluttered the factory and precluded machine layout according to the logic of the process. In theory, cycle times could be equalized in such a plant but the challenge of adjusting gearing ratios and machine speeds would have created gridlock with the clutter of power transmission devices.

[16] Ford gives an insight into an important secret to his success and a key aspect of technology management in reference to his coal gasification system. 'The processes are well known—most of our processes are well known. It is the combination of processes that counts' (1926: 172).

Flow meant redesigning machines to incorporate unit drive motors. While electrical power had become commonplace in factories in the first decades of the twentieth century, its delivery system was unchanged. A 1928 textbook indicates only a 'trend toward incorporating the motor as an integral part of the machine tool' even though the concept had been understood since the turn of the century (Devine 1983: 369).

Why the slow growth in distributed electrical drive systems? Answer: the limited diffusion of the principle of flow. The fusion of the electric motor with machines offered enormous potential to expand productivity but only with a prior commitment to a radical reorganization of the factory. Ford systematically pursued innovations in processes, procedures, machines, and factory layout to exploit the productivity potential of the principle of flow. The electric motor was a tool in the process.[17] Technological change in electric power awaited organizational change. Unit drive, in turn, created unforeseen opportunities in advancing productivity when integrated with production redesign.[18]

In short, technology management for Ford meant integrating technology and production in pursuit of the principle of single-product flow. While followers of Ford could take advantage of innovations developed by technological leaders, the synchronization requirement will always demand a technology management capability.

With hindsight, Ford, from the perspective of technology management, is a story of both productivity leaps and limits. The challenge of high throughput forced Ford's engineers to integrate a range of technologies, apply new ones, and continuously adapt others to facilitate flow. At the same time the organizational practices associated with single-product flow place limits on other forms of technological advance and erect constraints to the introduction of new technologies. Toyota, not General Motors, exposed the limits of single-product flow.[19]

Like interchangeability, the concept of synchronization is simple but implementation demanded a revolution in the organization of production and the management of technology. This was so even though Ford simplified the coordination problem by constraining the production system to one basic product and even though Ford's engineers did not

[17] Ford's earlier experience as chief of engineering at Detroit Illuminating served him well.

[18] For a more extensive treatment of the relationships between energy and manufacturing processes, see Best (1997*b*).

[19] General Motors moved from the organizing concept of material flow, developed by Ford, to that of functional departmentalization and the concept of 'economic order quantity'. In terms of throughput efficiency, GM was a step backwards; they did multiple products without multiple-product flow (Best 1990: 151).

go the whole way (the cycle times were not equalized for all fabrication activities).[20]

Ford's revolution was practical; the principle of flow was not conceptualized into a theory of production. Cycle times on the final assembly line regulated flow and established timing targets. But the Ford system was not a pure JIT system for reasons explored in the next section.[21] The completion of Ford's system was limited by the failure to conceptualize the principle of flow.[22]

Again, as in interchangeability, the refinement in both concept and application was a multi-decade affair. The concept of flow penetrated into management thought and, less often, practices, in the early 1990s masquerading as 're-engineering' and 'lean production'.

A final word. Ford, unlike American industrial followers, had no interest in measuring labor productivity, conducting time and motion studies, or devising piece-rate systems. The rate of production depended on throughput efficiency and associated cycle times. Ford increased the rate of production by technology management: bottlenecks were eliminated and standardized cycle times were driven down. Unfortunately, the principle of flow was not written into industrial engineering manuals which, instead, adopted the 'scientific management' paradigm. Less surprising was the complementary practice in economic research of focusing on capital and labor to the exclusion of production and organizational issues. Both obscured the sources of productivity gains in America's most celebrated production system for roughly a half-century after Ford's engineers first applied the principle of flow. Toyota forced the issue back onto the manufacturing agenda by extending the principle of flow to multiple products.[23]

[20] Ford seemed to worship his original product design. Sorensen writes: 'In all the years with Model T no one worried or bothered Mr. Ford with design changes, and it was hard to be told he should adopt something else for the Model A' (1957: 224). Ford adamantly refused to modify even the brakes although the Model T was banned in Germany and at risk from newly emerging state safety boards in the United States (Williams, Haslam, and Williams 1992).

[21] For example, some of Ford's machines processed more than one piece-part at a time which meant that inventory crept into the system and all material was not kept in motion. The point is not that such inventories were uneconomic, but that they were not deemed a challenge to be addressed as in the Toyota Production System.

[22] Ford rules were to keep material in motion and to eliminate waste. These rules produced the effect of equal cycle times without the concept. The tendency of perfect markets to produce the allocative efficiency rule of P = MC is an analogy from neoclassical economic theory. Producers' actions are consistent with the rule even though their actions are guided by maximizing profits and not allocative efficiency.

[23] As noted, neither the principle of flow nor system was widely diffused in American business until the 1990s. Deming often remarked that what he took to Japan was the 'theory of the

TOYOTA AND MULTI-PRODUCT FLOW

When Toyota developed JIT, engineers were not aware that they were triggering a sequence of organizational innovations in production that would create the conditions for a new trajectory of industrial growth. They were just in time.

Japan had wrung the growth out of the early post-war trajectory driven by labor-intensive and raw-material-intensive products, processes, and sectors. The high growth rate of the old trajectory had undermined its own preconditions: wages were driven up and imported raw material inputs were constraining critical industries such as steel. Equally important, Japanese success was not lost on business enterprises in nearby nations with lower wages and indigenous raw materials and aspirations to develop the same industries. Sustained growth, for Japan, depended upon the establishment of more complex production products, processes, and sectors.

The new production system known variously as just-in-time (JIT), the Toyota Production System, and lean production was not the consequence of large investments in capital. Nor was it about the introduction of new hardware-related technologies or lower cost production methods. But it was an organizational prerequisite to both. The new system was based on the development, application, and diffusion of new principles of production and organizational capabilities that enabled Japanese manufacturing enterprises to compete on more comprehensive performance standards combining cost, quality, time, and flexibility. The new performance standards put industrial enterprises and regions throughout the world on notice, much as Henry Ford had done a half century before: failure to adapt to, or counter, the new production system would lead to industrial decline.

The central organizing concept of Toyota can be described as multi-product flow. The major difference with Ford, and it is a major one, is that Toyota was not constrained to one product. Toyota applied the principle of flow to a range of products: different models go down the same line. For Henry Ford, this idea was an anathema: the timing task would have been overwhelming as the product range proliferated. It would have implied an unacceptable compromise to the production

system' (1982; personal conversations). He meant, in part, that much of American business enterprise was organized into profit centers and the associated logic of local optimization; the Japanese management system came to embody the idea of managing interrelationships or interfaces across business activities, hence the idea of process integration or global optimization.

goals of minimal throughput time and of low inventory targets. Finally, it would have meant de-linking the conveyor lines and all this implied for labor discipline.

Nevertheless, Toyota, the JIT standard setter, achieved an inventory turn (ratio of sales divided by work-in-process) approaching 300. It is unlikely that Ford ever achieved above 200 and was probably considerably below. When General Motors began to measure work-in-process turns the rate was in the neighborhood of six to eight.[24]

Toyota took Ford's challenge of synchronization two steps beyond Ford. The first step, as noted, was to introduce multi-product flow. The second was more fundamental: equalization of the cycle times for every part. Taiichi Ohno, who is to JIT what Ford was to mass production, describes the difference between Ford and Toyota in the following words: 'where the Ford system sticks to the idea of making a quantity of the same item at one time, the Toyota system synchronizes production of each unit. . . . Even at the stage of making parts, production is carried out one piece at a time' (1988: 96).

Thus, Ford did not achieve complete synchronization.[25] This would require one-piece flow or transfer lot sizes of one throughout the production system. But in certain fabrication stages, Ford's shops produced in large lot sizes. Lot sizes of more than one entail inventory if a single car absorbs less than the lot size. In these cases the process was fragmented into separated operations with the resulting interruption in flow and throughput inefficiencies.

The reasons that Ford did not produce each of the 6,000 distinct parts in the same cycle time are not hard to understand. Engineers can direct the practice of equalizing cycle times, but it is best accomplished by a management system in which workers take on a quasi-technology management role. This necessitated a revolution in management philosophy. Consideration of such a move was completely alien to Ford.

[24] The low inventory turn ratio for GM is because GM did not take on board the challenge of equalizing cycle times. Product flow was deeply congested by the mass batch system in which plant layout was organized by machine function. Instead of sequencing machines in the order dictated by the sequence of operations required to make a part, they were grouped by machining function. Material moved back and forth from department to department in large 'optimized' batches. Inventory adjustments were used in lieu of synchronization even at the final assembly line. Plant layout by machine function was common in US plants, hence the big impact of 're-engineering' which represented a return to flow principles. Ironically, functional departmentalization was consistent with 'scientific management' and Taylorism but not with Ford and flow.

[25] As noted, Ford's engineers aggressively attacked inventory waste and clearly saw it as an interruption to flow. But they did not make the next step to equalize cycle times for every single piece-part. A stamping machine, for example, may stamp 100 pieces at a time. This meant that all pieces would not be in motion; some would be waiting.

The work organization ideally suited to the challenge of multi-product flow is cellular manufacturing. The idea harks back to the concept of group technology in which work 'cells' are organized by the logic of the product. The reason? Multi-product flow requires equalizing cycle times and the flexibility to have different, but equal cycle times. This enables the product mix to be varied in response to demand shifts. While cycle times vary according to the product, they are the same for each specific product.

Flexibility comes from first, being able to adjust the number of workers in a cell; second, quick set-up and changeover designed machines; and third, multi-skilled workers. Each worker must operate not one machine, but three or four machines, and also do set-ups (and maintenance activities) on the machines. What was revolutionary at Toyota was not just-in-time production but the idea of single-minute exchange of die (SMED). To produce multiple products on the same line, it is necessary to make the machines capable of being programmable (mechanically or electronically) for different products. The challenge at Toyota was to go beyond multiple products on the same line to the idea of multiple products on the same line in batch sizes of one. This meant the worker had to be able to set up the machine and, in certain circumstances, set up several machines.

By establishing cellular production, Toyota was able to achieve the same high performance standards in terms of equal cycle time as Henry Ford, but with multiple products.[26] Machines, as along Ford's assembly line, are laid out and reconfigured according to the dictates of the routing sheet or flow chart but in U-cells and without a conveyor line.[27]

The new management paradigm makes possible the organizational capability of continuous, incremental innovation in the form of an

[26] The benefits of the Toyota production system do not stop with shorter production lead times. Mass batch production methods are extremely costly in finance because of low working capital productivity. JIT plants require much less inventory and indirect labor per car. See Abegglen and Stalk (1985) and Cusumano (1985) for comparative measures of indirect to direct labor and inventory per car.

[27] Group technology developed in England in the 1950s by, among others, John Burbidge was a forerunner of cellular manufacturing. Ironically, the concept was probably developed first in the Soviet Union in the 1930s even though it was never used in the Soviet Union to achieve high throughput efficiency (probably because it reeked of capital productivity, an oxymoron to Marxian ideology and Soviet thinking). Burbidge believed that group technology was applied successfully in at least eleven UK engineering plants in the 1950s and 1960s. Preliminary research, based primarily on conversations with Burbidge, suggests that the experiments were successful but did not survive the transition to finance-dominated management and the merger activities of the 1970s. Burbidge himself, a brilliant engineer who authored several books on production, did not integrate the principles of production with those of organization. Here we have to wait for Taiichi Ohno and the Toyota Production System for the first systematic treatment.

accumulation of thousands of tiny improvements and an unrivaled persistence to production detail built into the organization of production. The plan-do-check-act management paradigm of W. Edwards Deming was an organizational corollary to the principle of multi-product flow. While Deming's focus was not on innovation but on continuous improvement of product and process, his approach to integrating thinking and doing on the shopfloor introduced a new dimension to the management of technology.

For Deming, the discovery of knowledge is not the preserve of science just as thinking is not the preserve of management; the business challenge became to build the discovery process into every level and activity of the organization. For example, the workers involved can discover knowledge about the causes of product defects if the organization is properly designed. The purpose of statistical process control was not only to distinguish systemic from special causes of defects but also to focus attention on improvement of the organization as the means to advance quality and productivity. The idea was to design quality into the system, not inspect it into the product. This required innovation capability on the shopfloor. It created whole new possibilities for decentralized technology management that will take us beyond Toyota.

Multi-product flow is the mirror image of a new organizational principle which appears in a range of variants and goes under the popular names of continuous improvement, TQM (total quality management), *kaizen*, small group activity, and self-directed work teams.[28] Deming considered each of these management practices to be aspects of the 'theory of system' which, for him, meant replacing the hierarchical, up/down, vertical information flows and functional departmentalization with cross-functional relations, and horizontal, interactive information flows of process integration.[29]

The new principles of production (multi-product flow) and corollary organizational capability (*kaizen*) are interdependent and self-reinforcing; neither can be successfully applied without the other. Successful implementation, however, depended upon a prior or simultaneous development of specific organizational capabilities and investments in the skills required to apply and convert the new production

[28] Each of these management orientations are secondary to the fundamental principle of systems integration (see below).

[29] Deming inspired managers to focus on the management of interrelationships as well as the plan-do-check-act (PDCA) paradigm of total quality management. The idea of system or process integration spread from the material conversion process in the factory to the business enterprise which became understood, not as a collection of profit centers but as an integrated set of interrelated processes such as material flow, order fulfillment, new product development.

principle into production capabilities and pursue the new technological opportunities. Equalizing cycle times in production and driving down throughput times had an even more powerful induced, however unintentional, side effect: it created the possibility for driving down new product development cycle times and introduced a new form of product-led competition—and, to yet a new model of technology management.

CANON AND NEW PRODUCT DEVELOPMENT

Driving down manufacturing process times (increasing throughput efficiency) lowers costs, improves quality, and shortens delivery times. But the methodology of cycle time analysis and process simplification is not limited to the transformation of material in production. It can be extended to, and linked into, other business processes such as new product development (NPD). Extending cycle time analysis to NPD highlights the multiple facets of technology in production. The implications for technology management are profound.

While the Toyota Production System laid the foundation, consumer electronics companies applied and extended technology management into a source of competitive advantage. Canon, for example, uses the multi-product flow platform to institutionalize the dynamic integration of production with ongoing technology improvement and adoption. In fact, incorporation of technology management as an ongoing feature of production operations has fostered the emergence of a new business model designed to take full advantage of technology management to drive product-led competition. The result gives new force to product-led competition. Technology is put in the service of continuous product redefinition as never before.

The starting point of cycle time analysis is to identify the sequence of activities required from beginning to end of the process. Reducing new product development process time means redesigning and integrating every activity in the product development process (see Box 2.1).

Aspects of technology management enter into every activity category. Cycle time analysis as applied to the material transformation process suggests organizational practices for reducing cycle time which have analogues in the integration of new product development and production. For example, members from the various functional activities constitute work teams. Furthermore, occupational categories

Box 2.1. New product development process

- **product concept**
  conceptual design
  product architecture
  technology search and analysis
  target market

- **product planning**
  model building
  structural testing
  technology design viability testing
  technology R&D and integration
  investment/financial projections

- **product/process engineering**
  detailed design of product
  tooling/equipment design and specification
  building/testing prototypes
  master technology and engineering interfaces
  setting standards
  supplier tie-ins

- **pilot project/scale-up**
  initial production runs
  establish work skills and activities
  volume production tests

- **production**
  factory start-up
  volume ramp-up
  establish performance standards (cost, quality, time)
  maintain standards
  master engineering and work team interfaces for continuous improvement

are defined to be more inclusive.[30] These changes are reinforced by a perhaps more powerful force. Shorter new product development cycles means more product introductions. But it has a secondary, powerful benefit: integration of NPD and new technology introduction cycles. For any given product life cycle, product and process architecture are locked into place. To change any part requires new tooling, supplier specifications, testing, work task definitions, etc. Each new product introduction, however, is an opportunity for the adoption of new technologies and technology ideas (Gomory 1992).[31]

The shorter the NPD cycle, the greater the opportunity and organizational capability to introduce both discontinuous or radical technological innovations and new combinations of existing technologies into production. A company that is capable of reducing the NPD cycle to one-half that of a competitor can introduce technological innovations at twice the rate. Being first to market with a new technology is important, but having the shortest NPD process time is also important in that technology adoption and adaptations can be introduced more rapidly.[32]

The potential for rapid technological introduction induced a complementary organizational change: the shift of laboratory technicians from the laboratory onto the shopfloor. Laboratory technicians conducting research on the shopfloor discover new technological knowledge. What can appear as the elimination of R&D may be the development of cross-functional product development teams integrated into the production process.

In another application of the organizational principle of system integration, the Deming critique of the functional division of labor can be applied to the science-push model of innovation. The science-push model is one of central laboratories doing R&D and pushing it on to design engineer departments and on to production managers. In the

[30] The description by Ian Gibson, Managing Director of Nissan, UK, of national differences in the activities included in an engineer's challenge captures the point: An American or British engineer concentrates on design issues (product concept and product planning categories); the German engineer will seek to carry out pilot projects and participate in production ramp-up (all four categories); the Japanese engineer will do both of the above and participate in achieving world-class production standards for cost, quality, and time as well (personal interview, July 1985).

[31] Ralph Gomery makes this point in distinguishing 'the cyclic process' from a 'ladder' type of innovation. 'Ladder' refers to the step by step process by which an innovation descends from science downward 'step by step' into practice. 'The cyclic process' refers to 'repeated, continuous, incremental improvement' built into a series of dynamic design/manufacturing cycles.

[32] The engineering change orders and other changes required to implement rapid new product development are not conceivable under the scientific management paradigm.

interactive model responsibility for discovering new technological knowledge is spread from the central corporate laboratory to functionally integrated production groups. The chain-linked metaphor for technology innovation has been elaborated by Stephen Kline to capture the interaction and feedback loops common to many revolutionary new products and industries including, for example, the jet engine (1985).

The NPD pull, interactive model seeks to permeate R&D throughout the organization in a way that draws the customer/user into the definition of the problem and the solution. The concept of customer here is not only the final customer, but the chain of customers in which each producing link treats the next link as the customer. Decentralizing technology management for purposes of NPD mirrors the displacement of the responsibility for quality control from a central department into the operating activities of work teams on the shopfloor.

Teruo Yamanouchi, an ex-Canon Director of the Corporate Technical Planning and Operations Center, distinguishes a range of technology categories (1995). Discovery-driven knowledge and pre-competitive knowledge are at the base of a technology pyramid and overlap with the domain of science. Yamanouchi argues that technology management with the Japanese business enterprise has not made contributions to these areas of technological knowledge. Rather, the pool of scientific knowledge is tapped by Japanese enterprises for purposes of identifying a third layer of generic technologies to institutionalize a Schumpeterian innovation process. Here is where the Japanese technology management system has made significant contributions. Generic technologies form the foundation for ensuing layers described as core technology, product technology, engineering technology, and environmental technology.

Technology management at Canon is not a linear process beginning with generic technology. The process begins with developmental research for purposes of product innovation on technological categories near or at the top of the technology pyramid. This research is conducted on or next to the shopfloor. Findings at this level feed into applied research in design centers or business level labs which, in turn, leads to modifications in core technology; where applied research is not enough, fundamental research in corporate laboratories is conducted at the generic technology level. Contributions here lead to technological advance that can feed back into scientific knowledge. The Japanese technology management system has been particularly strong at recombining generic technologies and integrating these with process technologies. But, to date, most of the Japanese contributions to fundamental knowledge have been at the generic technology level as distinct from the more narrowly defined levels of scientific knowledge at the bottom two layers of the pyramid.

The technology management model is consistent with Deming's underlying concept of system and, as in production, led to the replacement of a push for a pull analogy.[33] However, such a small conceptual step represents a paradigm shift in the power relationships within an existing business enterprise. In the process of creating a knowledge-discovering business organization, the activities of work, management, and R&D are profoundly redefined.[34] The new business model connects Deming's focus on continuous redesign of the product to Kline's chain-linked model of technological innovation.

The new model of the business enterprise not only achieves continuous innovation built on a Deming inspired organizational method but combines continuous innovation with the capability to combine and recombine technologies in support of rapid new product development. Canon, for example, redefined the camera by rethinking the camera as a computer with a lens. The means was to combine the electronics and optical technology (generic technologies) with precision machinery technology and component assembly technology (process engineering technologies).

Canon did not simply combine generic technologies. It adopted, adapted, and refined generic technologies and recombined them in unique ways. The result was the emergence of specialized, proprietary product technologies that were not easily imitated. Firms without the Deming type organizational capabilities could not meet the time and quality standards; companies without the expertise across the range of technologies could not match the production performance standards.

Canon did not stop here. The emergent technological capabilities gave the company sophisticated resources to target technologically related areas. Canon moved first into the electronic office equipment business by developing electronic calculators which, in turn, led to the development of digital technology capabilities. The big hit came in the photocopier business in which Canon established a unique

[33] Combining the concepts of chain-of-customers and interactive or chain-linked R&D results in an organization in which each production link is also a customer to central R&D units. The resulting NPD-pull is analogous to *kanban* or pull-scheduling in which decisions to produce are governed not by a centralized scheduling department but by the demand of succeeding units.

[34] The Wagner Act which governs U.S. labor relations, was not set up to deal with quality, productivity, or innovation. The plan-do-check-act model of work organization is a prerequisite as is the development of a quality system.

cartridge product technology by combined technologies transferred from the camera and office equipment businesses with new technologies such as electrophotographic process technology, photosensitive materials technology, and toner technology.[35]

Combining Deming and Schumpeter in the same business enterprise has led to the development of an organizational chart that is unique in that two organizations function side by side within the same company. One accommodates the cost, quality, and delivery time performance standards associated with Deming. The other accommodates technological management to drive innovation and competitive strategies based on ever shorter product life cycles.[36]

The organizational structure is designed to establish layers in the R&D process to target product development at the business unit level and the development of long-term core technologies at the company level. The concept of the company is defined in terms of the core technologies and associated organizational capabilities. Separating the organizations enables the company to engage in both incremental and breakthrough innovation. The company has relatively open channels for internal technology transfer to new business units and core technologies are revitalized as new products and business units are developed.

To summarize: product-led competition has engendered new organizational capabilities that involve the redefinition and integration of four processes:

(1) manufacturing: the cell is the building block of the whole edifice; without cellular manufacturing the rest of the business system cannot drive product-led competition and continuous improvement;

35 The next technological transition was to combine laser-imaging technologies to what were now core technologies and develop a laser printer business. In each of these transitions Canon combined existing proprietary (or at least uniquely adapted) product and engineering technologies with new generic technologies to establish innovative products. The technologies are embedded in organizational and personnel capabilities which must be transferred and recombined in many cases into new business units specially designed to fabricate the new range of products. For discontinuous innovations, Canon developed a process of internal technology transfer into new business units rather than developing the new product technologies and products in plants that had been successful in pre-existing technologies. See Yamanouchi (1995).

36 The chief technologist of each center or laboratory does not report along a one-dimensional chain of command; instead, he/she reports to a technology strategy committee with the vice president of R&D as chair. The central labs, in turn, are hubs that network with the product-specific research centers with dotted line responsibility to their respective business groups.

(2) design/manufacturing cycle: companies need to compete on the basis of rapid new product development or they will fall behind in technology adoption;

(3) technology adoption: technologies are pulled by the first two processes as distinct from being pushed by autonomous R&D activities;

(4) technology R&D: increased technology knowledge is generated by developmental research, applied research, and generic technological research.

INTEL AND SYSTEMS INTEGRATION

In 1987 America's Defense Science Board, a governmental advisory board of distinguished scientists, claimed that the United States was in the lead in only three of more than a dozen critical semiconductor technologies (*Economist* 1995: 4). America's semiconductor industry was suffering. It was symbolic. The loss in industrial leadership was not expected in high-tech industries. Scientific research in the great industrial laboratories of AT&T, DuPont, General Electric, IBM, and Xerox was not being converted into a stream of commercially successful products.[37] Many warned of a 'hollowing out' of American industry given the capability of the Japanese model to engage in rapid new product development, absorb technologies, diffuse innovations, and achieve new comprehensive production performance standards. Manufacturing firms that had built American industry such as General Electric and Westinghouse were downsizing and outsourcing manufacturing and diversifying into financial services and the media.

But by 1996 the United States had established dominant position in microprocessor chips (the most technologically complex semiconductor) and a strong leadership position in personal computers, telecommunications including Internet-related activities, and software. Sales in information and communication technology (ICT) related industries grew from $340 billion in 1990 to $570 billion in 1995, a period during which Japanese ICT related industries grew less than one-quarter as much, from $450 billion to $500 billion (*Economist* 1997).

[37] Seven Nobel prizes were awarded for science breakthroughs at Bell labs. Most of the major labs were associated with breakthrough innovations that had redefined whole industries such as the transistor at Bell labs or nylon at DuPont. Nevertheless all have suffered loss of support.

Why the resurgence? The resurgence can be explained, in part by the development and diffusion of a new model of technology management. The new model has reinvented production by integrating manufacturing and continuous technological change within a business model of focus and network. The old American Big Business model of technological change driven by stand-alone industrial laboratories did come up short against the Japanese competition. But instead of ossifying, American industry has been revitalized by a business model that extends the technology management capabilities of the Japanese production system in three ways. First, systems integration is incorporated both as a driver of new product development and as a characteristic of production activities. It is mirrored in multi-disciplined teams. Second, networked groups of firms are linked by 'open systems' product architecture. In fact, the diffusion of systems integration has fostered new regional-based industrial dynamics with the widely decentralized design capabilities celebrated in internationally competitive light industries of the 'third Italy'. Third, basic research has been integrated into new product development in the form of a regional model of innovation and technical skill formation. The first two topics are explored here; the third is addressed in Chapter 4.

At the core of system integration, in American success stories, is the integration of hardware and software which, in turn, creates new potential for product design and process integration. Put differently, the new technology management model uses information technology to tap the potential of systems integration for rapid new product development. The new technology management capability is perhaps less alien to the machining shop that has always produced custom-designs but in limited volume. It expands the possibility of systematic design changes without violating the principle of flow.

Flow production has evolved from Ford's application to a single product to multiple products at Toyota and to new product development with multiple technologies as in the Canon model; but it has always been based on set designs. Relaxing the design constraint is an ongoing challenge in production; the integration of software and hardware is creating new opportunities to jointly custom-design products and processes in high-volume industries.

Custom-design is the competitive advantage of the fashion industries of the industrial districts of the 'third Italy'. Intra- and inter-firm flexibility in production combine with great design to produce leadership in a range of 'light' industries. The idea of integrating custom-design with flow in industries that combine and recombine complex and interactive technologies is not a completed project but a destination point on a map in which the organizational pathways are taking shape.[38]

The trajectory is toward one-piece flow applied to product design. Mass production at Ford and Toyota held design constant; Canon demonstrated the potential of combining technologies to strategically redefine products and markets. But the integration of software and hardware, both within the chip and across chips and control devices, opens the custom-design frontier as surely as the compass did to navigation. Product engineering is as crucial to the new frontier as it was to mass production, but it is software engineering that opens 'heavy' industry to the design imagination.

New and old firms alike, in a range of industries, have seized opportunities offered by information technology to radically redefine products and processes. They do not, in leading cases, simply add information technology to pre-existing products and processes. Instead, they integrate software and hardware to invent new products, or radically redesign old ones much as Henry Ford used unit-drive electric motors to redesign the production system according to the principle of flow.

The idea of integrating custom-design with flow is not simple in industries that combine complex technologies. But the principle can be operative even though its application may be incomplete. In fact, the goal may not be achieved for decades, much as one-piece flow took decades to implement after Ford successfully applied the concept of synchronization to single products (in the form of PS 3 and PS 4 in Table 2.1).

Intel is symbolic of America's manufacturing recovery, as Ford was for the introduction of mass production. The microprocessor is as fundamental to the new model of technology management as the machine tool was to interchangeability and as distinctive to the new era as the car was to mass production. Intel's production challenge is to combine the integrated design flexibility historically limited to machine shops with the throughput efficiency of the mass producers in an environment of technological complexity and rapid change.[39] Intel's

[38] Route 128 is particularly strong on system integration but relatively weak on volume production and associated engineering technologies. Success stories such as air defense and air traffic control systems are strong on custom-design and system integration but weak on production. Silicon Valley has a competitive advantage in the integration of all three.

[39] It is no secret that most of the world's chip-making plants are not organized according to the principle of flow, even Intel's. This is changing. Ford and Ohno would have understood the following quote in *Business Week* (4 July 1994): 'Rethinking the plant floor and grouping equipment in clusters should cut the time required for wafers to jump through some 200 processing

distinctive competence is not custom-designed microprocessors but leadership in volume production of a product whose performance requirements are advancing at double-digit rates. This involves combining fast-changing technologies with leadership in chip design and production.

Intel's process integration challenge is reminiscent of Ford's. But whereas Ford pursued process integration and synchronized a range of machines, Intel pursues systems integration and integrates over 600 activities embodying an array of technologies with deep roots in various technology and science research programs being conducted outside the company.

The production challenge addressed by Intel is not to achieve economies of scale for a given technology but to achieve continuously higher productivity and lower costs by sustained technological change. The historic productivity curve for chips has doubled every eighteen months for three decades, following Moore's Law.[40] The challenge is to manage manufacturing processes involving a range of technologies to satisfy productivity advances of this dimension. Systems integration is the response. It is about building the organizational capability to incorporate rapid technological change in components into complex products. This involves simultaneous advances in integrated circuit design tools, production technologies, and miniaturization capabilities. But it also involves sustained technological innovation, which, at Intel, led to the development of a business model constituted by a leadership and design dynamic described in Chapter 3.

Systems integration is to system integration what multi-product flow is to flow: an adaptation in a fundamental principle of production that has profound implications for business organization and competitive performance. Ford did system integration, but not systems integration. Ford was acutely aware of the opportunities offered by redesigning a whole system to fit the requirements of a seemingly independent technological innovation. As noted above, Ford redesigned the production system to take advantage of new electric power technologies. The dynamo was not seen as a means to reduce the cost of power but as a means to redesign production to apply the principle of flow. The result was an order of magnitude leap in productivity.

hoops from the present 60–90 days to just 7. That's because wafers wouldn't spend 90% or more of their shop-floor time being shuffled between operations and sitting in queues.'

[40] For example, in 1960, the average selling price for a transistor was $5.00; by 1985 an integrated circuit containing 500,000 transistors sold for $5.00 (Dahmen 1993: 32).

In this Intel does not break with earlier models of technology management. Henry Ford and his chief engineer, Charles Sorensen, understood the challenge, and rewards, of *system* integration.[41] But Intel, unlike Ford, designed a business model with the organizational capabilities to integrate new technologies on a continuous basis. Ford's system redesign was a one-off, once and for all commitment after which further fundamental technology change was ruled off limits.

Therefore, system integration does not capture Intel's uniqueness. System integration is a static concept with respect to *component design rules*; it does not imply organizational openness to innovation or technological change. Worse, the challenge of system integration exerts pressure to freeze technological change. *Kaizen*, or continuous improvement management, pursues experimentation and technological improvement but *holds basic technology design rules constant.*

The domain of systems integration encompasses two sets of design rules: those at the level of individual components or sub-systems and those that integrate sub-systems into a single production system. Systems integration pulls into the production organization the challenge of ongoing integration of technology design rules at both component and interface levels. The challenge is to co-manage manufacturing processes with processes of integrating and reintegrating technologies themselves being independently redefined. Further, the process of integrating sub-systems is not an additive one, particularly when sub-systems have independent design and development dynamics. Interactions amongst sub-systems have dynamic feedback effects. This was an organizational challenge that led Ford to freeze technological change. It enabled him to achieve high throughput efficiency but at a cost in sustained innovation.

The development of Intel's extraordinary technology management capabilities did not mean investment in stand-alone R&D laboratories. Strikingly, Intel has never owned a stand-alone R&D laboratory (Moore 1996: 168). This company policy decision was based on lessons gained from experience in the semiconductor industry by Intel founders. Gordon Moore observed that the premier semiconductor firms that invested in central research laboratories suffered from two major barriers to successful technology transfer and commercialization. The

[41] Ford's engineers revamped machines to fit the cycle time standard by adjusting, for example, tooling, material, and machine speeds. Rapid cycle time competition in new product development also involves an application of system integration. Here it entails redesigning the product from inside out and outside in to enhance flow. Popularly known as concurrent engineering, new products (inside) are designed simultaneously with production (outside).

result was slow 'time to market', an issue of paramount importance to Intel. The first barrier was resistance by manufacturing. Ironically, the barrier became greater as companies with stand-alone laboratories upgraded their production organizations. In Moore's words:

> the more technically competent a receiving organization becomes, the more difficult it is to transfer technology to it. . . . As the production organization became more successful and began to recruit more technical people . . . technology transfer became more difficult. Production, it seemed, had to kill a technology and reinvent it in order to get it to manufacturing. (167)

The second barrier was resistance to technological change by companies with success in earlier generation technologies. In fact, an inherent disadvantage is built into their very success at past technological advance.[42] Again, in the words of Moore: 'Because these companies are large, successful, and established, they tend to have difficulty exploiting new ideas. . . . Running with the ideas that big companies can only lope with has come to be the acknowledged role of the spin-off or start-up' (171). Does this mean that Intel does not engage in R&D? Quite the contrary. Intel's R&D budget exceeds $1 billion annually. Instead of stand-alone laboratories, Intel opted for the co-location of development research and manufacturing: 'development would be conducted in the manufacturing facility' (168).

Intel's integrated manufacturing focus requires the construction of full-scale experimentation plants.[43] For Intel, new product development is simultaneously new process development. Experimentation is carried out under full-scale manufacturing facilities under actual, not simulated, operating conditions. In the words of Moore:

> With a product as complex as semiconductors, it is a tremendous advantage to have a production line that can be used as a base for perturbation, introducing bypasses, adding steps, and so forth. Locating development and manufacturing together allows Intel to explore variations of its existing technologies very efficiently. (1996: 168)

Intel's concept of integrated manufacturing in which research experimentation and manufacturing are co-located is a response to the challenge of (complex) systems integration: changes in individual

[42] Moore's argument is not that such laboratories have not contributed to the dynamism of the semiconductor industry or been highly successful in developing new technologies. It is a free rider problem. 'The large, central research laboratories of the premier semiconductor firms probably have contributed more to the common good than to their corporations' (p. 171).

[43] For details on Intel's approach to technological development, see Iansiti and West (1997: 69–79). Other references include *Economist* (1997) and *Business Week* (26 May 1997: 170).

components will have system altering effects some of which cannot be identified or measured except in actual operating conditions.

The experiment plants are enormously expensive for microprocessors. But instead of a 'lean' production team driving high throughput, technology integration teams operate the experiment plants. The teams do not conduct fundamental research but collectively team members are familiar with a whole range of technology domains educated in a range of engineering and science disciplines.[44] The experiments may involve an entirely new chip in which case many of the technologies will be novel applications, some of which will have never been used before (Iansiti and West 1997: 70). Or a team may be developing a new version of an existing chip. Intel, for example, produces some thirty different kinds of the 486 chip (*Economist* 1996: 21). Here, too, experiments will be conducted on novel applications and combinations.

Intel addresses complexity with an 'open systems' business model that combines systems integration internally and design modularization externally. Modularization in production goes back to interchangeability of parts, an early application of modularity. The implementation of interchangeability required precise measurement that was facilitated by the development of gauges, an original and integral feature of the 'American System'. Modularization of components is a standard feature of mass production. Modularization in design is new. It enables systems integration and the incorporation of rapid technological change for partnering firms specializing in complementary capabilities. Common interface platforms unleash design potential in every component supplier by enormously expanding the potential market size for the assembled product.

Instead of designing its own equipment or complementary components for the various uses of microprocessors, Intel establishes and publicly discloses parameters for makers of chip-making equipment and for users of Intel chips *for the next generation of microprocessors.* Following the precepts of design modularization, equipment manufacturers build to published interface design rules and performance requirements established by Intel. Equipment makers, in turn, independently and privately design machines that will be inserted into Intel's chip fabrication plants. The challenge is to meet interface design rules which themselves incorporate Moore's Law rates of performance improvement.

[44] Iansiti and West (1997) point out that a number of the technology-integration team members will be recent graduates who have done dissertations on fundamental science.

Why do component suppliers and equipment manufacturers play the game and invest heavily in design? In part, because Intel is the standard setter. Intel, along with Microsoft, establishes the technology platform for the PC. The computer makers, Microsoft, and applications software producers must design next year's products according to the performance parameters of the central processing unit. Similarly, the equipment manufacturers must fall in line. With open systems the American PC industry has developed a networking model of inter-firm organization that has demonstrated unprecedented rate of technological innovation and diffusion. The risk to component suppliers of not participating, even as a bit player, overwhelms the risk of loss of intellectual property.

Intel depends upon, and reinforces, an industrial district constituted by multiple design nodes. Intel not only partners with a vast array of specialist producers and research institutions; Intel draws upon an extended industrial high-tech district with an extraordinary capacity to conduct experiments, carry out innovations, and conduct research.

The semiconductor manufacturing industry in the United States has more than 1,000 firms, most with sales between $1 million and $10 million per year. In contrast, Japan's semiconductor manufacturing industry is highly concentrated with twelve companies accounting for 75 percent of sales (Dahmen 1993: 34–5). Most of the Japanese semiconductor manufacturing companies are members of *keiretsu* supplier arrangements. The five largest semiconductor producers in Japan (NEC, Toshiba, Hitachi, Fujitsu, and Mitsubishi Electric) have built-in customers in the form of consumer electronics, computer, and communication divisions. This business model was designed for purposes of just-in-time or 'lean' production; it lacks the decentralized and diffused design capabilities associated with systems integration.

Turning to sales, distributors in America service a customer base of over 150,000 firms 'which are generally small and medium-sized companies in the computer, telecommunications, aerospace, instrumentation, and defense industries' (Dahmen 1993: 35). A number of distribution firms have differentiated themselves by establishing design centers. This has been associated with a dramatic growth in the application specific integrated circuit (ASIC) market.

Intel is also adept at technology management associated with PS 4 (see Table 2.1) in terms of defining research projects and networking to tap existing technology bases in the integrated process of pulling technologies into the production system. Moore describes Intel's transition in primary sites for identifying relevant research:

In its early years, the company looked to Bell laboratories for basic materials and science related to semiconductor devices; it looked to RCA's Princeton labs for consumer-oriented product ideas; and it sought insights into basic materials problems and metallurgy from the laboratories of General Electric. Over time, Intel found that most of the basic R&D relevant to its needs was being done by companies such as Fairchild and Texas Instrument, which had evolved into the product leaders in semiconductors.

Today, Intel looks to Universities for much of the basic research . . . the Semiconductor Research Corporation (SRC) established in the early 1980s by the Semiconductor Industry Association (SIA) . . . taxes large numbers of firms and users and then deploys the monies [*sic*] raised to promote university research. . . . (1996: 170)

In summary, for Ford and Toyota, the challenge was to synchronize by equalizing cycle times. For Canon, the challenge was to reduce new product development cycle time which involved enhancing the introduction of established technologies but new to Canon. For Intel, the challenge is to integrate all of the technologies required to make a chip along an emergent technology trajectory in which productivity is advancing 50 per cent every eighteen months. This is not simple, as many of the activities are rooted in distinctive science and technology domains. Intel alone, of the three, built a business model based on the principle of systems integration. Canon and Toshiba have substantial system integration capabilities. They, like Intel, integrate new product development with process reorganization. But the path breakers of technology management embedded in PS 4 have not redesigned their business systems to capture the innovation potential offered by the principle of systems integration. To do so would mean moving from a closed network to a business model organized around the leadership and design dynamic internally and open systems externally.

CONCLUSION: PRODUCTION CAPABILITIES AND INDUSTRIAL STRUCTURE

In this chapter we have introduced the concept of production systems, representing one of three domains in the Productivity Triad. Labor productivity is linked to the development of production capabilities which, in turn, are anchored in fundamental principles of production. Box 2.2, titled 'Production capabilities spectrum', summarizes the

Box 2.2. Production capabilities spectrum

- **Pre-flow, pre-interchangeability**
  Craft production, by itself, offers no basis for flow. Each drawer is custom fit. The task is to develop product-engineering skills. Jamaica and Honduras.

- **Interchangeability** (PS 1)
  Product engineering without process engineering, hence low inventory turns and working capital productivity. Cyprus and Slovenia in the 1980s.

- **Single-product flow** (PS 2)
  Plants with economies of speed for a single product or range of products with dedicated lines. Workers are not multi-skilled and attend to a single machine. Training does not include continuous improvement, rapid changeover, or blueprint reading skills. Multinational corporation (MNC) electronics production in Indonesia.

- **Single-product flow with continuous improvement** (PS 3)
  Involves problem-solving, *self-directed* work teams. Common training programs include Plan-Do-Check-Act diffused by the Japanese Union of Scientists and Engineers, the seven problem-solving tools of TQM (total quality management) at shopfloor level.

- **Single-product flow with process innovation** (PS 3)
  Personnel include maintenance and process control technicians with skills to identify, fix, and redesign machinery and production lines. Bottleneck analysis determines priorities. This may involve reconfiguring product design parameters at main office as required by DFM (design for manufacturability). MNCs in Singapore in the mid-1980s, MNCs in Malaysia in the early 1990s.

- **Multi-product flow** (PS 3)
  The Toyota system. *Kanban*, JIT (just-in-time), and SMED (single-minute exchange of dies) are introduced in large plants. High throughput and flexibility are combined. Cellular production with self-directed work teams.

- **Multi-product flow and product development** (PS 4)
  Japan and Taiwan both excel at concurrent engineering and design for manufacturability. Skills include reverse engineering, prototype development, and pilot runs.

Box 2.2. Production capabilities spectrum—*continued*

- **New product design and technology fusion** (PS 4)
  Japan's Toshiba and Canon are leaders in linking development to operations at the plant level and linking research in generic technologies to product development. Core technologies are developed, often via fusion in generic technology labs. Technology management involves worldwide sourcing of the existing technology base in pursuit of regularized, novel applications.

- **Systems integration and disruptive innovation** (PS 5)
  3M, HP, and Motorola use cross-disciplinary teams to identify new technology drivers for product development. Disruptive or breakthrough innovations are pursued but within an organizational context of process integration and HPWSs (high-performance work systems). Hardware and software integration assists product concept development.

- **Open systems and design modularization** (PS 5)
  Standard interface rules and diffusion of design capability support focus and network strategies. Fosters technology deepening R&D and techno-diversification.

historical evolution of production capabilities that lie behind the production systems sketched in this chapter.[45]

The sectoral transition diamond of Figure 2.1 illustrates the development of a region or nation's production capabilities including technology management. Each pole is associated with the production capabilities required to achieve competitive advantage in a distinctive set of products. Movements of the diamond in an upward and left direction represent a shift of resources from less technology and skill-intensive sectors to more complex and knowledge-intensive applications. Such reallocations involve transitions to technology management capabilities based on more advanced principles of production (from interchangeability, to single-product flow, to multiple-product flow and systems integration). Lack of movement over time in the sectoral pyramid suggests limited organizational change capability at the regional and enterprise levels.

[45] Many of the examples cited in Box 2.2 are elaborated in Chs. 4–7. Others are drawn from the author's personal experiences in the countries described.

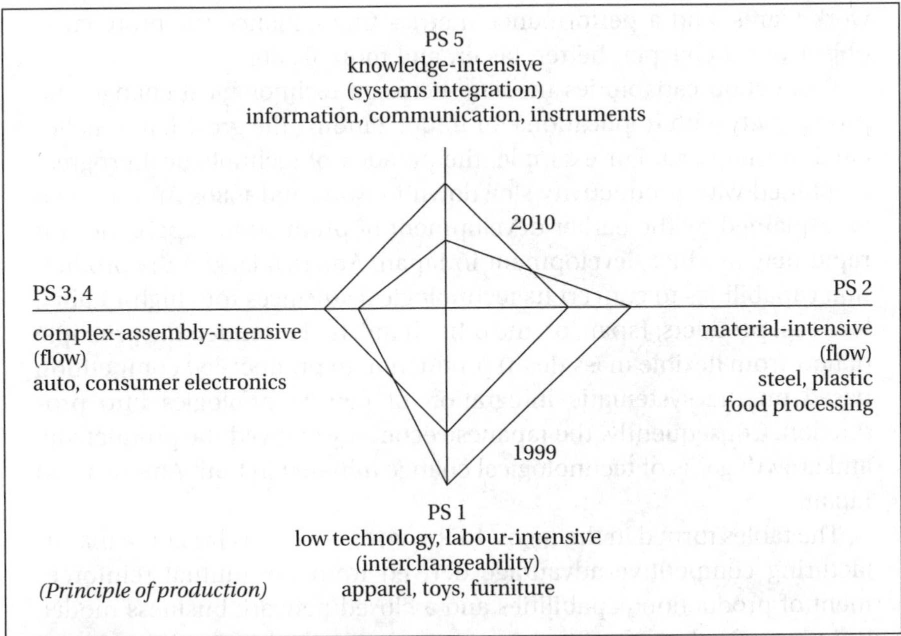

Fig. 2.1. Evolution of industrial structure

Rapid industrial growth can be depicted in terms of a movement of a region's diamond away from unskilled, labor-intensive activities and sectors (bottom corner) and raw material, scale economy activities (right-hand corner) to skilled labor, complex production process activities (left-hand corner) and knowledge-intensive sectors and activities (upper corner). An organizational x-ray of successful transitions captures movement along the production capabilities spectrum of Box 2.2 and the development of regional technology management and innovation capabilities.

Regions in which knowledge-intensive activities, firms, and sectors are the drivers of growth, the PS 5 pole in Figure 2.1, have a range of common regional capabilities which will be examined in later chapters. These include systems integration (starting with hardware and software), open systems networking, industry/university partnering models for integrating product development and R&D, decentralization and diffusion of design, and technological diversity and new firm creation. A similar examination of complex-process production activities at the PS 3, 4 pole reveals a range of management practices and organizational capabilities such as flow analysis, cellular manufacturing, self-directed work teams, and a performance metrics that enhance the production objectives of cheaper, better, faster, and more flexible.

Production capabilities mediate between technological change and productivity with implications for understanding the growth anomalies cited in Chapter 1. For example, the paradox of technological progress combined with productivity slowdown in 1970s and 1980s America can be explained by the earlier development of production capabilities for rapid new product development in Japan. America lacked the production capabilities to convert its technological advances into high-quality, low-cost products; Japan, on the other hand, had extended the principle of flow from flexible mass (lean) production to product-led competition based on the systematic integration of new technologies into production. Consequently, the Japanese economy enjoyed the productivity and growth gains of technological change initiated in both America and Japan.

The tables turned in the 1990s. In the 1970s and 1980s Japanese manufacturing competitive advantage derived from the mutual reinforcement of production capabilities and a closed network business model. But a new Productivity Triad was emerging in the high-tech regions of the United States. Companies like Intel were reinventing production around a new 'open systems' business model (see Chapter 3). A business policy of 'focus and network' facilitated the implementation and diffusion of the principle of systems integration in both technology and business organization. Both have been inputs into a new regional model of innovation based on the decentralization and diffusion of design, a concept taken up in Chapter 4.

Appendix 2.1. THROUGHPUT EFFICIENCY AND WASTE

Throughput efficiency is a measure of material flow in production. The rate of flow can be measured by applying the following formula:

$$TE = \frac{VA}{(VA + NVA)}$$

in which TE = throughput efficiency measured in time, VA = value adding time, and NVA = non-value adding time.

Mass batch and job shop production systems will rarely have throughput efficiencies above 5 percent; flow production systems, on the other hand, can achieve over 50 percent. A company with high throughput efficiencies will easily out compete a low throughput efficiency company because it has the advantage of production lead times that are only a fraction of the time.[46]

A corollary of the principle of flow is that anything that slows the flow of material is a form of waste. Waste is a concept for which multiple distinctions are made in the process of making it operational. For example:[47]

- waste of overproduction
- waste of waiting
- waste of transportation
- waste of processing itself
- waste of stock on hand (inventory)
- waste of movement
- waste of making defective products
- waste of underutilized worker earning power caused by bad methods

Each form of waste can become a target for improving throughput efficiency.

[46] The flow chart is a tool for tracking the flow of material through the production process. It is to the flow of material what a time and motion study is to labor for scientific management. The total time that material is in the production system is broken down into five categories: Operation, Transportation, Inspection, Delay, or Storage. Anyone can carry out a flow chart exercise by tracking the material from the time it enters into the factory until it is shipped to the customer. The hundreds of activities can be all designated into one or another of the five categories. Only Operations add value to the customer, the other four categories are non-value adding time which reduces throughput efficiency. Each of the non-value adding time activities is a form of waste which can become a target in a waste reduction program.

[47] The first seven items on the list are taken from the originator of JIT, Taiichi Ohno of Toyota, see Ohno 1988. The last is taken from Henry Ford's entry titled 'Mass Production' in the 1929 edition of *Encyclopedia Britannica*.

CHAPTER

3

Cluster Dynamics

In Chapter 2 models of technology management were anchored in production systems. Issues of business organization were not ignored but addressed indirectly. In this chapter I focus attention directly on business organization including inter-firm relationships as they relate to technological change and growth. The chapter has two parts.

The first part examines the intellectual genealogy of the 'entrepreneurial firm' beginning with Adam Smith, the father of economics. Technological change and business organization have not always been outside the mainstream of economic analysis. In fact, Adam Smith's principle of specialization is as much the precursor to a theory of innovation and wealth creation as it is to one of efficient resource allocation.

The second part elaborates upon a set of regional growth or 'cluster dynamics' that mediate between the entrepreneurial firm and regional growth. Business historians working in the strategy and structure perspective developed by Alfred Chandler have explained American industrial leadership in terms of the development of organizational capabilities associated with the rise of Big Business. More recently, Michael Porter has extended this strategy and structure framework from a focus on individual firms to clusters of enterprises and supporting institutions. Competitiveness remains a property of firms but firms operate within a 'home base' that is critical to their success. Porter reintroduces a regional dimension into business performance concerns. In the second part the idea of a cluster will be extended to that of cluster dynamics driven by entrepreneurial firms. This move will generate an understanding of the origins of successful clusters and criteria for distinguishing different patterns of inter-firm relations.

THE PRINCIPLE OF INCREASING SPECIALIZATION

Adam Smith began his famous book by drawing linkages between division of labor and wealth creation. He writes, 'The division of labor is not a quaint practice of eighteenth-century pin factories; it is a fundamental principle of economic organization' (Stigler 1951: 193). Wealth, for Smith, is created through a process of increasing specialization and division of labor. Specialization involves the decomposition of the commodity into an ever-greater number of constituent activities; each activity, in turn, is targeted for a refinement in skills and technique. Every increase in the extent of the market increases the number of activities that are subject to 'new improvements of art'.

In a resource coordination reading of Smith, changes in production methods, skills, and technology are outside the theory. But this violates Smith's view of production as an unfolding adjustment process. An increase in demand does not simply lead to an increase in production but to adjustments in production activities that are at the heart of the wealth creation process. An increase in demand, in Smith's words:

> though in the beginning it may sometimes raise the price of goods, never fails to lower it in the long run. It encourages production, and thereby increases the competition of the producers, who, in order to undersell one another, *have recourse to new divisions of labour and new improvements of art*, which might never otherwise have been thought of. (A. Smith 1976: 748, emphasis added)

It is critical to note that lower prices are not a consequence of increasing returns to scale for an unchanging process of production, but due to the *adaptation of process* to meet the *opportunities* of an expanded market. Smith suggests an interactive dynamic between the emerging opportunities and evolving activities of production. With each increase in the extent of the market the subdivision of activities proliferates and ever more activities become subject to specialization and increasing returns.[1]

Mechanization, technical change, and invention are part of the process of increased specialization.[2] In the opening chapter of *The Wealth*

[1] 'In consequence of better machinery, of greater dexterity, and of a more division and distribution of work, all of which are the natural effects of improvement, a much smaller quantity of labour becomes requisite for executing any particular piece of work' (A. Smith 1976: 260).

[2] Brian Loasby uses the term 'discovery process' to encompass a series of innovation activities described by Smith (Loasby 1997: 3). The term 'continuous improvement' is the English translation of *kaizen*, Japanese for a problem-solving model of work organization also referred to as 'incremental innovation' (Best 1990: ch. 5).

of Nations, Smith describes how increasing specialization leads to simplification of production activities which, in turn, creates search opportunities for improvement and innovation in methods and machines: 'A great part of the machines made use of in those manufactures in which labour is most subdivided, were originally the inventions of common workmen, who, being each of them employed in some very simple operation, naturally turned their thoughts towards finding out easier and readier methods of performing it' (Smith 1976: 20).

And, specialist machine-making trades join in the division of labor and technical change process:[3]

> What takes place among the labourers in a particular workhouse, takes place, for the same reason, among those of a great society. The greater their number, the more they naturally divide themselves into different classes and subdivisions of employment. More heads are occupied in inventing the most proper machinery for executing the work of each, and it is, therefore, more likely to be invented. (A. Smith 1976: 104)

Allyn Young, writing in 1928, adds a complementary aphorism to Smith's principle: 'the division of labor depends upon the extent of the market, but the extent of the market depends upon the division of labor' (1928: 539–40). Young's aphorism means, quite simply, that Smith's wealth-creating process has a potent feedback loop. An increase in the market leads to further division of labor and further division of labor leads to increased markets. The mediating variable is resource differentiation or increased specialization of activities and skills. An increase in the market triggers further specialization, a process that simultaneously increases the size of the market for specialist skills and activities.

Edge-banding, a specialist activity in furniture making, illustrates the idea.[4] A specialist edge-bander can supply the entire industry—no longer is edge-banding activity distributed across all firms in which the market for each edge-bander is limited by the sales of the individual firm; instead, the size of the market for the edge-bander is the entire furniture industry. The edge-bander enjoys increasing returns and so does the district; organizational productivity has advanced by a reallocation of resources not by an accumulation of capital or labor.

[3] 'Many improvements have been made by the ingenuity of the makers of the machines, when to make them became the business of a particular trade' (A. Smith 1976: 21).

[4] An edge-band is the strip of material that seals the edge of a table or desktop. An edge-banding capability requires knowledge about, for example, adhesives, substrate and banding materials, and edge-shaping tools. For a case study of two furniture districts, one of which firms specialize by capabilities and the other that combines capabilities, unsuccessfully, within the same enterprise, see Best (1990: chs. 7–8).

Marshall and the Fourth Factor of Production

Alfred Marshall extended the principle of increasing specialization from skills to businesses and industrial districts. Firms in industrial districts benefit from localization cost economies derived from specialist suppliers, a specialist labor pool, and local knowledge diffusion. Marshall added organization as a fourth factor of production to labor, land, and capital and put knowledge central to the wealth creation process:

knowledge is our most powerful engine of production; it enables us to subdue Nature and force her to satisfy our wants. Organization aids knowledge; it has many forms, e.g. that of a single business, that of various businesses in the same trade, that of various trades relatively to one another, and that of the State providing security for all and help for many. (Marshall 1920: 138–9)

In addition, Marshall sought to construct a theory of supply that connected with, and could inform, his observations of industrial activity. He proposed a concept of the firm but with the condition that it was consistent with the assumptions required for an equilibrium theory of price.[5] This move rendered his concept of *constant* returns to scale, required for an equilibrium theory of price, inconsistent with the concept of *increasing* returns engendered by increasing specialization and innovation encoded in his notion of knowledge creation and Smith's 'discovery principle'.[6] Constant returns to scale are also inconsistent with a limit to the size of the firm required by the assumption of numerous producers required for markets to induce an optimal allocation of resources.[7] To accommodate an equilibrium theory of price,

[5] Marshall's construct of the representative firm became the archetypal or textbook approach to economic theories of the firm: a Platonic mode of representing full systems by a single essence or exemplar—and then studying how this entity adjusts to external parameter shifts. The assumption of homogeneous firms and products yielded an elegant theory of price and a powerful teaching tool, but at a cost. From that time on the importance of technology to understanding economic performance and growth has not been denied, but it has been treated as a residual, outside the theoretical framework of economics. Strategy suffered the same fate: textbook firms have one goal, profit maximization; one strategy, price competition; and one organizational means, cost minimization (see Best 1990: 139).

[6] Following Loasby (1997), the discovery principle refers to Smith's 'recourse to new divisions of labour and new improvements in art' as driving incremental innovation (A. Smith 1976: 748).

[7] In the 1930s, Chamberlin and Robinson sought to integrate equilibrium with increasing returns to scale. Demand, not diminishing returns, limited scale of output (it was assumed that firms produced a single product). This approach was short-lived. The existence of increasing returns drove a wedge between the equilibrium and optimum allocation of resources. Without diminishing returns the optimality rules are violated: price and marginal cost are neither equal

Marshall's concept of knowledge creation was shifted outside the firm and the idea of innovation, central to a theory of wealth creation, was cut loose from the production. Smith's 'discovery principle' was assumed away. Innovation was separated from production in economic theory.

Penrose: Theory of Growth of the Firm

Young's extension of Smith's principle of increasing specialization into a concept of self-sustaining growth has remarkable resonance with Edith Penrose's theory of the growth of the firm. The enterprise growth dynamic derives from an extension of the principle of increasing specialization from skills to 'productive services' (think capabilities) of enterprises.[8] Penrose draws a distinction between resources, which are homogeneous, and productive services which are heterogeneous: 'it is never *resources* themselves that are the "inputs" in the production process, but only the *services* that the resources can render' (Penrose 1995: 25, emphasis in original).

The services of resources derive from the unique experience, teamwork, and purposes of each enterprise. Consequently, every enterprise is unique: 'The services yielded by resources are a function of the way in which they are used—exactly the same resource when used for different purposes or in different ways and in combination with different types or amounts of other resources provides a different service or set of services' (Penrose 1995: 25). Productive services are potentially dynamic: 'the process by which experience is gained is properly treated as a process of creating new productive services available to the firm' (48). And the generation of new productive services is a knowledge-creating process: '[t]he very process of operation and of expansion are intimately associated with the process by which knowledge is increased' (56). Production involves both the making of products or services and the creation of new production-related knowledge.

nor proportional across the economy. A more acceptable solution to preserve the equilibrium perspective was to assume diminishing returns to management. In the words of Hicks: 'the only reason why marginal costs should increase is the increasing difficulty of controlling an enterprise, as its scale of production grows' (1939: 83).

[8] Penrose's term for capability was 'productive service'. Richardson (1972) suggested the change in terminology.

The new production-related knowledge is a form of unused productive services; it creates both an imbalance and an opportunity.[9] The source of the imbalance is inherent in the execution of business plans: 'the execution of any plan for expansion will tend to cause a firm to acquire resources which cannot be fully used . . . and such unused services will remain available to the firm after the expansion is completed'. However, the act of deploying unused resources will eventually set in motion the process whereby new knowledge is created and, with it, unused resources which, in turn, creates a new round of pressures to seek yet new activities. Once again, as with Young's aphorism, the resource creation process is endless.

Realization of the growth process, however, is an entrepreneurial challenge. In an uncertain world, management must recognize and successfully pursue 'productive opportunities'. The pursuit of 'productive opportunities' links the firm to the customer in an interactive relationship in which new product concepts are developed. The advances in productive services can extend the firm's 'productive opportunities' by enlarging the members' capacity to recognize and respond to new product concept possibilities in the environment. 'Experience . . . develops an increasing knowledge of the possibilities for action and the ways in which action can be taken by . . . the firm. This increase in knowledge . . . causes the productive opportunities of a firm to change' (Penrose 1995: 53). From the Penrosian perspective, the firm shapes the market as much as the reverse but within a moving, historically contingent environment. As firms develop and respond to productive opportunities, they alter and further differentiate and, in the process, re-characterize the parameters (technological, product, organizational) of the 'market'.[10]

Penrose's case study of Hercules Powder illustrates the productive services and market dynamic. The company's base in 'extensive know-

[9] The process of creating new productive services, a by-product of goods production, engenders a balancing or coordination problem: 'only by chance [will] the firm . . . be able so to organize its resources that all of them will be fully used' (1995: 32). The coordination problem, however, is partly the outcome of planning limitations: 'In general there will always be services capable of being used in the same or in different lines of production which are not so used because the firm could not plan extensively enough to use them.'

[10] In contrast, technology is exogenous to the resource coordination treatment of the market and firm. The production challenge is to squeeze the maximum amount of output from a fixed pool of resources; the challenge can be met by satisfying a set of optimality rules involving inputs, outputs, and prices for a *given* technology. 'Waste is economic sin'; optimality is the elimination of waste. Unused resources are not seen as part of a dynamic process of increasing a firm's productive services.

ledge' of cellulose technology leveraged a strategy of moving into and developing promising markets. This, in turn, led the firm to invest further in the advance of cellulose technology.

But limits are part of the same process. Just as the scope for expansion on the basis of the firm's existing productive services comes up against market opportunities, so movement into new areas comes up against the problem of extending the firm's unique productive services to meet market opportunities, that is of 'building up an experienced managerial and technical team in new fields of activity'. Internal coordination needs set a brake on the rate at which market opportunities can be pursued: 'the rate of growth is retarded by the need for developing new bases and by the difficulties of expanding as a coordinated unit'.

The reference to 'bases' is to the 'basic position' a firm must establish and protect (as distinct from merely achieving efficiency in production):

> In the long run the profitability, survival, and growth of a firm does not depend so much on the efficiency with which it is able to organize the production of even a widely diversified range of products as it does on the ability of the firm to establish one or more wide and relatively impregnable 'bases' from which it can adapt and extend its operations in an uncertain, changing and competitive world. It is not the scale of production nor even, within limits, the size of the firm, that are the important considerations, but rather the nature of the basic position that it is able to establish for itself. (Penrose 1995: 137)

The drive to establish a basic position limits the productive opportunities that any single firm can pursue. But in an open system of firms (see below), such opportunities are not lost but instead are shifted into market 'interstices' and become opportunities for other firms, existing and new. In this way the growth dynamic is propagated to the larger population of firms. The interstices represent new opportunities for expansion that develop out of industrial change and innovation but which cannot be pursued by the originating enterprise: they are inconsistent with reinforcing the basic position, or unique productive services, of the firm in which they emerged.

Richardson: Networking

George Richardson replaced Penrose's resources and productive services terminology with that of activities and capabilities. The result is an extension of Smith's specialization principle to account for inter-firm partnering. In Richardson's words:

It is convenient to think of industry as carrying out an indefinitely large number of *activities*, activities related to the discovery and estimation of future wants, to research, development and design, to the execution and co-ordination of processes of physical transformation, the marketing of goods and so on. And we have to recognize that these activities have to be carried out by organizations with appropriate *capabilities*, or, in other words, with appropriate knowledge, experience and skills. (1972: 888, emphasis in original)

The concept of capability illuminates the process view of production and competition. It gives integrity to organization as an economic concept. Capabilities can be neither reduced to individual skills nor purchased in the market. The concept of capability can be extended to address a range of issues in industrial organization.

The growth process, from the capabilities perspective, is simultaneously a networking theory of industrial organization.[11] Firms specialize in activities that utilize a similar capability and partner with other enterprises that specialize in complementary activities. The boundary between the firm and the market becomes blurred as the firm takes on resource creation functions; the firm and the market are no longer simply substitute means of resource coordination. Networking emerges as a means of coordination that can enhance the resource creation activities of enterprises.

Open system dynamics, or networking adjustment processes, in turn, foster capability specialization, decentralization and diffusion of design, and technological experimentation. The consequent regional diversity of enterprises and technologies, in addition, increase the opportunity for local innovation based on new combinations of existing technologies.

Production and inter-firm relations are no longer offstage. The production of a commodity involves hundreds if not thousands of activities. Increasing specialization and further decomposition of the commodity reveal a dynamic population of firms themselves connected by 'markets'. The market in which the end-user receives a completed product is but one market in a long continuum of 'markets' in the form of relationships between producers and users of intermediate products and services between raw material and end-user.

[11] Instead of firms as islands in a sea, Richardson's image is of industry as a 'dense network of co-operation and affiliation by which firms are inter-related' (1972: 883).

The principle of increasing specialization is inconsistent with a static image of industry. The new image is one of a moving picture of increasing specialization within networked systems of enterprises each specializing in complementary but distinctive activities. This has far-reaching implications for understanding the dynamics of industrial organization including the mutual adjustment processes amongst firms, regional competitiveness, and industrial growth. For example, the concept of an industrial sector of replica firms producing replica products, and deploying replica production methods, a facilitating assumption of the economics of a stationary economy, denies a role for entrepreneurship or the identification of new product concepts from emerging market opportunities. But it also limits understanding of the processes of enterprise specialization and inter-firm integration, which are central to understanding capability development and economic progress.

Schumpeter: Internal/External Dynamic

In the history of economic thought, Schumpeter came close to the formulation of a dynamic between intra- and inter-firm organization. This was a logical outcome of his rejection of the ideal of perfect competition: 'perfect competition is not only impossible but inferior, and has no title to being set up as a model of ideal efficiency' (Schumpeter 1942: 106). His critique of perfect competition was that it could 'spread the bacilli of depression'. Fighting for survival, homogeneous firms would resort to cut-throat competition (selling at prices that only covered variable costs) and without investment capitalism has no dynamism.[12]

The capability and innovation perspective gives explanatory power to the concept of an internal/external dynamic and anchors Schumpeter's innovation in business and industrial organization. It creates conceptual space for the idea of product-led as distinct from price-led competition. Just as price-led competition and closed system models of industrial organization are conceptually linked, so too are product-led competition and open system models of industrial organization. The

[12] Profit in the Schumpeterian perspective is not simply a trigger for the invisible hand to coordinate demand and supply but a return to innovation, a source of investment, R&D, growth, and, in Schumpeter's term the source of 'future values'. This is a variation on the resource creation theme.

textbook ideal of perfect competition presumes the first structure and denies the second. Real world economies offer both as possibilities. The fact that at least two possibilities exist offers a further possibility: competition across regional business systems with distinctive regional capabilities. Regional business systems, like Penrose's enterprises, are organizational entities with unique patterns of 'experience and teamwork'.

OPEN SYSTEM DYNAMICS

Schumpeter is justly famous for explaining long-term growth in terms of waves of technological innovation. But if the strength of Schumpeter and the neo-Schumpeterian perspective is its focus on the role of technology in industrial growth and change, its weakness is how business organization fits into the story. Schumpeter explained innovation in terms of the role of entrepreneurs as individual inventors not as instituted processes or organizational capability. Neo-Schumpeterians risk explaining growth in terms of technological determinism.

Perspectives on business organization, on the other hand, focus on the origins of success of individual enterprises not on regional growth. Porter's concept of the cluster makes progress by linking the success of individual enterprises to the 'home base' in which they operate. But Porter's Diamond is a description of advanced clusters not an explanation of cluster development. Enterprises in the poorest regions of the world tend to co-locate with like enterprises but all are stuck at a low level of productivity. The links between clusters and growth still need to be worked out. The dynamics between technological change and business institutions and practices are at the heart of the matter.

The concepts of technology management and production system were developed in the last chapter. In the first part of this chapter we traced the genealogy of the idea of the entrepreneurial firm back to Adam Smith and the principle of increasing specialization. We can now pose the idea of the entrepreneurial firm as the driver of cluster dynamics and regional growth.

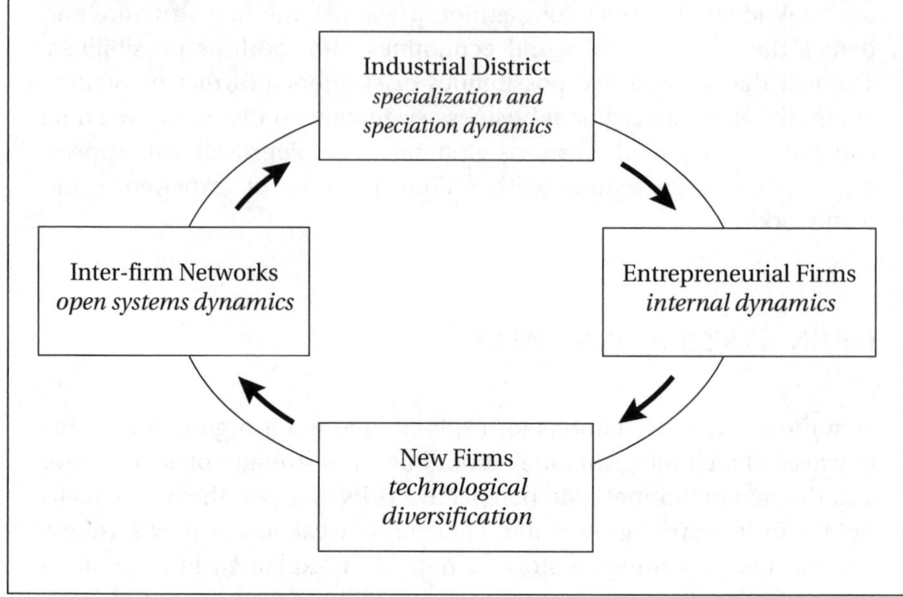

Fig. 3.1. Model of cluster dynamics

Entrepreneurial Firm

The starting point is the concept of the entrepreneurial firm. The internal growth dynamics of entrepreneurial firms lie at the core of a set of regional growth dynamics or cluster dynamics shown in Figure 3.1. The right-hand box represents the entrepreneurial firm.

The entrepreneurial firm does not take the market or the product as given, but as objects of strategic reconstitution. The challenge is to be able to identify market opportunities and respond with products with superior performance characteristics. Rapid and effective response to market opportunities involves developing production capabilities including, for example, rapid new product development and technology management.[13]

But responsiveness to market opportunities is only one side of a mutual adjustment process. The ability to read or identify market opportunities depends, in part, on a firm's production capabilities. The

[13] It is, at the same time, an extension of Adam Smith's principle of increasing specialization from skills and occupations to capabilities as mediated by business and industrial organization. This theme is elaborated below.

actions involved in advancing a firm's production capabilities to meet market opportunities is simultaneously a discovery process that may turn up new product design possibilities. New design ideas precipitate the identification of market opportunities not otherwise perceptible. The double interaction between market opportunity and production capability is mediated by and fosters new product concepts.

This internal dynamic fosters new applications of technology and technological innovation, powerful sources of productivity growth. The interactive process is potentially endless.[14] New 'market' opportunities feed back to precipitate changes in technological capabilities, setting in motion a new technology/market dynamic and fostering new product concepts.

The dynamic builds on and advances the enterprise's technology trajectory. Firms develop distinctive technological knowledge bases, which facilitates their ability to turn market opportunities into new products. These knowledge bases are anchored in the firm's unique technological capabilities and are shaped by the technology/market dynamic.

Firms that simply purchase technologies do not have the same capacity to respond to market opportunities and shape the market. In contrast to entrepreneurial firms, such firms lack unique production capabilities and thereby the capacity to anticipate emerging market opportunities. Unable to differentiate their products, they are commodity producers governed by the 'market'. They enjoy little productivity-advancing and growth-driving force.

But sustaining growth is not a simple matter for entrepreneurial firms. While the technology/market dynamic can drive growth, impediments to the dynamic in a region's business enterprises undermine the productivity growth process. This focuses attention on the sustainability of the underlying technology trajectory. As the boundaries of the 'market' are continuously being redrawn, the underlying technology trajectory is advancing. Sustainable growth demands that the technology trajectory and the evolving product designs in the market are in sync. The technology trajectory is not static; it is highly uncertain. Long-term growth requires technological continuity and change.

[14] Individual firms may be entrepreneurial for a long or short period. From a regional policy perspective it is not important that individual firms survive but that the technology/market dynamic be ongoing as firms exit and enter. In this, the entrepreneurial firm functions like runners in a relay race, handing the baton on after having done their job in advancing the region's technological capabilities and redefining the market.

The technology/market dynamic that defines the entrepreneurial firm suggests a criterion for distinguishing real world business models in terms of their technology management capability. Business models, in turn, are important determinants of regional competitive advantage.[15] Three examples follow. In each case, organizational capabilities that harness the technology/market dynamic enable an advance in business performance.[16]

First, the development of flexible production methods enables firms to achieve higher product quality, lower costs, and faster delivery times. Technology management is integrated into shopfloor work practices in the form of incremental and continuous improvement of the process of production; this involves the development of agile (cellular) manufacturing methods, self-directed work teams, and continuous improvement work practices.

The development of the *kaizen* or continuous improvement work system established a Japanese variant of the entrepreneurial firm. This organizational capability enabled Japanese manufacturing enterprises to rapidly gain market share in many industries in the 1970s and 1980s. It was achieved by designing and diffusing an *incremental innovation* capability into production. The problem-solving, self-managed, team-centered work system gave the new business model a flexible production platform for integrating design and production. It set a new global standard in time-to-market for new product development.

In the 1980s and 1990s, many American firms undertook a transition to another variant of the entrepreneurial firm increasingly referred to as 'high-performance work systems' (HPWSs).[17] HPWSs combine quality-improvement teams, problem-solving skills, and group incentive pay schemes. 'Scientific management', a work system designed for price-led competition could not survive the new performance standards in

[15] The responsiveness of a firm to market opportunities is a determinant of its competitiveness. Success goes to firms able to respond more rapidly and effectively. The same is true for regions. Changes in industrial leadership and competitive advantage are often based on a critical mass of firms within a region developing and new business models with superior technology management capabilities.

[16] In Ch. 2 a similar range of business models are contrasted in terms of their technology management capabilities by anchoring each in a fundamental principle of production.

[17] The proportion of employees in firms that 'made some use of self-managed teams increased from 28 percent in 1987 to 68 percent in 1995'. 'A plant that has adopted a cluster of practices that provides workers with the incentives, the skills, and, above all, the opportunity to participate in decisions and improve the plant's performance has an HPWS' (Appelbaum et al. 2000: 9). They continue, 'Workers in an HPWS experience greater autonomy over their job tasks and methods of work and have higher levels of communication about work matters with other workers, managers, experts (e.g., engineers, accountants, maintenance and repair personnel), and, in some instances, with vendors or customers' (7).

cost, quality, or time-to-market for new product development. Team-centered rather than supervisor-centered work organization delivered superior performance and higher productivity.

Second, the integration of product design and manufacturing into a seamless process enables firms to alter product designs on a regular basis and compete on the basis of rapid new product development. The business model is organized according to the logic of process integration rather than functional departmentalization. New product development teams meld into a single unit individuals that specialize in, for example, product design, product and process engineering and manufacturing. These teams reflect new product development capabilities that enable the firm to introduce new or modified technologies on a regularly scheduled basis.

Third, a top-down leadership and bottom-up design dynamic enables firms to proliferate experiments to foster technological change but still focus on core technological capabilities. Technological change is uncertain but incessant. Firms, which are successful with one technology, can lose out to firms that develop alternative technologies. Therefore, anticipating technological change is an organizational challenge. Firms can enhance their technological flexibility by developing an organizational capability to combine recurrent phases of bottom-up experimentation and top-down direction (Grove 1996). Intel is an example.

Andrew Grove, a co-founder, argues that Intel is internally organized to combine phases of experimentation, which stimulate new ideas and innovation, with the focus required to sustain unique technological capabilities. Experimentation and new design ideas are fostered by decentralization of decision-making. The challenge of leadership is to allow enough time to stimulate the development of new ideas before managing a new phase during which the most promising ideas are pursued and the weaker ideas are abandoned. Grove writes: 'a pendulum-like swing between the two types of actions is the best way to work your way through a strategic transformation' (1996: 161). The swings of the pendulum are made possible by a 'dynamic dialectic' between bottom-up and top-down actions (1996: 159–61).

The challenge is to balance the phases of experimentation and direction so that the enterprise can benefit from the advantages of both bottom-up initiatives and top-down decision-making. Too much experimentation can result in chaos; too much direction can stultify innovation. Built into the challenge of leadership is the ability to manage organizational change; leaders must gain personal commitment to new directions, technologies, processes, and products. Without personal commitment from top to bottom, human energies will not be mobilized to drive the redirection of organizational resources. While experimentation demands turning everyone into a designer, direction demands that everyone enthusiastically accept the winning designs. This is no small organizational challenge. It involves aligning individual intentions and actions to common purposes. It stretches the concept of the entrepreneurial firm.[18]

The leadership and design dynamic at the level of the firm can have a counterpart at the level of the region. In these cases, the entrepreneurial firm is part of an internal/external dynamic based on *open systems networking*. This dynamic fosters the internal decentralization and external diffusion of design and thereby enhances regional innovation. Each of these characteristics, in turn, reinforces and replenishes entrepreneurial firms.[19] We turn next to a series of internal/external dynamics that are fostered by the unfolding of the technology/market dynamic of the entrepreneurial firm.

Techno-diversification

The link between the boxes at the right and bottom in Figure 3.1 represents a 'techno-diversification' dynamic between entrepreneurial firms and 'new firms' or new activities within companies specializing in the requisite capabilities. In the process of pursuing its goals, the entrepreneurial firm propagates new productive opportunities that can be either pursued internally or pushed outside the firm.

The firm faces a dilemma: unique capabilities are both the source of competitive advantage and a constraint on future development. Firms that experiment and develop unique and/or new capabilities simultaneously must choose which of the new possibilities to pursue as the

[18] The technology-driven firm is a predecessor in the evolutionary chain and close cousin of the entrepreneurial firm. A technology-driven firm seeks to compete by advancing its technological capabilities as manifest in distinctive products in the marketplace. But it does not have the organizational capabilities to harness the technology/market dynamic. Consequently, its technology trajectory is more prone to getting out of sync with evolving market opportunities. A technology-driven firm becomes an entrepreneurial firm by developing technology management capabilities that enable it to harness the feedback effects from market changes.

[19] Information technology, alone, will not create the entrepreneurial firm. But digitization is a great facilitator of the entrepreneurial firm, much as electrification was a great facilitator of mass production (see below).

basis of their competitive advantage. Given the inherent uncertainty regarding technological change, firms are required to place bets on which technological possibilities should be pursued and which abandoned. No firm, no matter how big, can pursue all technological possibilities. New opportunities, which require activities that are not consistent with reinforcing the firm's basic position, risk devaluing the firm's unique capabilities. Those not pursued internally become 'market' opportunities for other firms to advance their productive capabilities.

The originating firm can generate three types of new opportunities for other firms that can, in turn, foster secondary internal dynamics in follow-up firms. First, because of the inherent uncertainty about future technological pathways, the entrepreneurial firm must place its R&D and new product development bets on specific opportunities and forsake the internal development of others. The choice to abandon certain opportunities may say less about the odds for future success than about sustaining the value of a firm's existing knowledge base.

Gordon Moore, a co-founder of Intel, illustrates the point as follows:

> Integrated circuits, MOS transistors, and the like proved too rich a vein for a company the size of Fairchild to mine, resulting in what came to be known as the 'Silicon Valley effect'. At least one new company coalesced around and tried to exploit each new invention or discovery that came out of the lab. (1996: 167)

Intel was itself a spin-off from Fairchild, along with dozens of other successful firms (Saxenian 1994: 25–6).[20]

Second, the new opportunities may not offer the scale required by the existing organization. Clayton Christensen labels the mismatch between the sales required to sustain an established firm and the market size of an emerging technology as the 'innovator's dilemma' (1997). But what is an innovator's dilemma for the established firm is an innovator's opportunity for the new entrant.

Third, if the entrepreneurial firm is part of a networked group of firms each specializing in a complementary capability, a technical change at one link in the chain will create new pressures and opportunities for specialists in each of the complementary capabilities. In this way, advances in design and technology are both diffused and interactive across production networks. In some cases, the effect may be one of induced technical change which, in turn, may set off a secondary

[20] The process of increasing specialization in technology capabilities is an application of Smith's principle of increasing specialization as described above.

internal dynamic and consequent pressure for change across the network.

In all three cases, productive opportunities that have been created by technology-driven firms represent market opportunities in the market 'interstices'.[21] New, small-scale entrants can harness new technology capability and market opportunity dynamics in ways that simultaneously advance the emerging technology and develop the new market. They are potential productive opportunities for new enterprises, spin-offs, or existing enterprises with capabilities in similar activities.

New firms are often the path to techno-diversification. In some cases, new firms and spin-offs can trigger the emergence of new industry subsectors. Classic examples are the transistor, the telephone, the laser, and the personal computer. The companies that sponsored the original research developed none of the key technological innovations even though all became the basis for the emergence of a vast range of new enterprises better positioned to read and seize the opportunities. In most cases, the new companies were not saddled with already existing capabilities in competing technologies. Unlike the originating enterprises, they were not forced to make a decision between supporting core technologies and associated skills and new technologies and the new skills.

The process of techno-diversification can operate on a much smaller scale. In any case, new firm creation is often critical to the emergence of new industrial sectors and business models. For example, new firms pursuing new technologies with new business models drove the resurgence of Massachusetts' Route 128 following the demise of the minicomputer industry. The new open system business model fostered much greater technical diversity and industrial 'speciation', or the creation of new technology species (see next section).

In these ways the growth dynamic of entrepreneurial firms feeds into the larger industrial system. But the story does not stop here. A growth impact is not automatic; it depends on choices made within the originating firm, inter-firm organization, and extra-firm infrastructure. Furthermore, the relations between firm and regional growth dynamics are not one way. They too are interactive.

[21] Interstice is Penrose's term for niche-market opportunities that have not yet been pursued.

Networking

The box at the left of Figure 3.1 represents inter-firm networking. Three types of inter-firm relations can be distinguished: market, closed system or Japanese *keiretsu*, and open system networking. Inter-firm relations are structurally linked to intra-firm organization: Big Business and arm's length, market-driven supplier relations, the *kaisha* (Japanese) business model and *keiretsu*, long-term supplier relations, and entrepreneurial firm and open systems networking. The *kaisha* business model fostered the principle of multi-product flow and achieved performance standards (cheaper, better, faster) which established the New Competition of the 1970s and 1980s.

The third type is open systems networking, commonly referred to as 'horizontal integration', multi-enterprise integration, cooperation, networking, or affiliated groups of specialist enterprises. Open systems networking is the inter-firm counterpart to increasing specialization of the entrepreneurial firm. It has proved effective at both rapid new product development and innovation and, consequently, became the New Competition of the 1990s. The open systems model depends upon inter-firm networking capabilities.

Inter-firm networking has evolved with the shift from price-led to product-led competition. This entails integration of manufacturing and new product development processes. But rapid new product development is not simply adding a product (multi-divisional diversification); increasingly, it involves a whole group of specialist companies operating at different links along the product chain or nodes in the value networks.

Open system networks convert the inescapable dilemma of the individual entrepreneurial firm into a growth opportunity for a region's collective enterprises. Abandoned possibilities are simultaneously opportunities for new divisions within subsidiaries or spin-offs or for new firm creation. The pursuit of new capabilities also opens new inter-firm partnering possibilities for complementary capabilities. Ease of entry, as well, enhances the regional capability for firms, existing and new, to respond to new market and technological opportunities.

Open systems networking is a model of industrial organization that fosters specialization and innovation. Historically, open systems prevailed in the design-led industrial districts of the 'third Italy' (Best 1990: chs. 7–8). More recently, the emergence of systems integration capabilities in technology has both fostered open system networks and developed because of them. In both cases, the business model of specialization and inter-firm networking form an internal/external dynamic that fosters innovation and growth.

The starting point remains the technology capability/market opportunity dynamic that drives the entrepreneurial firm, the source not only of the growth of the firm but of a derivative set of regional growth dynamics. But the internal dynamics of entrepreneurial firms simultaneously enhance *regional* growth potential. Whether or not the potential is realized depends, in part, upon strategic choices made within the entrepreneurial firm and the extent of inter-firm networking capabilities.

The firm's dilemma is either a cluster's constraint or its opportunity. The firm's dilemma is a *cluster constraint* in a region populated by enterprises that are vertically integrated.[22] But the firm's technology choice dilemma is a *cluster opportunity* in a region with 'open system' networks.

The goal of the entrepreneurial firm is to develop the organizational capabilities to differentiate its product in the marketplace and establish a market niche and ongoing relationship with customers. Success requires product redesign and development capability. To the extent that firms are successful, the mode of competition shifts from price-led to product-led. The rebounding pressures of product-led competition in the market on the internal organization of the firm reinforce the drive to develop unique products and production capabilities. A new dynamic between internal organization and inter-firm competition is established. Regions that make the transition to product-led competition can enjoy a competitive advantage over regions in which the dominant mode of competition is price. Product-led competition engenders the entrepreneurial firm. The entrepreneurial firm, in turn drives the new internal/external dynamic. Success in the marketplace increasingly depends upon product development, technology management, and innovation capabilities.

Inter-firm networking offers greater flexibility for new product development and innovation than does vertical integration.[23] Ironically, networking can foster the social relations necessary for effective colocation of specialist but complementary activities more easily than can vertical integration. While a vertically integrated company operates

[22] Externally integrated enterprises are defined as productive units coordinated within 'closed system' inter-regional networks or value chains directed by global enterprises.

[23] Horizontal integration, the term used by Andrew Grove of Intel to describe open systems networking can be considered an inter-firm consequence of Intel's production concept of integrated manufacturing (Grove 1996; see Ch. 3 below).

under a single hierarchy that can direct departments to co-locate, it does so within a bureaucracy and a set of technologies that were originally designed for different purposes. They become embedded in social systems and individual career paths within the firm that can offer resistance to organizational change. Open systems networking offers a range of co-design possibilities without locking an enterprise into any single design possibility. The open system organizational model is fostered by open systems in the form of standardized interfaces and shared design rules at the technological level.[24]

The Internet, which marries telecommunication and information technologies is a great facilitator of the open systems networking. In fact, the Internet is an archetypal open systems technology. It establishes interface rules that enable design modularization. The Internet makes it possible to manage supplier relations by seamlessly integrating information across different computer systems, parts lists, and even design programs.[25] Virtually seamless integration across businesses enhances the simultaneous increase in specialization and integration that Adam Smith identifies as the principle of increasing specialization.

As an easy plug-in system for specialist companies, the Internet lubricates the internal/external dynamics that spawn entrepreneurial firms. But it can also be seen as a metaphor for networking in general and thereby a target for policymakers seeking to increase entrepreneurial firms. In this, the Internet is a new 'invisible hand' but one that can assist the creation of entrepreneurial firms and regional innovation. In both cases a self-organizing supply response improves economic performance.

Regional Specialization and Innovation Processes

The upper box in Figure 3.1 signifies the extent of capability specialization and diversity within a regional population of industrial enterprises.

[24] The idea of system integration suggests a common design principle that enables the integration of independently designed components. The term 'open system' suggests that the system design rules are openly published. A closed system, in contrast, suggests the challenge of integration is achieved by an overarching design principle which leaves no space for independently designed components. The IBM 360 computer, for example, was a closed system before an anti-trust ruling forced the publication of the system design principle and thereby began a process that led to an open system. The embedded and private operating system of Massachusetts minicomputer companies is another example.

[25] The HPWS variant of the entrepreneurial firm has been one that more fully exploits the opportunities of information technologies. The result has been a deepened integration of manu-

Specialization has regional and inter-regional dimensions. Greater specialization internally is a measure of technological diversity within a region. Greater specialization externally, or across regions, is a measure of uniqueness of regional capability and thereby regional competitive advantage.

Regional specialization results from cumulative capability development and the unique combinations and patterns of intra- and inter-firm dynamics that underlie enterprise and regional specialization. Successful industrial districts are the outcome of historical processes of capability development often of a technological character.[26]

To contribute to economic growth, technologies must be embedded in production systems. The processes by which technological capabilities are embedded in a company's and a region's production system are an extension of the ongoing operations of entrepreneurial firms. The technology capability and market opportunity dynamic that drives the entrepreneurial firm is, simultaneously, a single step in a *cumulative* sequence by which a region's technological capability is extended.

A region's technological capabilities are like a seabed or industrial ecology, in which entrepreneurial firms are spawned, grow, and die. At the same time, however, entrepreneurial firms, driven by a technology capability and market opportunity dynamic, are forever advancing their own capabilities. In the process, the region's technological capability seabed is revitalized by the ongoing activities of its inhabitants.

The variation amongst technologies within a regional system of enterprise is critical to the fecundity of the seabed. Adam Smith's principle of increasing specialization, applied to capabilities, engenders greater variation of capabilities within a system of networking enterprises.

Greater technological diversity is particularly relevant to innovation in the form of industrial speciation, or the creation of new industrial sub-sectors. Speciation, a metaphor borrowed from the natural world, refers to innovation that emanates from new combinations

facturing and design that enhances design experimentation and incorporates various R&D activities into production. In the entrepreneurial firm, information technology is not a separate department but integral to new capabilities in rapid product development, technology management, and networking. Here, as in the Japanese variant, the entrepreneurial firm is characterized by the move from supervisor centered to team centered work organization. But the leadership/design dynamic is associated with a model of innovation that combines continuous improvement with technology integration (see Chs. 2 and 4).

[26] An example, developed in Ch. 5, is the success of New England in jet engine production, a technology that has a technological genealogy that goes back to water turbine innovations in the 1850s to power the region's textile mills.

of technologies that lead to new product applications and industrial classification categories.[27]

Speciation is a consequence of increased specialization. Greater specialization leads to increased variation of capabilities within a system of networking enterprises. Variety fosters ingenuity and innovation. Sometimes the variation fosters a metamorphosis of the district itself as new species of technologies emerge with new product applications. These become, in turn, market opportunities for refining technological capabilities and, perhaps, further specialization and variation.

An industrial district, unlike any single firm, offers the potential for new and unplanned technology combinations that tap a variety and range of research and production-related activities. This protean character of technological capability, particularly evident in high-tech sectors, is a feature of industrial change even in the oldest sectors. The electronics industry metamorphoses into, for example, an information and communications sector. Furniture becomes interior design and furnishing. In most cases, the process of industrial speciation cannot be done within a single firm. Speciation involves new combinations of technologies.

Thus, a region's technological capabilities are an outcome of a *cumulative* and *collective* history of technological advances embedded in entrepreneurial firms. Just as individual entrepreneurial firms develop unique technological capabilities, a virtual, collective entrepreneurial firm extends a region's unique technological capabilities. The regional process of technology capability advance will likely involve a succession of firms, with new firms building on advances made by previous innovators. Regional specialization, in the form of industrial districts or clusters, is the outcome of the technology/market dynamic played out at the level of the collective entrepreneurial firm.

Cluster dynamics and the development of regional technological capabilities are not limited to high-tech regions. They lie behind the competitive advantage of 'low-tech', high-income industrial districts common to the 'third Italy'. Such districts have developed a competitive advantage in design capabilities that have fostered industrial leadership in a range of design-led and fashion-oriented industries. In fact, the existence of cluster dynamics addresses the anomaly of high-income and 'mature' industry regions.

[27] Stephen Jay Gould (1996) argues that progress comes from variety not complexity. Gould uses the analogy with a full house in poker to make the point that excellence is a property of all parts together. Trends are better read as changes in variation within full systems rather than 'things moving somewhere'.

Recently, high-tech regions have developed similar capabilities for rapid design changes and industrial innovation that integrate basic research into production. In fact, regions such as Silicon Valley and Route 128 have developed regional innovation capabilities embedded in virtual laboratories in the form of broad and deep networks of operational, technological, and scientific researchers which cut across companies and universities. Silicon Valley project teams are continuously combining and recombining across a population of 6,000 high-tech firms, making it an unparalleled information and communication technology industrial district.[28]

Models of innovation are associated with different business models. The *kaisha* variant of the entrepreneurial firm decentralizes design and continuous change into the operating units. The rapid gain in Japanese market share in many industries in the 1970s and 1980s was achieved, in part, by designing a complementary incremental innovation capability into production. It fostered a technology-pull model of innovation. An American variant, and perhaps advance, is the leadership and design dynamic which combines top-down and bottom-up actions captured by Andrew Grove's leadership/design dynamic.

The regional model of innovation derives from the open system, regional growth dynamics (the diffusion and development of a range of growth dynamics ensuing from the entrepreneurial firm). Techno-diversification, technology integration, new technology combinations, and industry speciation are all elements in processes that advance the technology capabilities of a region.

The regional growth dynamics model fosters combined development and diffusion of innovation. Regional innovation refers to processes that not only trigger the regional growth dynamics but also which reshape it via the process of industrial speciation. Thus, the regional growth dynamics are an infrastructure for new industry incubation and formation.

The concept of regional innovation dynamics suggests a *collective entrepreneurial capability* as a basis for regional competitive advantage which, like its enterprise level counterpart, can be conceptualized as a technology market dynamic but at the regional level. Industrial districts compete against one another. Given different paces of technological development or a shift by one region to a higher model of technology

[28] Intel is not the only driver of new products. Approximately one in five of the Silicon Valley (and Route 128 in Massachusetts) publicly traded companies were gazelles in 1997, which means they have grown at least 20% in each of the last four years (the number for the United States is one in thirty-five). See MTC (1998).

management or a new technology platform, the losing region risks losing a whole swathe of enterprises.

As the networking capabilities of a region become more robust, the region takes on more the semblance of a collective entrepreneur. The virtual collective entrepreneurial firm is a self-organizing agent for change composed of networked groups of mutually adjusting enterprises.[29] The collective entrepreneurial firm is a composite of networking firms that collectively administer the regional growth dynamic processes of Figure 3.1.

While the high-tech districts are unique in terms of specific technologies and research intensity, they exhibit regional innovation characteristics in an exaggerated form that are common to the virtuous circle of regional growth. Examples follow.

First, the technology/market dynamic of the entrepreneurial firm drives the 'Silicon Valley effect', a *new firm creation process* which produces yet more entrepreneurial firms. The regional capability to create new firms can be measured in terms of the ratio of new to total number of firms. One study estimates that nearly three-fourths of Silicon Valley firms have been created in the last fifteen years compared to less than one-fourth in German 'high-tech' regions (Kluge, Meffert, and Stein 2000: 100). New firms engender regional techno-diversification that increases technological specialization and the variety of distinctive technology capabilities within a region. As already noted, this is an extension of Adam Smith's fundamental principle of economic organization from skills to capabilities and, in the case of Silicon Valley, to capabilities which themselves embody the principle of systems integration.

Second, the high-tech, open system industrial district is, as well, a *collective experimental laboratory.* Networked groups of firms are, in effect, engaged in continuous experimentation as the networks form, disband, and re-form. Both the ease of entry of new firms and the infrastructure for networking facilitate the formation, demise, and re-formation of technology integration teams. However successful the industrial district as a mode of economic coordination has been in international competition, heretofore, it has been considered appropriate only to 'light' industry such as the design-led, fashion industries of the 'third Italy' and the machine tool and metalworking regions of Baden-Württemberg in Germany.

Third, an open system district expands the number of *simultaneous*

[29] See Best (1990: 207–8).

experiments that are conducted. A vertically integrated company may carry out several experiments at each stage in the production chain, but a district can well exploit dozens simultaneously. In this way, a district counters the barriers to introducing new ideas in firms that already have well-developed capabilities around competing technologies.

Fourth, an open system district fosters the *decentralization and diffusion of design capabilities.* Design modularization in the personal computer industry is an example. IBM got the process underway in response to an antitrust ruling to publish its system design rules. This was greatly enhanced when Microsoft and Intel developed the design modules for the operating system and the microprocessor.[30] The resulting standards have created enormous market opportunities for specific applications software. But, in addition, the concept of design modularization combines common interface design rules with decentralization of component design. This diffusion of design capability increases collective innovation capacity. It can also strengthen the district model of industrial organization, and even encourage conversion from a closed to an open system.[31]

Fifth, the diversity of technologies within a dynamic district creates potential for innovations as '*unplanned confluences* of technology from different fields' (Kostoff 1994: 61).[32] In a survey of innovation, Ronald Kostoff finds that the first and most important factor associated with innovation is a broad pool of advanced knowledge. In Kostoff's words 'an advanced pool of knowledge must be developed in many fields before synthesis leading to innovation can occur'. This advanced pool of knowledge is the critical factor, not the lone entrepreneur:

> The entrepreneur can be viewed as an individual or group with the ability to assimilate this diverse information and exploit it for further development. However, once this pool of knowledge exists, there are many persons or groups with capability to exploit the information, and thus the real critical path to innovation is more likely to be the knowledge pool than any particular entrepreneur. (1994: 61)

[30] See J. Katz (1996: 15). Katz also describes network economies and increasing returns. The value of a network is roughly proportional to the square of the number of users.

[31] The regional innovation processes can be referred to as the 5Ds: disruptive (internal/internal dynamic), dip-down (fast new product development), design diffusion (leveraging creativity), dispersed (laboratories for experimentation), and diversity (new technological combinations).

[32] Kostoff's survey supports Rosenberg's historical research on the inherently uncertain dimension of innovation and the role of confluence of trends in shaping the effects of any specific innovation on productivity and growth (1976, 1982). The point here is that an open systems model of industrial organization counters the inherent uncertainty of technology with the potential for the confluence of trends.

The knowledge pool is developed through non-mission-oriented research in a range of fields 'by many different organizations'. Kostoff does not underestimate the role of planned research, but stresses the combination: 'mission-oriented research or development stimulates non-mission research to fill gaps preceding the innovation'.[33]

From this perspective, an industrial district, unlike any single firm, offers the potential of a technological full-house with a variety and range of research and production-related activities which can foster creativity, fill gaps, replenish the knowledge pool, link needs to research, and incite unplanned confluence of technologies.[34] The district itself is an organizational structure that fosters a focus and network business model.

CONCLUSION

The models of production systems derived in Chapter 2 suggest that technological and organizational change are part of the same process. The Springfield Armory, for example, was a pioneer in the application of the principle of interchangeability and in a series of organizational innovations in 'factory management'. Henry Ford introduced the principle of flow and a work organization and plant layout designed to maximize throughput efficiency. In both these cases innovations in business organization were necessary to institutionalize the new process technologies.

Firms exist, according to Penrose, because they can accomplish activities that cannot be done alone or at once.[35] The concept of the

[33] Following the broad pool of advanced knowledge, the second critical condition identified by Kostoff is *recognition of technical opportunity and need*. 'In many cases, knowledge of the systems applications inspires the sciences and technology that lead to advanced systems'. The third, fourth, and fifth critical factors are a technical entrepreneur who champions the innovation, financial, and management support. The final, sixth factor is *continuing innovation and development over many fields*. In the words of Kostoff: 'additional supporting inventions are required during the development phase preceding the innovation'. At least three of the six critical factors for innovation success identified by Kostoff point to networking capabilities.

[34] The regional model of innovation offers a decentralized, self-organizing explanation of the success of high-tech regions, but of industrial districts in general as an alternative to the linear, science-push model of innovation. In the latter, technology is thought of as applied science; in the regional model, technology is part of the industrial process. It is built into the process by which firms establish unique capabilities and network with other firms. The science-push model, in contrast, fails to capture the extent to which research is woven into the production, technology, and networking fabric of a region's industrial system as distinct from being an external, autonomous sphere of activity.

[35] The two perspectives treat the firm and market asymmetrically: in the wealth creation

entrepreneurial firm unifies production and business organization. Both the Springfield Armory and Henry Ford's business model hinted at the organizational features of ongoing technological change and market development dynamic captured in the concept of the entrepreneurial firm. The entrepreneurial firm is a firm that pursues market niches by developing unique production capabilities, often of a technological form, and the process of developing such capabilities precipitates new market opportunities to guide new product development. The entrepreneurial firm is driven by a technology/market dynamic; an endogenous process built into the ongoing operations of the firm.[36]

The idea of the entrepreneurial firm captures a link between technological change and industrial growth. The perpetual pursuit of 'improvement of art' motivates innovation and engenders perpetual change. The combination of increasing specialization in capabilities and the discovery of new production methods generates increasing returns, higher productivity, and industrial growth.

Penrose put Adam Smith's 'discovery principle' back into the wealth creation perspective by developing a theory of the growth of the firm. Learning, or advances in knowledge, becomes central to the operations of the entrepreneurial firm as conceptualized by Penrose. But knowledge is not separable from other 'factors of production' as in the case of Marshall; instead knowledge creation is integral to the production process. Increasing specialization in technological capability fosters innovation as firms seek to develop and sustain unique capabilities in the market. In the process they differentiate technologies and products and reshape the market. The performance standard that explains competitiveness is not measured in cost alone. Firms can compete on the basis of cost, product design, quality, or delivery time.

The entrepreneurial firm integrates Adam Smith's discovery principle into the operations of the firm. The sources of productivity are improvements in organizational and technological capabilities triggered by increasing specialization. Given the entrepreneurial firm, capability is

perspective, the market is defined in terms of the firm; in the optimal resource allocation perspective, the firm is defined in terms of the market. In the former the firm drives knowledge creation; in the latter the firm exists to counter market failure.

[36] The term 'technology/market dynamic' is an abbreviation of technology capability/market opportunity dynamic and a variant of Penrose's resource/productive service dynamic taken up in the intellectual heritage section of this chapter (Penrose 1995). The idea of the entrepreneurial firm as an extension of the entrepreneurial function from an individual attribute to a collective or organizational capability is introduced in Best (1990: 11–14).

the unit of specialization. Success is achieved by developing distinctive organizational, technological, and production capabilities.[37]

Organization and time are integral to the capabilities and innovation perspective. The entrepreneurial firm drives a cumulative technological capability trajectory that advances with each consecutive technology and market dynamic.[38] This is a process of increasing capability specialization.

A theory of the wealth creation process implies an account of industrial organization that starts with the learning dynamic built into the production operations of the entrepreneurial firm. The capabilities and innovation perspective extends the internal dynamic that drives the entrepreneurial firm in three ways that have implications for a complementary theory of industrial organization.

First, the technology capability and market opportunity dynamic internal to the firm can combine with inter-firm networking to drive an internal/external growth dynamic. Increasing firm specialization fosters open system networks which, in turn, feed back and enhance opportunities for further specialization and innovation within the constituent firms, as well as create opportunities for new firms. In this way the technology/market dynamic internal to the firm deepens inter-firm networking and inter-firm networking creates new market opportunities for specialist firms to advance their technological capabilities. The external dynamic fosters the internal dynamic and vice versa.

The state of the internal/external dynamic points to a distinction between static and dynamic industrial districts. A static industrial district lacks the internal/external growth dynamic. Such districts can enjoy Marshall's locational economies, but they do so within an unchanging 'production chain'. Dynamic districts, in contrast, are continuously upgrading, redefining, and reconstituting the 'production chain'. Most of the world's industry is conducted within static industrial districts that lack entrepreneurial firms. Capabilities are not advancing and innovation is limited. They do not drive growth.

[37] The concept of the firm required for understanding wealth creation must account for more comprehensive performance standards than cost minimization (Lazonick 1990; O'Sullivan 2000). The idea of the entrepreneurial firm is that firms can succeed by product-led competition as well as price-led competition. In contrast, the concepts that define the firm that populates the resource allocation perspective are constrained by consistency with the assumptions required for a theory of optimal resource allocation. These assumptions include cost minimization as the determinant of success in the marketplace and that capabilities are commodities that can be bought and sold in the marketplace.

[38] The examples of precision machining and turbine technology as examples of continuity and change in technology capability are developed in Ch. 5.

Second, the capabilities and innovation perspective extends the technology/market dynamic at the entrepreneurial firm level to a collective technology/market dynamic at the regional level. The internal/external dynamic enhances specialization both within and across industrial districts. A consequence of increased intra-regional technological specialization is the development of increased inter-regional technological specialization. A regional technology/market dynamic is like a collective entrepreneurial firm dynamic between a region's unique technological capabilities and worldwide market opportunities. It is the basis for regional competitive advantage.

As noted, many regions have Marshallian industrial districts; few develop the regional growth dynamics associated with increasing capability specialization. But in competition between the two regions, the higher productivity of the dynamic districts will create regional competitive advantage. The example of competition between a Marshallian industrial district and a dynamic industrial district explains the rapid decline of the East and North London furniture districts once barriers to competition with Italian furniture districts were removed (Best 1990).[39]

Regional cluster dynamics are a virtuous circle. New technological possibilities inspire new entrepreneurial firms, which upgrade regional technological capabilities, which inspires new entrepreneurial firms. The entrepreneurial firm start-up system is particularly strong in the Silicon Valley and Route 128/495 high-tech regions in the United States and in the design-led and the fashion industries of the 'third Italy'. Taiwan, Ireland, and Israel have all established variants, if on a smaller scale.

Most attention has been focused on financial markets as the enablers of entrepreneurial firm emergence and development. Venture capital and 'initial public offering' capabilities are certainly contributors to the high new firm creation rates in both Silicon Valley and Route 128/495. Important as financial commitment is, however, the driving force must be the technological and market opportunities for establishing a firm with the profitability to make an attractive return to suppliers of finance.

Third, the capabilities and innovation perspective extends the concept of the entrepreneurial firm to account for principles of produc-

[39] The idea that regional or cluster competition accounts for the decline of Route 128 relative to Silicon Valley in the late 1980s is developed in Ch. 5. The uniqueness of clusters in the same industrial sector is explored in the case of three regional electronics clusters in Malaysia in Ch. 6. The form of networks is also stressed in Lazerson and Lorenzoni (1999).

tion.[40] The level of a region's productivity can be explained in terms of the development of its production capabilities. The principle of interchangeability, for example, goes a long distance to explaining the regional competitive advantage of New England manufacturing in the nineteenth century. Increasing precision, a corollary of interchangeability, became a regional production capability that was sustained across technological domains. But the development of the principle of flow in the American mid-west meant the emergence of production capabilities in throughput efficiency that could not be matched by New England's volume producers.

The capabilities and innovation perspective is also an account of innovation and growth. In the next chapter innovation and skill formation, the third domain of the Productivity Triad, are integrated into the story.

[40] Thus, the capabilities and innovation perspective is an account of industrial organization that explains performance in the marketplace in terms of the comparative organizational and production capbilities. This contrasts with the 'structure-conduct-performance' approach to industrial organization in which enterprise performance is predicted by market structure and measured in terms of divergence of output levels and price and cost ratios that would satisfy the optimal allocation of resources rules.

CHAPTER

4

Innovation Capabilities and Skill Formation

The organizational characteristics of a new competitive advantage are taking shape. These include a technology management capability linked to systems integration elaborated in Chapter 2 combined with the open systems business model and cluster dynamics described in Chapter 3. These two organizational developments are enabling conditions for a new model of innovation.

Much is known about the history of radical technological innovations.[1] The first task in this chapter is to examine the interface between innovation and models of business organization. These linkages are important to the growth process. When innovation is embedded in a business model that fosters mutual adjustment processes between innovation and production it becomes an instituted process. Innovation, as a one-off activity, becomes an innovation capability. The term 'capability' signifies an ongoing institutional process central to the strategy and performance of the business enterprise. The New Competitive Advantage is about the emergence of business models and production systems that seamlessly integrate technology management and innovation (PS 5 in Table 2.1).

However, for new business models and production systems to drive growth a third condition is required: a skill formation process must be instituted that matches the skill requirements of the rapidly growing firms. An examination of skill formation processes, the third dimension

[1] Leading examples include research done at the Science Policy Research Unit at Sussex University by Freeman (1982), Hobday (1995*b*), Pavitt (1980), Perez (1983), Prencipe (1998), and von Tunzelmann (1995). Other major contributors include T. Hughes (1989), Kline (1985), Landes (1970), Mansfield (1980), and Nelson (1996).

of the Productivity Triad, is the second task of this chapter. The process of innovation is simultaneously the creation of new knowledge and new skills. Much can be gained by viewing these two activities as opposite sides of the same coin. This involves breaking down the concept of R&D to distinguish basic, developmental, and applied levels and to account for complementary skill formation activities at each level.

The process of skill *formation* is about the characterization, development, and diffusion of new skills which, in turn, enables innovation to spread from single applications in a lab or an enterprise to groups of firms and thereby fuel growth. Single firms can grow by pulling the requisite skilled labor from other firms, but for large numbers of firms to grow a skill formation process must be established. The regional growth process involves the development of education and training methodologies and programs in sync with technological advance and innovation.

BUSINESS MODELS AND INNOVATION CAPABILITIES

The practice of innovation has evolved along with the production system and business models. Innovation in the American System of Manufacturing was a decentralized and collective process carried out by specialist machine makers (Tull 2000). Important as the evolution of a specialist machine industry was to the development of industrial leadership in America, it was largely an invisible process of designing improvements in products, machines, and production processes.

More visible were the independent inventors credited with radical innovations that sparked the establishment of new industries in the early days of Big Business. At the turn of the century, independent inventors such as Bell, Edison, and the Wright brothers were the great innovators consistent with Schumpeter's vision. These men set the stage for a new age of organized, corporate innovation. Thereafter, innovation became institutionalized in corporate laboratories to feed new products into the production facilities of the large managerial enterprises that dominated national markets. While our story begins with Big Business, the new model of innovation shares certain features of the decentralized model associated with the earlier American System of Manufacturing which have relevance for development in technology-poor regions of the world today.

Big Business: Corporate Laboratories

The age of Big Business refers to the period in which the managerial enterprise came to dominate much of American industry. The term refers to a series of organizational innovations associated with the substitution of the visible hand of managerial hierarchy for the invisible hand of market coordination of economic activities (Chandler 1977). The Big Business model also signals the transition from an age of innovation led by independent inventors to the age of corporate laboratories in which the education of engineers and scientists was a critical component (T. Hughes 1989).

The production side of the managerial enterprise was the diffusion of the principle of flow from cars to supplier industries, including petrochemicals and steel, and a range of consumer durables.[2] The vertically integrated, managerial enterprise was the enabling business model. The new business model integrated the economies of mass production with those of mass distribution and ushered in the age of mass consumption.

The new business model, in turn, fostered the growth of industrial research activity as a means of identifying new products to plug into mass production facilities and mass distribution channels. The development of the multi-divisional organizational capability meant that laboratory breakthroughs could be converted into new product divisions and share the company's marketing and distribution channels. Mowery and Rosenberg estimate that the number of industrial laboratories in manufacturing companies increased from around 100 in 1900 to nearly 2,000 in 1940 (1989; cited in Mowery and Nelson 1996: 199–200).

The development of the industrial laboratories depended upon and fostered a huge expansion in engineering and science education. The employment of scientists and engineers in industrial research labo-

[2] In practice the principle of flow as developed at Ford was subverted by mass batch production which came to dominate American manufacturing. See Reid (1990) for an example of the difference between the two production systems as applied to Harley Davidson. Harley made a successful transition from mass batch methods based on the model of optimal inventory levels to mass production based on the principle of flow. CEO Vaughn Beals used the idea of a Productivity Triad to describe the turnaround. The elements were MAN (materials as needed, a variant of just-in-time), EI (employee involvement), and SOC (statistical operator controls, a variant of total quality management). Until changes in all three elements were simultaneously integrated into the transition process, Harley Davidson was not successful. See also Best (1990) for distinctions between the mass batch and mass production. Most commentators fail to distinguish the two and thereby fail to capture the core elements of mass production (see Ch. 2 above).

ratories in US manufacturing firms expanded by ten times between 1921 and 1940 (from 2,775 to 27,777) (Mowery and Nelson 1996: 196). US higher education degrees went from 48,000 in 1913 to 216,000 in 1940. The United Kingdom with a population 35 percent of the United States had only 6 percent as many students in higher education in the 1930s (Mowery and Nelson 1996: 225).

While the Big Business model of industrial innovation was established with a relatively minor role played by the federal government, this was to change radically with World War II. This war began a new era in US government R&D expenditures. In 1940 federal support of science was under $80 million of which nearly 40 percent went to the Department of Agriculture. If the military identified a scientific need it would draft personnel with the appropriate qualifications into public service (Sapolsky 1990). During the war federal expenditure mushroomed from $83 million in 1940 to over $1,300 million in 1945 (in 1930 dollars).

During World War II and thereafter federal agencies oversaw and funded a vast expansion in R&D. Federal government funding of R&D increased from around $10 billion in 1953 to nearly $30 billion in 1960 and over $38 billion in 1965; it slumped to $31 billion in 1975 before climbing to over $45 billion in 1985 and $50 billion in 1990. Industry invested only half the federal government totals in 1960 and 1965 but a roughly equal amount in the 1980s (Nelson 1993: 41, real dollars).

The industrial innovation system involved huge government funding of industrial labs and education. An indicator of the government/industry/university system is the twentyfold expansion in scientists and engineers in industrial research laboratories from 27,777 in 1940 to 45,941 in 1946, to 300,000 in 1962, and to 600,000 in 1985. In 1965 the United States had 65 scientists and engineers engaged in R&D per 10,000 workers; in contrast, France, Germany, Japan, and the United Kingdom had between 20 and 25 scientists and engineers engaged in R&D per 10,000 workers (see US National Science Board 1989, 1991: appendix table 3–19).

This explosive growth accompanied the development of American industrial leadership in the 'high technology' products of aircraft, electronics, and computers. University research and education of scientists and engineers were transformed in the process; they vastly expanded science and engineering programs to meet the demand for research and graduates from industrial and governmental laboratories. From an estimated level of $420 million in 1935–6, university research exceeded $2 billion in 1960 and reached nearly $14 billion in 1993 (Mowery and Nelson 1996: 204, in 1982 dollars).

The implications for industrial growth were not lost on policymakers. The logic appeared unassailable: funding science generates technological breakthroughs that usher in new products and new industries that, in turn, drive growth. Federal spending on R&D, including the underwriting of the huge increase in the education of scientists and engineers, became America's de facto industrial policy.

Industrial leadership, at the same time, was about more than promoting competitive industries. Scientific leadership not only created jobs in America but also created economic opportunities abroad. High-wage America would enjoy leadership in development and introduction of new products. Eventually technology would be transferred abroad to lower wage regions; the lowest income regions would specialize in mature designs and second-generation technologies.[3]

The loss of American market share in the traditional mass production labor-intensive industries to lower wage regions was a consequence of advances in production capabilities elsewhere. Japan's success in high-volume manufacturing industries such as cars and electric appliances was consistent with the spread of mass production technologies. But it came as a shock when American enterprises began losing market share in high-tech industries such as semiconductors. The publication of the MIT book *Made in America* in 1989 signaled the growing concern that American industrial leadership was under severe attack and American industry was threatened with a hollowing out process (Dertouzas, Lester, and Solow 1989).

The American business model came under competitive pressures. All too often, it seemed, the manufacturing arms of American business enterprises could not convert innovations developed in industrial laboratories into commercially viable products. Why? Part of the reason is that American Big Business had developed a 'linear sequence' model of industrial innovation from:

basic research → technological development →
product engineering and development → manufacture and sales.

The linear sequence was a consequence of the organizational principles of hierarchy and functional departmentalization. The business model engendered the separation of research laboratories from product design and development and both from manufacturing. A status

[3] The term 'mature' is not meant to imply the biological metaphor of the product life cycle, a concept which does not take into account production capabilities.

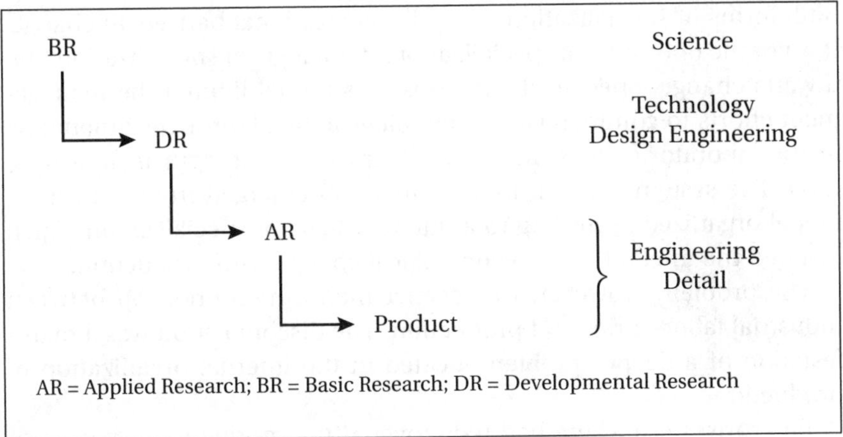

Fig. 4.1. Laboratory-push innovation: US big business
Source: Adapted from Methé 1995.

hierarchy of engineers mirrored and reinforced the sequence of activities. Basic research was deemed the most and manufacturing activities the least challenging.

The one-way flow of ideas between innovation activities, centered in research labs and production is shown in Figure 4.1. New technologies or product concepts were developed in R&D laboratories (BR) and passed on to process and product engineers to specify the production specifications (DR). The lagged task of production management was to convert the product designs and process specifications into manufacturing activities, procedures, and job tasks (AR) for which industrial engineers devised incentive systems. Supervisors, in turn, fit workers into the tasks and implemented incentive systems in pursuit of production targets.[4]

Introducing new product designs and/or new processes and technologies meant negotiating new methods, new ideas, and new practices conceived elsewhere for implementation in production. The business model was designed around a particular logic of specialization which departmentalized by functional activity and created an occupational divide which slotted individuals into activities of design or production, thinking or doing, and conception or execution, managers or workers.

[4] In fact, the problem was not so much functional departmentalization, as in reality the United States always had a 'chain-linked' model of innovation as defined by Kline (1985). It was more the failure to integrate production into the new product development process and thereby enjoy the benefits of an endogenous technology management capability (see PS 4 in Table 2.1).

Both forms of specialization erected organizational barriers to change. It is not the only logic of specialization. It is a logic of specialization that thwarts change. Specifically, the business model limited the management efforts to commercialize technological breakthroughs originating in the laboratories and undermined America's strength in industrial R&D. The system worked until competition emerged from a business model organized according to a different logic of specialization which fostered the integration of technological change with production.

The problem, however, was deeper than a disconnection between industrial laboratories and production. The disconnection was a manifestation of a deeper problem located in the internal organization of production.

Enterprises elsewhere had rediscovered the production principle of flow (originally developed but usually ignored in American industry) and the associated business organization principle of process integration (see Chapter 2). Furthermore, they applied the principle of flow not only to production but extended it to two new challenges: multiple products on the same production line and new product development. The challenge for management, engineers, and workers was to drive down cycle times for multi-product production and new product development. The new business model developed an incentive system and set of manufacturing practices to make it work.

The result was a systemic advance in manufacturing performance. The United States lost the manufacturing platform that it had used to establish industrial leadership. No matter how inventive the industrial laboratories, or low the wages of its workforce, American industry could not deliver the goods. The new production system, originated elsewhere, could.

Robert Forrant (1997) provides an example to illustrate the mediating role of skill formation in the innovation growth process. Computer-numerical control machine tools were developed at MIT's Servomechanism Labs (see Chapter 5). But they were first inputs into Japanese and not American industrial growth. The Japanese model of work organization made it easy to integrate the new technology and exploit its potential for flexible production. In the process they were refined, simplified, and diffused in Japanese industry. The American model of work, which at that time did not integrate design and mass production, was not organized to pursue applied research and shopfloor innovation. It was blind to the strategic opportunities of the new technology.

America had considerable industrial strengths. The combination of federal and industrial labs and higher education system fostered an unrivaled science community in the United States. Nowhere else did industrial enterprises enjoy such a broad and deep pool of basic research capability to which it could dip for talent and research assistance. But the system had an Achilles heel: without a world-class manufacturing platform the innovation capabilities could not be realized in production performance and industrial growth.

Incremental Innovation

As we saw in Chapter 2, American Big Business came under pressure from the emergence of a new model of technology management designed to facilitate product-led competition. The Japanese business model (*kaisha*) was capable of rapidly assimilating new technologies into the production system; this capability, in turn, provided the platform for extending rapid cycle time competition from manufacturing multiple products to new product development (PS 4 in Table 2.1). The success of the new model of technology management in converting new technologies developed elsewhere, into a stream of new products led to the dismantling of many industrial laboratories in America. All too often investments in R&D laboratories by functionally departmentalized American corporations were not being translated by their own manufacturing facilities into new products and commercial success.

The new business model involves an extension of the principle of multi-product flow (the Toyota Production System) to new product development (NPD). Reducing cycle time for NPD depends upon the production capability to introduce new technologies with each NPD cycle. Driving down cycle times was not simply a management directive; it involves a new team-centered model of work organization, which requires new roles for workers and managers. The supervisor-centered model of work proved ill suited to the problem-solving challenges of rapid NPD.

The strength of the new business model was in continuous improvement or incremental innovation. But *kaizen* is more than self-directed work teams (or 'lean production') and the development of the inclusive management philosophy led by the quality movement. It also altered the constitution of research, development, and associated engineering activities in production.

It was a small organizational step from the self-directed work team model of work organization to the integration of developmental research

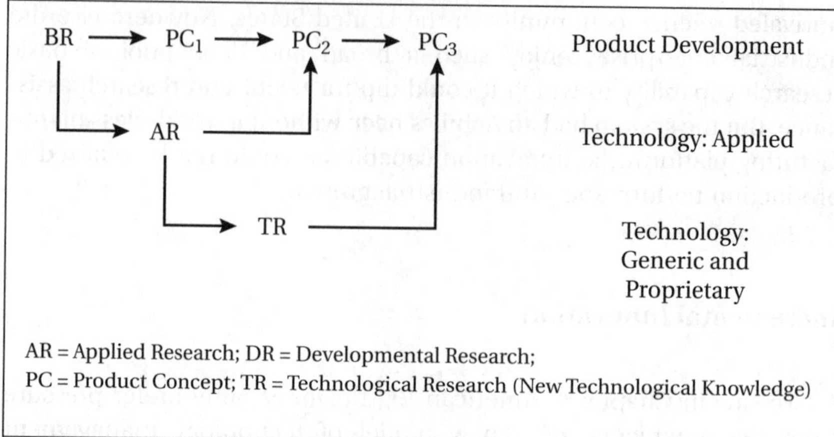

Fig. 4.2. Incremental innovation: Japan PS 4
Source: Adapted from Methé 1995

with production. As shown in Figure 4.2, developmental research triggers new product concepts (PC) that are progressively reinvented via feedback effects with applied research (AR). The *kaizen* work organization enables the integration of AR and production. The systematic introduction of new product concepts involves linking AR with technological research (TR) carried out in company laboratories which in turn, tap into worldwide technology knowledge bases.

The new model extended the technology/market dynamic into production: developmental research became interactive with technological research on the core technologies that define a company's uniqueness in the marketplace.[5] The business model involves the integration of production into the technology and market dynamic of the entrepreneurial firm. The manufacturing engineering challenge was profoundly changed. A design engineer's task is not finished with a new product design: he/she must design the product jointly with manufacturing personnel for purposes of manufacturability. In the case of the *kaisha* this often means an engineer stays with a new product development (NPD) project from initial design phases to prototyping, to pilot runs, and on through ramp up to full-scale production.

The organizational capability to assimilate new *product* technologies rapidly led, in turn, to an organizational capability to assimilate new

[5] For an organizational chart of Toshiba that illustrates the integration of applied research and operations, see Yamanouchi (1995: 217).

process technologies rapidly. Thus, developing rapid NPD cycle time capability was simultaneously the development of rapid technology diffusion capability. A primary example is the diffusion of CNC (computer-numerical control) equipment and reinvention of the Japanese machine tool industry. The diffusion of numerical control machine tools grew from approximately 10 percent to 70 percent of the market between 1974 and 1981 (Kodama 1986).[6] As noted, the numerical control machine tool was developed in MIT's Servomechanism Laboratory under a contract from the US Air Force (Forrant 1997; Noble 1977). Its pace of diffusion, however, was very slow in Massachusetts and throughout the United States. In America, the business model was not organized according to the principle of multi-product flow appropriate for small lot size production and firms were not competing on the basis of rapid new product development. The prevailing business model was not designed to take advantage of the new general purpose technology; where the new technology was introduced it was deployed to speed up batch production, not to integrate design and production in the pursuit of flexible production capabilities (Jaikumar 1986; Best 1990: 156–8).

But the integration of production and developmental research also represented a distinctive perspective on knowledge and knowledge creation including the relationship between science and technology. Production, in the second approach, is a laboratory for creating, advancing, combining, and diffusing technological knowledge. Myers and Rosenbloom (1996), following Kline (1985), argue that science and technologies were the enablers, rather than the drivers, of the innovation process.

> Therefore, science is depicted in two constituent parts: bodies of 'stored knowledge' and processes of research. Each part enters into the innovation process across its breadth. Thus science and technology interact with innovation in multiple ways, including learning from previous market engagements, continuing enhancement of innovative capabilities through the creation of new tools and instruments, and acquisition of new knowledge from the external technical infrastructure. The innovation process in this view is primarily a learning process in which knowledge has a central role as the key ingredient and the principle output. (Myers and Rosenbloom 1996: 214)

This concept of production as producing both goods and ideas resonates with the idea of the entrepreneurial firm as a learning firm.

[6] The typical technology adoption times were 25–50 years for the cumulative market adoption on new technologies to reach 50% (Freeman 1982 and 1991; Kodama 1986).

The superior technology management capabilities constituted in part by the incremental innovation model put the Big Business model of innovation under pressure. But it also undermines the implicit assumption that technology is applied science. The incremental model of innovation presumes, instead, that technology is an independent body of knowledge, which can be initiated in the sphere of production as well as in R&D laboratories.

Open Systems

The cell of the new production system is in all production systems the make-up of the teams in the production unit. The composition of the team reflects production principles in organizational capabilities and enables specific competitive strategies. In lean or flexible mass production the team must include members from the range of functional activities required to make the product. This facilitates continuous improvement of the production process. In the case of the Canon production system, the business model is designed to compete on the basis of rapid new product development and teams are constituted to integrate design and manufacture. The technology integration teams of the Intel model (PS 5 in Table 2.1) reflect the organizational capability to integrate technologies to drive high annual rates of productivity advance (30 percent in the case of Intel).

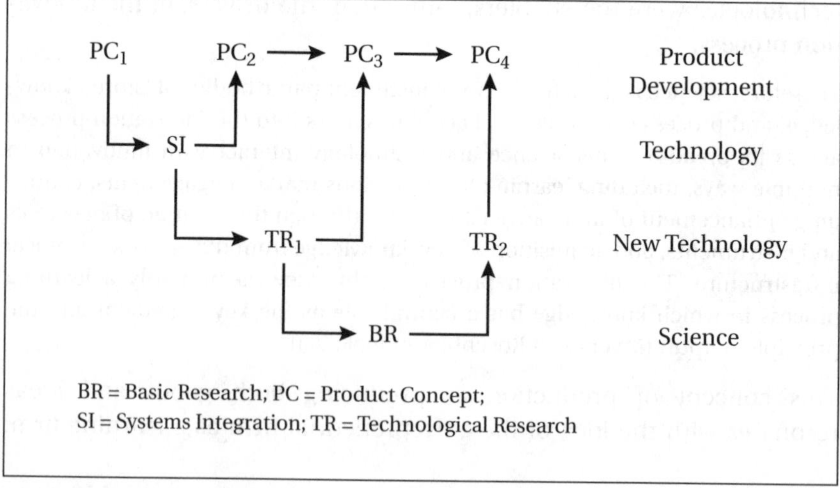

Fig. 4.3. Systems integration innovation: US PS 5

As shown in Figure 4.3, systems integration involves integrating technological research (TR) and basic research (BR). Technology integration teams are designed to foster the organizational capability to engage in communication across multiple technology domains and associated disciplinary languages.[7] It requires more. Technology management in production units that involve the incorporation of fundamental research into production, not as a driver but as a servant of technological advance, requires networking. As a feature of its systems integration capability, Intel's technology management process breaks with Henry Ford, Toyota, and Canon in a fundamental way: it is embedded in virtual laboratories in the form of broad and deep networks of researchers at the frontiers of scientific and technological research. For this, Silicon Valley has developed a unique competitive advantage.

Technology integration teams are organized to facilitate communication internally and externally. The challenge of rapid technological change continually generates technical challenges and the search for solutions. Teams 'dip-down' into the scientific and technological bodies of knowledge that are available in the universities and 'industrial districts'.[8] This involves identifying where specialized knowledge and expertise can be located. Companies form long-term relationships with university research groups and other technology-oriented firms to access it.

Intel divides research into two types: research 'that require[s] integrated manufacturing capability to examine' and 'chunks' that do not required state of the art semiconductor technology. Intel focuses on the former and networks with universities to get the latter. The research that is assigned to universities can be early-stage research with highly uncertain potential applications. It can also be research designed to anchor observed processes in science or at least repeatable patterns. Moore notes that a number of processes in semiconductor manufacturing are 'more of an art than a science': the plasma etching process, for example, is not well understood' (Moore 1996: 72).

[7] Each engineering and scientific discipline has a distinctive 'language' (see Ch. 5 for examples). Mechanical, electrical, and software engineering methodologies, for example, are based on different units of analysis and measurement. Systems integration involves technology teams that can combine the strengths of the disciplines to develop and produce new product concepts. Internal training programs at companies like Intel rely on software tools developed for each discipline to facilitate interdisciplinary communication. Nevertheless no functional equivalent short of experience and teamwork has yet been discovered to Douglas Adams' 'Babel fish', a device used to enable inter-galactic communication in *A Hitchhiker's Guide to the Galaxy* (1989: 42).

[8] The metaphor 'dip-down' to describe the process illustrated in Fig. 4.3 was suggested to me by Arthur Francis of Bradford University.

In this way the open systems business model (PS 5 in Table 2.1) stretches the concept of technology management to integrate production with basic research. Here technology management includes the pursuit of breakthrough innovations in technological knowledge.

The new model of innovation builds on an advanced set of production capabilities (see Box 2.2). It has involved moving from functional departmentalization to agile manufacturing, to systems integration and, in terms of research, moving from a linear sequence, to closed networks, to open networks. This is part of a process of implementing the principle of systems integration. It is also a model of technology management that combines incremental with breakthrough innovation.[9] University partnerships are also valuable for recruitment purposes and to access advances in the pool of technical knowledge as well as research expertise to solve problems.

University research laboratories are an important but not the only external knowledge pool. Intel depends upon, and reinforces, an industrial district constituted by multiple design nodes, which includes a vast array of specialist producers and research institutions. In this, it draws upon an extended industrial high-tech district with an extraordinary capacity to conduct experiments, carry out innovations, and conduct research. In fact, Silicon Valley project teams are continuously combining and recombining within a population of 6,000 high-tech firms. Thus, technology integration teams are the hubs of extended research networks in districts like Silicon Valley. They extend beyond the firm enabling project teams to participate in a highly innovative milieu for technology management.

As a model of industrial organization, Silicon Valley breaks with the tendency of ever increasing concentration of technological research within a few big labs during the heyday of Big Business (T. Hughes 1989). Certainly, R&D budgets can be huge, as in the case of new microprocessor chip-making plants. But big, centralized R&D labs are not the keys to understanding regional growth dynamics. Entrepreneurial firms and their cumulative and collective technology capability and market opportunity dynamics drive regional growth. Regionally distributed R&D activities interact with these dynamics.

The regional innovation model of industrial organization is not new.

[9] In contrast, the *kaisha*, closed network business model (PS 4 in Table 2.1) is not based on the principle of systems integration; it does not involve management of feedback effects between production and basic research. It is a one-way street, with a pull into production of technology and innovation rather than a push. This is not surprising. Just-in-time production is all about pulling materials through the production system, not pushing.

For example, the networked groups of small firms that collectively exhibit entrepreneurial firm capabilities in the highly productive furniture districts of the 'third Italy' are carriers and contributors to Adam Smith's principle of specialization and derived 'improvements of art' (A. Smith 1976). They even have systems integration capability to combine and recombine technologies and materials in pursuit of compressed new product development cycle times. Wood engineering, for example, is itself highly advanced and derivative of generic advances in engineering and transition in technological domain (see Ch. 5). Networked firms here, too, have innovative capabilities that extend into various domains of research without centralized R&D capability.

The light industries of the 'third Italy' are collectively entrepreneurial in that production involves both the decentralization and diffusion of design capability (in the forms of both AR and TR in Figure 4.3). But they do not force the pace of technological change as in industries associated with basic research. This requires systems integration capabilities that extend deeply into basic research.

This, in part, explains the anomaly of Italy as the lowest spender on corporate R&D but with acknowledged capabilities in new product development and industrial innovation.[10] Such regions may have limited formal R&D capability, but they have highly developed technology management and networking capabilities that combine to foster regional growth dynamics. They are not high tech and do not require the advanced science and engineering skills needed to manipulate material with micron and nanometer size dimensions (see Chapter 5). Here, the innovation networks of Silicon Valley set the standard; a range of regional innovation capabilities in their most advanced form has flourished.

The new open system model of innovation derives from the application and diffusion of the principle of systems integration. Systems integration often entails the fusion of multiple technologies, each of which is anchored in a different scientific discipline and associated language community, and which operates according to different design protocols; hence the organizational imperative of teamwork across scientific backgrounds.

Information technology has played a double role: enabler of systems integration and open systems in industrial organization. Computer-aided design, by integrating hardware and software, illustrates the role

[10] See 'Innovation in Industry Survey' (*The Economist* 1999: 12), in which Italy ranks bottom of a list of 14 industrialized nations with an R&D spend of 2% of sales. Denmark, the leader, is over 16%.

that information technology can play in systems integration. Information technology has opened the terrain of sub-micro-size dimensions at which nature constructs to research and manipulation. But even in 'old' industries, information technology expedites the process of continuously rethinking product concept by simulating design changes in materials and processes.

The Internet, which itself fuses information and communication technologies, has assisted the establishment of standard design protocols and thereby enhanced inter-firm networking. Consequently, barriers from the closed technology architectures and the bureaucratic inertia of vertically integrated business enterprises are lowered, and focused companies can integrate, dis-integrate, and re-integrate with other companies as technologies change. Thus, the open system cluster fosters an innovation dynamic involving systems integration within companies and networking amongst companies.

In fact, information technology is to the knowledge-driven economy what the machine-tool industry was to the diffusion of the principle of interchangeability, and unit-drive electricity was to the diffusion of the principle of flow, which ushered in the age of mass production (see Chapter 2). In each case, a new principle of production was associated with the development of a new business model capable of achieving a breakthrough in performance standards that redefined the basis of industrial leadership. As with the emergence of the machine-tool industry and fractionated electric power, information technology has fostered an entirely new approach to product architecture, production organization, and business models, which in turn has redefined industry boundaries.

To summarize, the evolution of the entrepreneurial firm has enjoyed a step change advance, firstly with the extension of the principle of flow to new product development, and secondly with the development of the principle of systems integration. These advances, in turn, have facilitated a new model of technological innovation that has given new meaning to the technology/market dynamic. Information technology, by fostering new capabilities in systems integration, has worked hand in glove in reinventing the industrial district as a model of industrial organization that is especially suited to rapid technological change. But it is an error to think of the advances in regional productivity in regions such as Silicon Valley and Route 128/495 simply as technological advances. They represent a New Competition that involves an advance in technology management capabilities. But without mutual adjustments in skill formation processes, innovation in firms will not translate into regional growth. Regional productivity growth demands a third condition: the development of a labor force with the complementary skills. We turn now to skill formation, the third element of the Productivity Triad.

TECHNOLOGY MANPOWER DEVELOPMENT

New capabilities and skills mediate between technological innovation and regional growth. As firms develop new technologies they need a skill base both to conduct research and convert the incipient capabilities into new products. Likewise, a region needs a skill base to amplify leading enterprise capabilities into regional capabilities, competitive advantage, and growth. The policy challenge is to foster a regional learning and skill formation process that reinforces the technology advance and multiplies a region's entrepreneurial enterprises.

The location of MIT and Stanford within high-tech regions has impressed policymakers the world over. Too often, however, the links between R&D conducted at research universities and industrial innovation and growth is defined in terms of technology transfer. While examples of technology transfer between basic research in universities and industrial enterprises have been important in both regions, focusing on technology transfer can obscure mediating links between education and growth. In any case, many prestigious research universities are not associated with regional growth dynamics just as most high growth success stories do not involve a technology transfer role for prestigious universities.

The Productivity Triad (see Figure 1.1) and the open systems model of innovation point to a more complex set of relationships between basic research conducted at universities and industrial growth than the technology transfer imagery. Successful technology transfer, in terms of the capability perspective, is often a consequence of these underlying and enabling relationships.

- Demand for and supply of graduates
- Engineering methodologies and curriculum development
- Enterprise capability and university research dynamic

The first two will be examined in this chapter. The third is examined in the following chapter.

Demand for and Supply of Graduates

Entrepreneurial firms are successful because they advance technology capabilities to develop emerging market opportunities in an ongoing interactive process. But the growth of firms will not translate into regional economic growth without the expansion of the requisite engineering/technological skill base. The regional growth dynamics depend as well upon a labor pool of engineers and technologists to convert the innovative ideas into production capabilities. As shown in Figure 4.4, 'Regional Growth and Skill Formation Dynamics', the role of tertiary education is critical for producing a pool of engineers and technologists. The challenge is to synchronize the supply of graduates with the demand. Synchronization means that innovative ideas sparked by the internal growth dynamics of entrepreneurial firms can be converted into viable products on the *scale* and in the form required for regional growth.

Matching supply of and demand for technical skills is a long-term, mutual adjustment process requiring institutional coordination. Regional growth, represented by the growth dynamics on the left side of the figure, will be choked if the requisite numbers and types of graduate engineers are not produced by the education system, represented by the demand for and supply of technical graduates on the right side of the figure. Two conditions must be met for success. The first involves characterization of the demand for specific technological skills. The second involves investment in technical education so that education institutions are successful at meeting the demand. (A third condition, complementary skill formation in the workplace, is examined below).

An inelastic skill base will translate into skill shortages and wage pressures thereby choking growth and eroding regional competitiveness. Industrial development depends upon an integrated process of labor supply development. Without a complementary growth in a labor force with the requisite skills, the innovation capabilities of even MIT would not have been translated into sustained regional growth dynamics.[11]

[11] Cambridge University researchers have developed many innovations, often in partnership with industrial labs and emerging companies. Rarely have these developments been translated into regional industrial growth. The development of engineering methodologies must involve methods for ramp-up in technical labor supply and the institutional capability to drive it. It is as if Cambridge, Massachusetts has had manpower planning capability and Cambridge, UK has not.

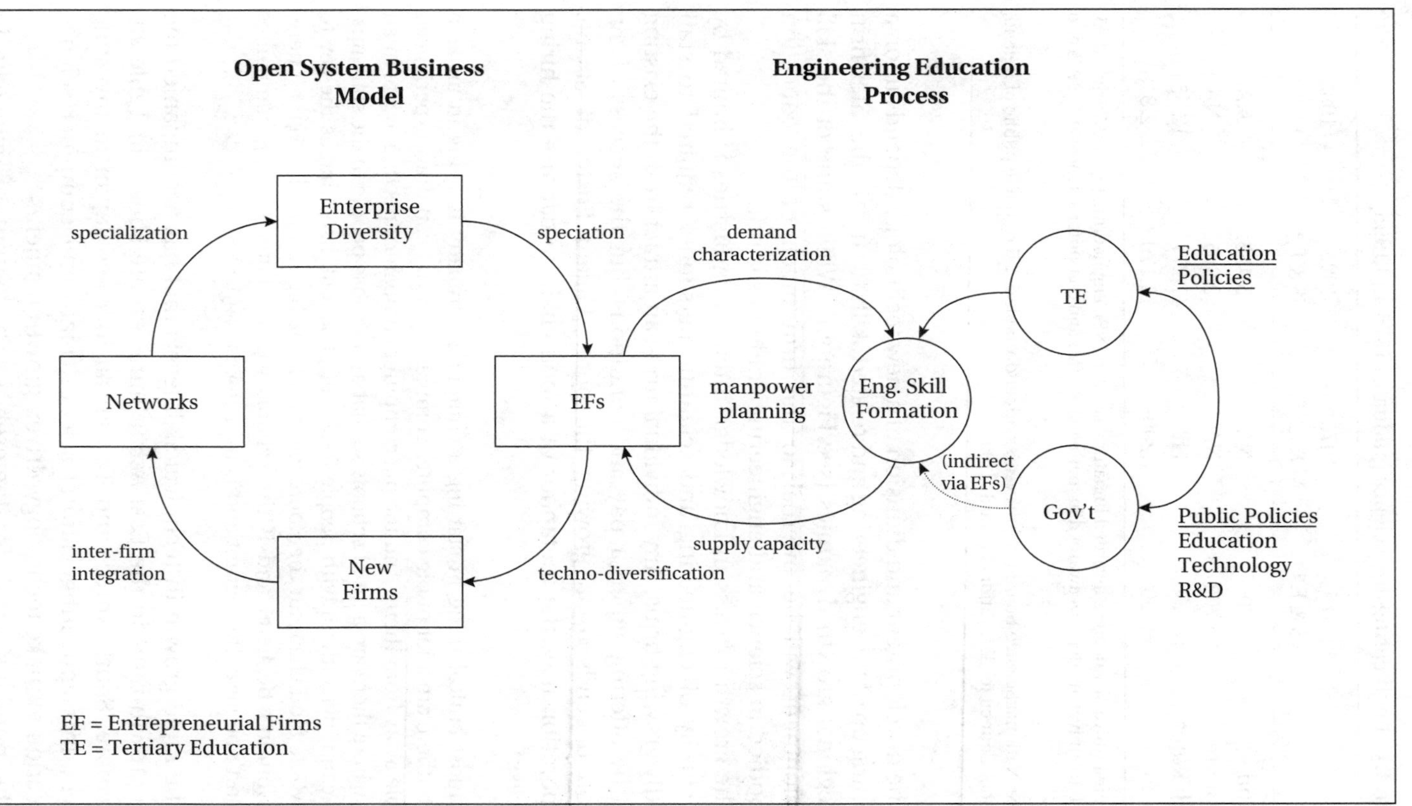

Fig. 4.4. Regional growth and skill formation dynamics

Table 4.1. Engineering and science graduates 1975 and 1995

	1975 NS & E [a]	1975 M & CS [b]	1995 NS & E [a]	1995 M & CS [b]
Ireland	706	NA	5,456	NA
Singapore	702	NA	2,965	NA
South Korea	10,266	Nil	47,277	12,351
Taiwan	6,700	1,200	15,170	2,818

[a] First university degrees awarded in natural science (NS), engineering (E) in 1975 and 1995.
[b] First university degrees awarded in mathematics (M) and computer sciences (CS) 1975 and 1995.

Source: National Science Board (various years): appendix table 2–2. For the Republic of Ireland, National Council for Educational Awards (1995).

The development and diffusion of a new technology depends upon a ramping up of the engineering and related skills to sustain the inter-firm or regional growth dynamics (see Figure 3.1). While some of the skill development will be internal to the firm much of the education embodied in science and engineering graduates is not.

The growth process in knowledge-intensive industries is limited by the supply of engineering and scientific personnel required to staff rapidly growing firms. Any individual firm can attract from the existing pool by offering superior pay and conditions, but the success of the region depends upon growing the pool. William Foster of Stratus Corporation uses the metaphor of a food chain to capture the hiring process:

> The most critical thing in starting a computer company is being in an area where there are a lot of big computer companies so you can draw experienced people away from them. And the big computer companies need to locate in an area where there are a lot of schools so that as they lose people to the start-ups, they can replace them with people fresh out of school. I see that as the key to the whole food chain for the Route 128 area. If the big companies weren't here, we wouldn't be here, and if the schools weren't here, the big companies wouldn't be here. (Rosegrant and Lampe 1992: 158–9)

The rapid growth in technical skill levels that has accompanied the high growth rates in the East Asian 'miracles' are shown in Table 4.1. Singapore, South Korea, and Taiwan all followed Japan in investing heavily in engineering, natural science, math and computer science education to make technology-driven growth happen.

The numbers speak for themselves. The output of engineers in

Singapore increased *seven times* between 1975 and 1995.[12] The graduates of scientists/engineers in South Korea increased by nearly *five times* over the same period. The Republic of Ireland,[13] the fastest growing region of Europe in the 1990s, is the same story.[14] Its output of scientists and engineers increased over *seven times* in the same two decades. These numbers all testify to the industry and education dynamics captured in Figure 4.4. In all cases, without the investments in skill formation, growth would have been choked. Instead, a virtuous cycle emerged that funded the advances in education by rapidly growing national income.

Technology Change and Engineering Curriculum

The challenge of engineering education is exacerbated by technological change. The link between entrepreneurial firms and engineering graduates is mediated by engineering curriculum. During normal times updating the engineering curriculum does not present a challenge. But at times of fundamental technology transition, such as from the age of mechanical to electrical technologies, the issue of curriculum becomes paramount. Firms seeking to advance their technological capabilities in opto-electronics, for example, seek graduates educated in photonics as well as electronics. This means that the challenge for educational institutions is not simply to increase the number of graduates but to increase graduates educated in a curriculum that includes emerging technological methodologies.

The mutual adjustment process between technology-driven enterprises and university curriculum is critical to an understanding of both Silicon Valley and Route 128. Silicon Valley and Stanford, in the words of Leslie and Kargon:

[12] The cases of Singapore and Malaysia are examined in Ch. 6. The success of Singapore suggests that the cause of Malaysia's skill gap is not due to heavy reliance on MNCs. Singapore, which has pursued a similar strategy attracting MNCs has, at the same time, developed indigenous production and technology management capabilities. Singapore, like Taiwan and South Korea, has major education programs to continuously upgrade their skill base. Unlike Singapore, Malaysia has yet to turn heavy reliance on technology imports into indigenous production capabilities. The critical factor is the development of a local skill base that can serve as a medium for absorbing and diffusing technology and technology management capabilities in local firms.

[13] Government led the growth with large investments in regional technology colleges.

[14] See Fig. 5.4 for a similar explosion in output of engineers accompanying the Massachusetts 'Miracle'.

had grown up together, gradually adjusting to each other and to their common competitive environment. Each helped the other discover and exploit new niches in science and technology.... In the proliferation of new technical fields and new companies that characterized the early evolutionary stages of these industries, the right kind of university could make a real difference in fostering horizontal integration and collective learning throughout the region. (1996: 470)

This regional dynamic did not begin with Stanford. This dynamic between technological advance and engineering methodology has a long history.[15] Engineering disciplines are not static. Each major technological transition has been accompanied by the development of a new engineering discipline that, in turn, became a vehicle for the diffusion of the new technology across the industrial spectrum. In the early days of American industrial development the agents of diffusion were machinists trained in interchangeability or Armory Practices. Today they are likely to be engineering and science graduates that have specialized in disciplines such as information technology, opto-electronics (photonics), or life sciences.

Examples include chemical engineering and the petro-chemical industries; electrical engineering followed by the electrical power and electric engineering firms such as GE; microwave technologies and the development of Raytheon. In all of these cases, the development of the technology and the industry shaping and market creating and expanding firms was not university technology spin-offs but partnerships in the co-shaping of emerging and unfolding technologies and engineering methodologies.

Many regional success stories in one technological age become the depressed areas in the succeeding period. Integral to the concept of the Productivity Triad is the mutual adjustment process between technology advancing, rapidly growing firms which, in fact, are driving a new technological trajectory, and engineering methodologies which make it possible to ramp up an engineer/technology skill base. These form a mutually interactive process in which technology capabilities in companies and engineering methodologies in the education system march forward together. This is particularly so with the application of the principle of systems integration and the development of the open

[15] Industrial technological history can be divided into a predominately mechanical period spanning the nineteenth century giving way to an electrico-mechanical period beginning at the turn of the last century and to an electronics period in the last half of the twentieth century. We are presently in the early stages of an opto-electronic or photonic-mechanical period (see Ch. 5 and Fig. 5.2).

systems business model which has opened up the terrain of knowledge-intensive industries.

With each historic development of new engineering methodologies, the earlier ones were redefined to take account of the new technological domain. Mechanical became electro-mechanical followed by integration with electronics and later, information technology. Information technology plays a double role as independent technology domain and enabler of technology integration. Each revolution fostered a regional ability to communicate across technological domains. Most techno-entrepreneurs are cross walkers, they are problem-oriented people who learn to read and converse in various technological languages. These are the vaunted communication skills that are often considered missing in engineering education.

The Invisible College

Much attention has been given, rightfully, to the links between education and growth. Less attention has been paid to informal, regional processes by which knowledge is created, adapted, modified, and diffused in the workplace and growth.

The concept invisible college underscores the shared creation and diffusion of knowledge within technical or occupation communities that cut across companies. Here knowledge is created and diffused in ongoing production activities as workers address challenges and devise new methods. The informal, skill formation dimensions associated with production are rarely examined and subject to improvement. Nevertheless they are important to understanding economic progress.

Figure 4.5, titled 'Plastics Industrial Food Chain' captures the extreme specialization and diversity of a low-tech sector in a high-income region. The second column lists nine plastics processing technologies used by firms in column 3 to develop specialist capabilities and supply unique inputs into a range of end use markets. Knowledge-intensive inputs come from a range of extra-firm agencies listed in the upper right-hand corner. Nevertheless, success depends upon innovation. But in this case, increased specialization is an application of Adam Smith's principle of increasing specialization. Increasing specialization enhances the 'art of discovery' and advances productivity. It also represents a vast pool of knowledge, much of which is not formalized. In fact,

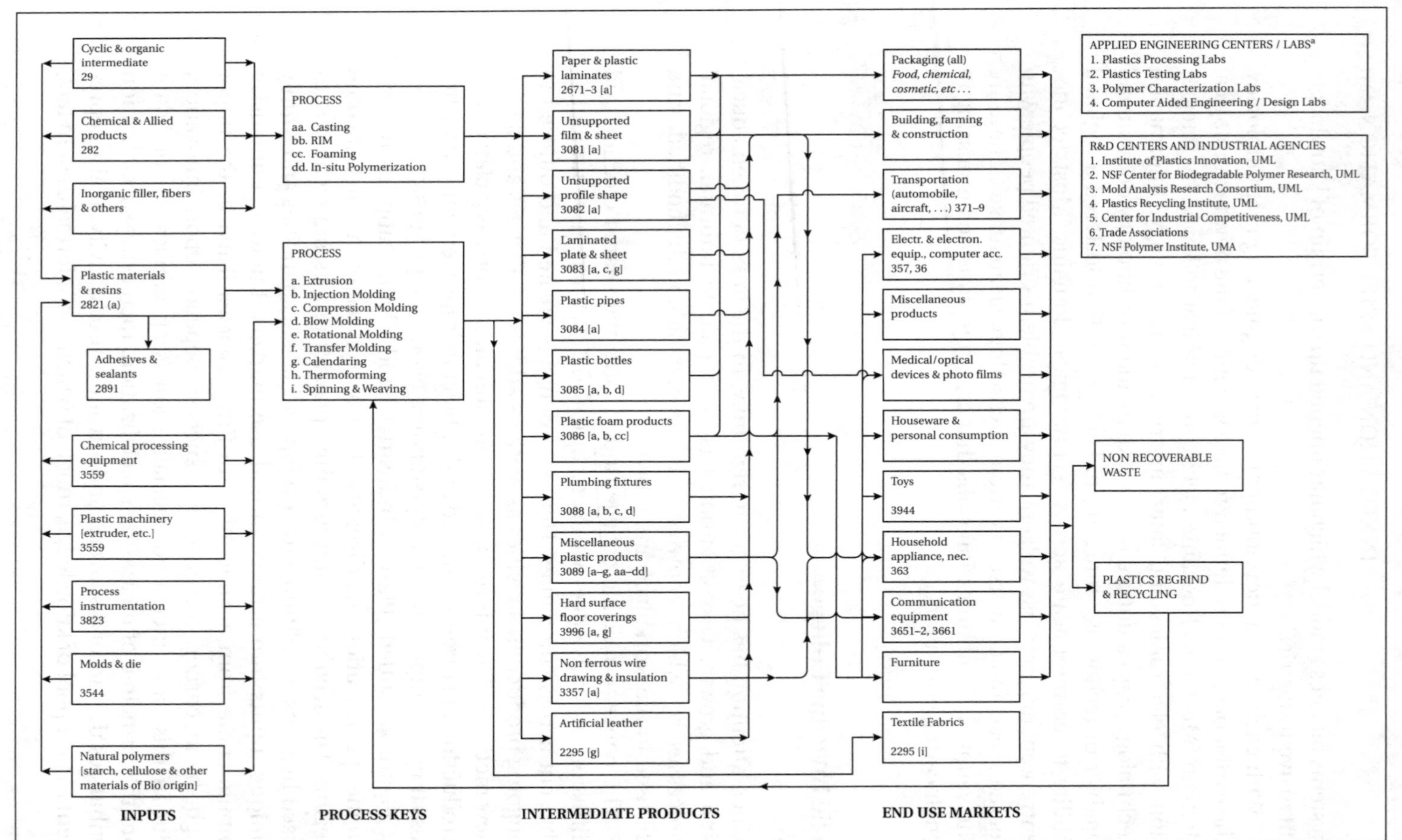

Note: [a] = Located at the University of Massachusetts Lowell (UML); UMA: University of Massachusetts Amherst

technology diffusion and skill-formation go hand in glove in industrial transitions. The technology diffusion process depends upon the skill formation level and capability built into the work organization of a region's enterprises. As a region's enterprises move up the production capabilities spectrum, these communities progressively advance in skills. The diffusion of technical knowledge takes place in hundreds of ways as individuals in different firms tackle common problems, share new methods, advance their skills, and move from firm to firm.

Every region that has made the transition to PS 3 (Table 2.1) has simultaneously incorporated a variant of the *kaizen* or continuous improvement model of work organization across a critical mass of firms. The pace is enhanced by a shared supplier base of small and medium-sized enterprises (SMEs) that can achieve world-class performance standards in cost, quality, and time.

Continuous improvement in work organization is a counterpart to process integration in material flow or just-in-time production. Multi-skilling, particularly across functions, is a by-product of making the transition from 'scientific management' models of work organization and functionally departmentalized models of factory organization to 'high-performance work organization' and production systems organized according to the principle of flow.

The revolutionary idea was to design quality into the system rather than inspect it in. It required the development and diffusion of problem-solving skills throughout the organization. Firms that make the transition from supervisor-centered to self-directed work organization enjoy a leap in direct labor productivity as many non-direct labor functions such as quality inspection, supervision, scheduling, and coordinating are increasingly internalized into work teams. But the effects of the revolution did not stop here. The new idea laid the foundation not only for the quality revolution but for rapid cycle time competition. The transition meant the extension of short cycle times in production to short cycle times in new product development (see PS 4 in Table 2.1). Short cycle time production capability entails the integration of design and production to quickly pull new generation technologies into production.

An array of terms is used to capture a set of organizational innovations that have emerged to institutionalize the learning process within

Fig. 4.5. Plastics industrial food chain

Source: Research conducted at the Center for Industrial Competitiveness, University of Massachusetts Lowell

production.[16] *Kaizen*, Total Quality Management, Plan-Do-Check-Act, self-directed work teams, and 'high-performance work system' are all methodologies to convert production into a learning system receptive to sustained improvements including technological advance. They share a view of work organization that runs counter to the set of principles embodied in 'scientific management'.[17] Breaking the dichotomy between thinking and doing in the workplace has profound implications for our views of skill formation, education, and theories of growth.[18]

CONCLUSION

Each business model links R&D to production in different ways. Indeed the concept of innovation depends, in part, on the business model. Innovation for Big Business meant basic research conducted in stand-alone labs. Pitted against the *kaisha* business model (PS 4 in Table 2.1), the linear sequence model of innovation associated with Big Business lacked technology management capabilities. The *kaisha* business model extended the concept of innovation to incremental changes in production processes. The resulting decentralization of design into the work organization enhanced the new product development production capability. This business model could rapidly introduce technological changes enabling product-led competition.

But just when the *kaisha* business model seemed invincible, a new open systems business model emerged to set yet a higher international performance standard in rapid new product development. The principle of systems integration enables enterprises to achieve higher

[16] The work organization revolution involves the extension of the organizational principle of co-locating power and responsibility throughout the organization. The principle of co-locating power and responsibility is the idea that those who have the responsibility for achieving certain goals must also have the authority to get the job done. Responsibility without power leads to alienation; power without responsibility fosters despotism. This principle is the starting point for the practice of inclusion that is universal to workforce involvement programs.

[17] Louis Brandeis, not Frederick W. Taylor coined the term 'scientific management' and Taylor's system was probably never applied precisely according to Taylor's principles. Nevertheless, the term has considerable meaning and does capture the approach to the management of production that distinguished the old competition.

[18] The examplar of 'scientific management' is that of Schmidt, the pig iron loader made famous by Taylor. By studying the loading of pig iron with the aid of a time watch, Taylor and his associates were able to locate the single best method which would maximize labor productivity. A pay incentive system could then be devised to motivate the worker to act according to the standard.

performance standards in innovation. Converting the principle into a production capability means having technology integration teams with the skills to capture advances in technology sub-systems but to redesign the production process to fully exploit such gains on an ongoing basis.

The research networks in districts like Silicon Valley extend beyond the firm enabling project teams to participate in a highly innovative milieu for technology management. The principles of flow and process integration which Japan applied to integrate production and new product development are present and reinforced at the district level to anchor a model of regional technology management and industrial innovation.

The focus and network business model is complemented by an open systems industrial structure that, in turn, fosters regional innovation capabilities. Interestingly, the development, diffusion, and deployment of innovations are, in fact, part of a single process of industrial innovation. This is because innovation for growth has cumulative and collective dimensions.[19] The networking capabilities act as diffusion agency for technological change. Partners in new product development make innovation available much as machine tool making companies spread innovation across sectors. Regions populated by enterprises without networking capabilities are regions that lack a critical means for diffusing technological change built into ongoing operations.

Open system networks mean that research is not limited to laboratories but becomes a regional capability embedded in a complex of regional institutions. Silicon Valley is an open systems industrial ecology that combines a range of sources of innovation identified in this and previous chapters. These include the effects of the decentralization and diffusion of design capabilities on innovation; of capability specialization within firms on the creation of new firms in the market 'interstices' (see Chapter 2); of techno-diversification on industrial 'speciation' or the creation of new industrial 'species'; of integration, dis-integration, and reintegration of networks enabling new product development projects; and of extending the variety of a region's technological capabilities leading to 'unplanned confluences of technologies from different fields' (Kostoff 1994).

These effects are sharply diminished in regions where firms lack ties to a strong and growing knowledge base in fundamental research and

[19] Innovation is a never completed project, a step in a 'continuum of inventive activity' (N. Rosenberg 1982: 12). As the technology develops it creates opportunities for applications in other firms that, in turn, offer new development possibilities for the technology trajectory.

the associated human resource development of research universities. This has implications for the skill formation process. Without the integration of the production system with skill formation, a region can have innovation without innovation capabilities and innovation with limited growth impact. The latter means innovation and production are mutually interactive.

Tertiary education has always been critical to educating the scientists and engineers that would populate the industrial labs. But the development of appropriate engineering methodologies within education institutions is not sufficient for regional industrial growth. The supply of engineering graduates must be in sync both in skill and quantity with the demand from technology-driven firms. The supply response depends both on the appropriate curriculum and the scale up capacity of the region's education institutions.

The policy challenge is to foster a learning dynamic which reinforces technological advances and diffusion within a region. As firms develop new technologies, they need a complementary skill base to realize them to convert new market opportunities into production capabilities and a region needs a critical mass of such skills to convert them into a basis for competitive advantage.

CHAPTER

5

The Resurgence of Route 128: The Triumph of Open Systems

THE ARGUMENT IN BRIEF

Massachusetts in the 1950s was suffering from the loss of its traditional industries, textiles and shoes, and its industrial future looked bleak. But by the early 1980s the 'Massachusetts miracle' heralded the emergence of America's first high-tech industrial district. The 'miracle' turned to dust with the abrupt loss of one-third of the state's manufacturing jobs between 1986 and 1992.

The simultaneous collapse of the minicomputer and defense industry, with the end of the Cold War, touched off a downturn which, added to the long-term rundown of traditional industries, suggested that industry in Massachusetts was in terminal decline. Combined with the drop-offs in these major markets was the emergence of Silicon Valley which fostered and commercialized innovations much faster than Route 128 and often in the same technologies. It appeared that the forces of decline were deeply entrenched. This is an old story in economic history. Once thriving regions get locked into obsolete products and technologies and lose competitive advantage. Clearly, few were willing to bet on the resurgence of Route 128. Nevertheless, the predictions of industrial gloom turned out to be wrong.

Instead of going into structural decline, eastern Massachusetts—symbolized by Route 128—became an 'innovative milieu' which has spawned new generations of companies, attracted innovative companies from around the world,[1] proliferated new product concepts,

[1] To signal the argument ahead, the innovation potential which attracts firms from around the world into Massachusetts is based on the skill base, the diversity of technologies which are

obliterated old industry boundaries, and, in turn, been reconstituted by the emergence of new sub-sectors. The resurgence has not been limited to high technology sectors. Increasingly, electronics is penetrating into previously non-electronics sectors, enabled by information technology.

Because of the range and depth of research universities and government-funded research laboratories, many have perceived the source of economic growth in terms of the traditional linear model of innovation (see Figure 4.1). Nevertheless, as important as universities and laboratories are to Massachusetts and to the innovation process, focus on them alone fails to capture the underlying growth dynamics of technology-driven firms and the regional heritage of technological capabilities and skills.

The argument in this chapter is that both the decline and the resurgence of Route 128 can be explained in terms of the emergence of a new competitive advantage based upon the principle of systems integration. The new principle has both fostered and been driven by a comprehensive reorganization of the business system.[2] The old business model of vertical integration has been transcended by an open system of specialist firms; open systems, working at both the technological and organizational levels, entail decentralized, diffused, and complementary design capabilities across a wide range of business enterprises. The result has been a regional capability to rapidly reinvent products, diversify technologically, create new market niches, and invent new industrial sub-sectors. These processes are part of a new regional model of innovation that gives the region a competitive advantage in the capability to rapidly create, develop, and commercialize new product and technology concepts and speciate new industrial sub-sectors. An understanding of these processes holds the key to understanding both the decline and the resurgence of growth in Massachusetts.[3]

potential inputs to systems integrators, and the time compression facilitated by the wide and deep supply base for doing new product development. For example, Michel Habib, Israel's economic consul in Boston, estimates that the number of Israeli technology firms in the Boston area grew from 30 in 1997 to at least 65 in early 1999. The companies span a range of technologies including optical inspection machines, medical lasers, digital printing equipment, scanning technology, and bio-tech. In the words of one Israeli manager, 'There are a lot of technological resources and knowledge in the area we can take advantage of' (Bray 1999).

[2] The concept of New Competition as industrial leadership based on the establishment of new principles of production and organization is developed and applied to Silicon Valley in Chs. 2–4.

[3] The severity of the decline of Route 128 following the Massachusetts Miracle is linked to the earlier development of the open systems business model in Silicon Valley. It was here that the open systems or horizontal integration model of industrial organization was first developed in a high-tech region.

But the entrepreneurial firm is about more than closed versus open business systems. It is also a driver of distinctive technological capabilities. What is perhaps unique about the industrial history of Massachusetts is the combination of technological continuity and change. The region's unique industrial and technological heritages have proven to be propitious for systems integration.

New England has never had a competitive advantage in mass production. The region converted its early leadership in precision machining into a competitive advantage in complex product systems. The emergence of a new open systems business model was ideally suited to reassemble the region's capabilities and resources in new pursuits. A series of cluster dynamics were set in motion that fostered new rounds of techno-diversification and industrial speciation.

A fascinating feature of New England industrial history has been a capacity to 'reinvent' its industrial system to take advantage of the emergence of new general purpose technologies. Information technology is the latest example. The integration of hardware and software has fostered applications in numerous and diverse industries, virtually reinventing many. Information technology has, in the process, been transformed from a separate industrial sector to a constitutive, multidimensional feature of industry itself. It is analogous to the process by which the machine tool industry in the early nineteenth century and electricity in the early twentieth century were handmaidens of industrial transformation. New England's industrial history and technological heritage offer unique opportunities for exploring concepts of economic development and change.

INDUSTRIAL HISTORY

Booms and Busts

Massachusetts has a rich industrial history. Two regions within Massachusetts can lay claim to being the birthplace of American industry. One surrounds the Springfield Armory where the principle of interchangeability was first applied and which, in turn, fostered the development of the world's first machine tool industry; the other is Lowell where the Boston Associates built a canal and waterpower infrastructure for America's first textile district. The machine tool industry fostered the growth of a range of industrial districts in Massachusetts such as watches in Waltham, footwear in Haverhill and Lynn, furniture in Gardner, jewelry making in Attleboro, and metalworking and specialist machine making in Worcester. The proliferation of industrial sectors, in turn, supported hundreds of small, highly specialized tool-and-die shops and foundries engaged in the production of fixtures, tooling, gauges, and made-to-order components in Massachusetts. Just as the consumer goods industries created a market for machine tool makers, the machine makers diffused innovations across the industrial spectrum (Best and Forrant 1996*a*).

In the twentieth century, Massachusetts has been on a roller coaster caught between the decline of industries with their origins in the last century and the emergence of new industries derived from a regional competitive advantage in research and development, and technological innovation. The machine tool industry was the source of new technologies and a skill pool which fostered the emergence and sustained the growth of new industries in nineteenth-century New England. An engineering and scientific skill base linked to and diffused by technologically oriented, research-intensive universities became the functional equivalent for the twentieth century. MIT, of course, is the exemplar. The Boston area has the highest concentration of colleges and universities, research laboratories, and hospitals anywhere in the world. The plethora of graduate research programs suggested that the industrial future of Massachusetts was secure in the emerging knowledge economy of the late twentieth century.

However, the research intensity of the region has not insulated the state from the forces of industrial decline. After enjoying a ninety-month expansion labeled the 'Massachusetts Miracle' in the years from 1976 to 1984, the Commonwealth lost one-third of its manufacturing jobs between 1985 and 1992. The country's first high-tech region had seemingly lost competitiveness much more quickly in the new industries of the late twentieth century than in industries first established in Massachusetts in the last century.

Symbolic of the decline was the sale of the Wang Towers in Lowell, Massachusetts, a building complex that had cost $23 million to construct during the Massachusetts Miracle, for $500,000 in 1992. The old textile mill buildings, many of which had been refurbished and converted, were no longer the symbol of regional decline; this role had shifted to the high-tech edifices built in the 1970s and 1980s. The simultaneous collapse of the minicomputer and defense industry, with the end of the Cold War, touched off a downturn which, added to the long-term decline in traditional industries, suggested that industry in Massachusetts was in terminal decline. Combined with the decline of these major markets was the emergence of Silicon Valley based on a different business model. The new model in which 'horizontal integration', 'institutions of cooperation', and 'collective learning' figured prominently, was fostering and commercializing innovations much faster than Route 128 (Saxenian 1994; Grove 1996). Clearly, few were willing to bet on the resurgence of Route 128.

Nevertheless, the predictions of industrial gloom turned out to be wrong, or at least premature. The Wang Towers, a new home to over three dozen companies, was sold in April 1998 for $120 million. A return to growth beginning in 1992 lasted longer than the Massachusetts Miracle. The downturn between the two expansions can be explained in terms of the decline of the minicomputer and defense industries plus the institutional problems highlighted in the account of AnnaLee Saxenian (1994). But why the upturn? It was not predicted and it has not been explained. Nothing in Saxenian's account of regional decline in Massachusetts suggested a return to growth.

An explanation should account equally for the decline and the resurgence. An account of the rise based solely on the plethora of research capability does not explain the severe downturn; an account of the decline in terms of horizontal integration, institutions of cooperation and collective learning, such as Saxenian's, does not account for the resurgence.

The Miracle Years: Techno-concentration and Closed Systems

The entrepreneurial firm was the driver of growth during both periods. During the Massachusetts Miracle a series of firms led by techno-entrepreneurs (often benefiting from government orders and research sponsorship) invested heavily in emerging computer-related technologies and established new markets. They joined others that were specializing in defense industry products and systems. The rapidly growing new firms organized according to the business model of vertical integration (Kuhn 1982). The new firms simply adopted the business model of the leading firms in the region such as GE and Raytheon, as well as those in more traditional industries such as textiles and footwear. This had a series of knock-on effects.

Both the business model and the technology architecture of the leading enterprises were closed system. The pyramidal organizational chart and functional departmentalization of the minicomputer companies had been designed for price-led competition in technologically stable markets. But functional departmentalization was a barrier to product-led competition which requires process integration in production, new product development, and technology management. The top-down hierarchies were alien to process integration and resistant to cross-functional communication and the decentralization of design into production operations and work organization.

Functional departmentalization in production is alien to agile production methods. Instead it supports batch production methods which cannot achieve the performance standards of throughput efficiency and quality of agile production. The business model was ill-equipped to compete against firms organized according to the organizational principle of process integration, the corollary to the production principle of flow. Process integration dictates that consecutive activities required to execute production tasks are co-located and interactive.

Furthermore, vertical integration and functional departmentalization foster closed systems in product architecture. A closed system architecture is one that cannot accommodate independently designed components. Digital Equipment Corporation's components, for example, were hardwired to one another. The microprocessor, the mother board, the memory chips, the disk drive, the operating system, the display screen, the software programs, the printer, the printer microprocessor, the printer engine software, all of the computer peripherals were designed according to a proprietary (and closed) architecture.[4] Likewise, Wang word processors were designed to accommodate Wang software and Wang printers only. The open system personal computer manufacturers, in contrast, were designed to run Word or WordPerfect software on Epson or Hewlett Packard printers. Sub-contractors to closed system computer companies made peripheral parts but were not encouraged to develop independent design capabilities. This is not surprising; it was the business model that had served the nation well for roughly a century (Chandler 1977). But the functionally departmentalized business model proved resistant to both bottom-up design initiatives and to ongoing technological change.

What was inconceivable was that these highly successful high-tech companies, the leaders in the rapidly growing markets, could stumble

[4] See Morris and Ferguson (1993) and Garud and Kumaraswamy (1993) for detailed examples.

on the technological side. They were first movers in rapidly growing markets and they were integrated into the innovative milieu centered on Boston's universities and research institutions. But they did stumble, collectively. Ironically, their weakness was technology management, individually and collectively. The leaders of the Massachusetts Miracle were innovative, but primarily in two industries, minicomputers and defense. The closed system business model was a barrier to technological diversification, to new firm creation, and to inter-firm networking.

The miracle years in Massachusetts were also a time during which new business models with superior new product development and innovation capabilities were being developed in other regions. The Japanese extended the Toyota production system to the Canon model that set new standards for rapid new product development and incremental innovation (see Table 2.1). This model established a technology management capability that integrated applied research and production in the service of product-led competition. The Canon model established new performance standards in time-to-market for new product development (see Figure 4.2). The Canon production system, however, did not pose the biggest threat to Route 128.

Route 128 companies rarely competed head-to-head with the Canon model. Industrial enterprises in Massachusetts had never developed high-volume manufacturing capabilities. Consequently, they were not vulnerable in industries like consumer electronics, automobile, and electrical products in which the Japan enterprises were rapidly gaining market share. The vulnerability of Route 128 was to the new focus and network business model that emerged first in Silicon Valley. The vertically integrated computer industry of Route 128 is contrasted with what Andrew Grove of Intel describes as the horizontal computer industry in Figure 5.1.

The 'open systems' model established new performance standards for combining disruptive and incremental innovation, for integrating basic, developmental, and applied research (see Figure 4.3). It was this vertically dis-integrated but systems integrated business model that exposed the weaknesses of Route 128's business enterprises and shut down the engines of growth in New England.

The 'open systems' or focus and network business model of Silicon Valley organizationally fits the principle of systems integration. The new business model unleashed the internal technology/market dynamic from containment within vertically integrated enterprises. Design was decentralized internally and diffused externally. Silicon Valley firms, such as HP, were early adopters of high-performance work systems

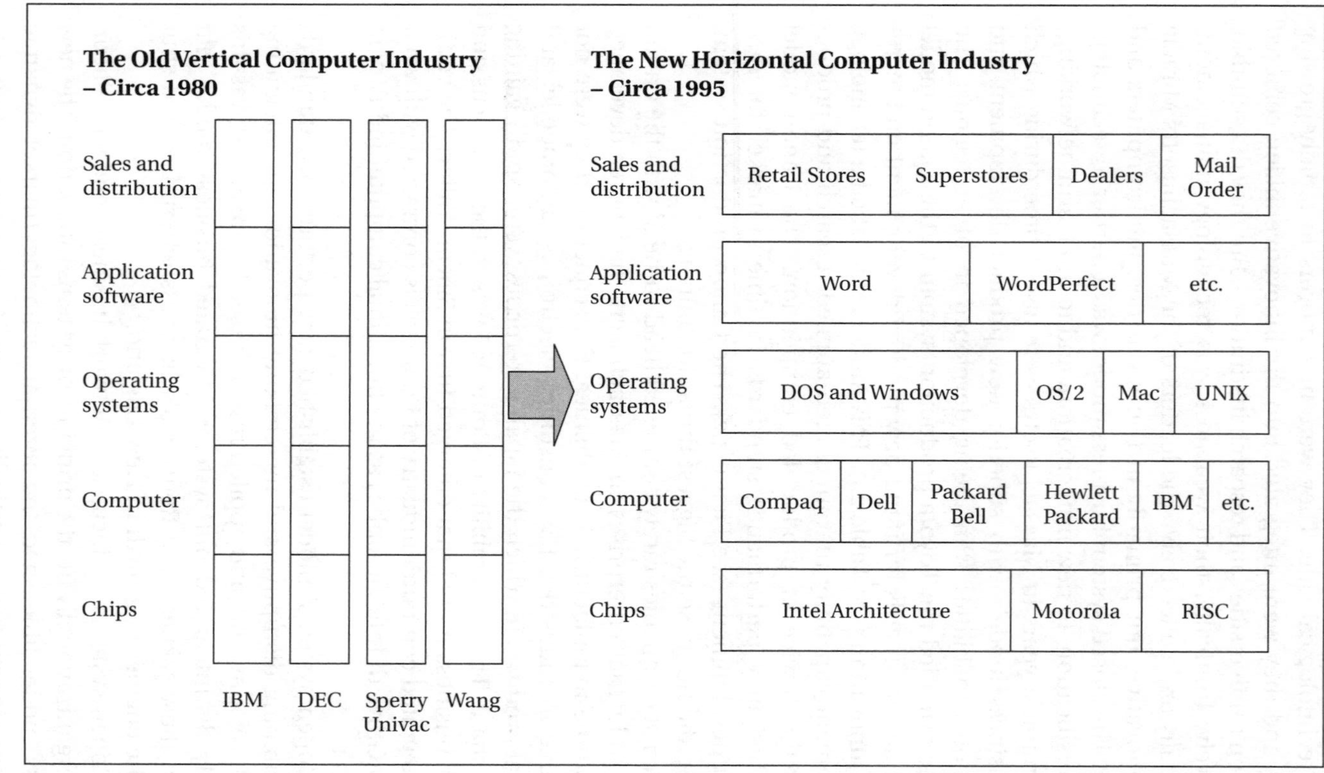

Fig. 5.1. Competing business models

Source: From *Only the Paranoid Survive* by Andrew S. Grove, copyright © 1996 by Andrew S. Grove. Used by permission of Doubleday, a division of Random House, Inc.

(HPWSs). HPWSs involve a cluster of practices that provide workers with the incentives, skills, and opportunity to shape decisions and to improve plant performance (see Appelbaum et al. 2000).

Open system networks are an organizational structure to foster a whole range of specialty component suppliers (not only those along the 'value chain' but across 'value networks'). Sun workstations, for example, were designed with common interface rules and operating system source code to plug in microprocessors from Intel, IBM, AMD, or Motorola; display screens from Sony or NEC; disk drives from Seagate or Quantum; memory chips from Hitachi or Samsung; printers from HP or Xerox. This, in turn, set in motion the processes identified in the regional growth dynamics model (Figure 3.1). The new business model, enjoying increasingly far-flung applications, has proven highly competitive against both the Canon (closed system) and the Big Business (vertical integration) models. In leading companies like Intel, HP, and Sun it combined a leadership/ideas dynamic with the technology/market dynamic.[5] It is the organizational cornerstone of a new competitive advantage.

In summary, the decline of Route 128 was not due to failure to cooperate, to cutbacks in government- or corporate-funded R&D, to high wages, to lack of 'clusters', or other conventional explanations. Put simply, Silicon Valley had established a new open systems business model with superior technology management and innovation capabilities. The top-down hierarchy, vertically integrated, closed system business model that had driven the Miracle could not achieve the performance standards in time-to-market for new product development or industrial innovation. Technology trajectories, it turns out, do not unfold according to natural law. They are dependent, in important ways, on the business model in which they are developed.

The Resurgence: Techno-diversification and Open Systems

Two competing accounts have emerged to explain the rise of Silicon Valley and the decline of Route 128 which began in 1985. One attributes the difference primarily to cultural and organizational features (Saxenian 1994), the other emphasizes distinctive technology trajectories.

[5] See Glossary for summary of both dynamics.

Table 5.1. Techno-diversification of Massachusetts manufacturers (January 1999)

Type of companies	*Number of companies in Massachusetts*	*Massachusetts (%)*	*United States (%)*
Factory automation	337	10.5	12.1
Biotechnology	151	4.7	3.5
Chemicals	95	3.0	4.1
Computer hardware	435	13.6	13.8
Defense	56	1.7	2.1
Energy	105	3.3	4.5
Environmental equipment	203	6.3	7.1
High-tech manufacturing equipment	421	13.1	12.6
Advanced materials	159	5.0	6.6
Medical	248	7.7	6.3
Pharmaceuticals	95	3.0	2.5
Photonics	240	7.5	5.0
Computer software	993	30.9	24.8
Subassemblies/components	530	16.5	17.2
Test & measurement	378	11.8	11.2
Telecom & Internet	415	12.9	15.5
Transportation	92	2.9	3.6
US holding companies	245	7.6	8.4

Source: CorpTech Directory of High Tech Manufacturers. CorpTech tracks America's 45,000 plus technology manufacturers with under 1,000 employees (90% are 'hidden' private companies and the operating units of larger corporations). Of 42,342 US entities, 3,242 or 7.7% are located in Massachusetts. These are independent companies, subsidiaries of major US corporations, and American operating units of foreign companies. Data extracted with permission from CorpTech/Web <www.corptech.com>.

For Kenney and von Burg (1999), the explanation of the divergent growth experience is the difference between the semiconductor and the minicomputer. The semiconductor is an 'input into every product with an electronics function, whereas the minicomputer was a much more limited artefact' (68). This fact, for Kenney and von Burg, explains vastly different rates of new firm creation. But neither camp has explained how and why Route 128 recovered so quickly and powerfully beginning in 1992. In fact, both accounts presume the continued decline of Route 128.

Why the resurgence? An explanation must account for a striking difference in the industrial organization between the Miracle years and

Resurgence years. In the 1990s, industrial diversification had replaced industrial concentration.

What is remarkable is the extraordinary sectoral diversity of the resurgence. Table 5.1 illustrates the theme. Massachusetts is once again a diversified industrial economy, much as it had been in the early days of industrial development. In the intervening decades, industry was concentrated in few sectors. Textiles and shoes were the big employers, followed by aircraft engines and defense (Browne and Sass 2000). Minicomputers dominated the Miracle years.

The short answer to why the resurgence is that the region made a rapid transition from a closed to the new open systems business model. The resurgence was a consequence of replacing the missing element of the Productivity Triad of business model, production system, and skill formation. Route 128 was strong in both the technology and skill sides; it lacked a business model to achieve the performance standards established elsewhere. When it adopted such a business model, the decentralization and diffusion of design triggered the transition to a more advanced Productivity Triad. It is like the missing piece of a jigsaw puzzle: once in place it leveraged the region's other advantages.

The leaders of the Massachusetts Miracle (1976 to 1984) were technology-driven, engineering-led companies. They were semi-entrepreneurial firms, strong on the technology capability side but weak on the interactive dimensions of the technology capability and market opportunity. Ultimately, the lack of mutual adjustment between technology capability and market opportunity led to a technology trajectory that lacked customer feedback, denied the firms refined guidance, and ultimately left them with technologies and products that missed the market target.

But even had the technology-driven firms read the market opportunities correctly, individually and collectively, they lacked the production flexibility to respond quickly with new products based on refined technological capabilities. This was not a consequence of strategic choice alone, but of organization. The predominant organizational structure of leading Route 128 companies was top-down, design was centralized and production capabilities were neither lean nor agile. They were not organizationally designed to integrate technology management with production to pursue emerging market opportunities on an ongoing basis. They had achieved rapid growth without focusing attention on the business model. The model was not adaptive to market and technology shifts. Its weakness was exposed by the emergence of the focus and network, open systems business model of Silicon Valley.

This transition is a prerequisite to the integration of applied research with production, or design and manufacturing (see Figures 4.2 and 4.3). It is an organizational platform for product-led competition. The key to the resurgence was not the transition to 'lean production' or other variants of high-volume, high-throughput efficient production. Mass production has never been the basis of competitive advantage in New England.[6] This weakness, as shown below, is the basis for the region's strategic advantage in complex product systems and precision equipment. Here the region's absolute disadvantage has historically been least. In the age of industrial, as distinct from consumer, electronics the region's comparative advantage in complex product systems (see below) has combined with 'agile' manufacturing to engender a return to industrial competitiveness.

Cluster dynamics illustrated in Figure 3.1 were released by the new business model. The technology capability and market opportunity of entrepreneurial firms generated enterprise growth and new technological opportunities which, in turn, fostered firm creation in emerging sub-sectors followed by new patterns of inter-firm networking. In the process regional innovations dynamics are engendered as the techno-diversity of the region increases and with it the probability of new technological combinations to inspire the emergence of yet new entrepreneurial firms.

Examples of the repetition of the cluster dynamics leading to enterprises specializing in new technological 'species' in different technological domains are commonplace in Massachusetts of the 1990s. An example is that of data storage systems, the 'file cabinets of the electronics age'.

EMC is an entrepreneurial firm that has simultaneously developed a unique capability and spawned a new industrial sub-sector. The company began as a supplier of add-on memory boards for the minicomputer market in 1979, moved into mainframe storage a decade later, and 'added software to help manage its boxes as it made the switch to

[6] New England manufacturers have advanced up the production capabilities spectrum to higher levels but not as applied to high-volume production. The production capabilities of the minicomputer companies were pre-Ford, or at the level of 'Interchangeability' on the Production Capabilities Spectrum (see Box 2.2). Few New England manufacturers had high inventory turns or were organized for throughput efficiency. Instead they pursued either job shop or mass batch production methods. Performance standards were uniformly low by world-class manufacturing standards. Without the integration of design and manufacturing, these companies had little chance of success against companies that had made the transition. This is critical to explaining the decline.

open systems in the middle of this decade' (Degman 1998: 1). EMC has achieved the leading edge in storage technology with an engineering staff which, in 1998, totaled 1,200 and an annual research budget of one-third billion dollars. In the same year the company opened a 682,000 square-foot facility in central Massachusetts to test, qualify, and assemble computer storage systems.

EMC has 'spawned a new generation of software and service companies providing ways for corporations to monitor and manage data, back up and protect it, find and fix disk-storage bottlenecks, and warn desktop computer users to clean out their hard drives before they run out of space' (R. Rosenberg 1999: 1). For example, a co-founder of EMC and a ten-year employee have formed StorageNetworks, a company that offers businesses data storage services on the networking model of telephone switches or electric power generators. Other nearby companies that are driving and redefining the data storage business, each with a unique specialty are Astrum Software (monitor disk storage usage at each PC and server within a department), HighGround Systems (storage research management), Connected Corp., and Network Integrity Inc. (backup systems) (R. Rosenberg 1999).

The eleven firms that have spun out of Cascade Communications in the optical switching equipment sector are another example. All are located north of the Massachusetts Turnpike on I-495, a Boston ring road outside but paralleling Route 128.[7] The emerging firms specialize in a range of products and services unified by the integration of hardware and software required to move data, voice, and video over networks. While the region has historically been a center for communication switching equipment (ex-AT&T's Lucent Technology 2 million square-foot manufacturing site is in North Andover), many of the new firms can be traced to the technological capability and skill base created at Cascade Communications. Cascade specializes in frame relay technology for 'efficiently directing the congested streams of data flowing across phone lines'. Sycamore, likewise, combines networking and optical technologies. Each of the companies, however, specializes in a distinctive technological capability and uses open systems architecture. Principals in nine of eleven of the start-ups had been employed at

[7] The companies are ArrowPoint Communications Inc. of Westford, Astral Point Communications of Westford, Cadia Networks Inc. of Andover, Castle Networks Inc., Convergent Networks of Lowell, Equipe Communications of Acton, Ignitus Communications of Acton, Omnia Communications Inc. of Marlborough, Redstone Communications of Westford, Sonus Networks of Westford, and Sycamore Networks Inc. of Chelmsford.

Cascade (Zizza, Pelczar, and Eisenmann 1999). Several principals had been members at each of the Advanced Network Group at MIT's Lincoln Laboratory, Motorola/Codex, and DEC.

The examples of data storage equipment and telecommunications switching equipment are leading cases. But they represent a large class of business enterprise genealogies in which the emergence of regionally networked groups of firms can be traced to the technology and market dynamic of an entrepreneurial firm. Other examples in the Route 128 region include semiconductor equipment manufacturers (Eaton Semiconductor, Varion Ion Implant, Teradyne, Micrion); electronic test equipment suppliers; digital signal processing semiconductors (Analog Devices, Mercury Computer Systems, Alpha, BKC Semiconductor, C. P. Clare); electro-medical products (over twenty companies led by HP, now Agilent); biotechnology; genome industry (nearly 200 Massachusetts companies in 1998); enviro-technology; pump laser equipment (MIT Lincoln Labs, Lasertron); infrared imaging systems ('Lab 16' Raytheon, Honeywell Radiation Center, Lockheed Martin Infrared Imaging Systems, Telic Precision Optics, Inframetrics Inc.); and industrial automation (Foxboro Instruments, Groupe Schneider's Amicon Division).

CorpTech, a data processing company, categorizes America's small and medium-sized (under 1000 employees) 'technology manufacturers' (most of which are privately held) in seventeen industries as shown in Table 5.1. The dispersion is indicative of the diversity of industries associated with Route 128. The mix of high technology manufacturing in Massachusetts, with approximately 2 percent of the nation's population, is remarkably similar to the nation as a whole. CorpTech estimates that over 8 percent of America's small and medium-sized high-tech companies are based in Massachusetts with a total of over 200,000 employees.[8]

These data support the theme that a process of techno-diversification has driven the 'resurgence' of the Massachusetts economy. Technology management in the 'Massachusetts Miracle' growth industries of minicomputers and defense was locked up in vertically integrated enterprises. The downturn was critical to the upturn, as the demise of these enterprises facilitated the transition to an open system, multi-enterprise model of industrial organization. The accompanying decentralization and diffusion of design combined with a heritage of technological capabilities and skills to fuel the internal growth dynamic

[8] Massachusetts had 6.2 million people in 1999, 2.3% of the country.

of entrepreneurial firms which, in turn, fostered techno-diversification and regional innovation dynamics.

The new business model, in turn, enabled the region to make the transition from a research-push, linear sequence, to a product concept-pull, dip-down, model of regional innovation (see Figures 4.1 and 4.3). Now, as never before, the region could exploit its strengths in basic research to advance its industrial competitiveness. This meant developing a model of innovation that played on the region's technological heritage and unique production capabilities.

REGIONAL TECHNOLOGY CAPABILITIES

To contribute to economic growth, technologies must be embedded in production systems. The process by which technological capabilities are embedded in a company and a region's production system is an extension of the ongoing operations of entrepreneurial firms. The technology capability and market opportunity dynamic that drives the entrepreneurial firm is, simultaneously, a single step in a *cumulative* sequence by which a region's technological capability is extended.

The concept of collective entrepreneurial firm extends the idea of the technology capability and market opportunity dynamic that drives the growth of the firm to the region. Regions can be thought of as developing specialized and distinctive technology capabilities, which give them unique global market opportunities. The successful pursuit of these market opportunities, in turn reinforces and advances their unique regional technological capabilities. Regional specialization results from cumulative technological capability development and the unique combinations and patterns of intra- and inter-firm dynamics that underlie enterprise and regional specialization.

Thus, a region's technological capabilities are an outcome of a cumulative history of technological advances embedded in entrepreneurial firms and internalized in the skill formation systems. But the historical process is also *collective.* Just as individual entrepreneurial firms develop unique technological capabilities, a region's entrepreneurial firms will collectively extend their unique technological capabilities. The regional process of technology capability advance will likely involve a succession of firms, with new firms building on advances made by previous innovators.

A region's technological capabilities are an industrial ecology, in which entrepreneurial firms are spawned, grow, and die. At the same time, however, entrepreneurial firms, driven by a technology capability and market opportunity dynamic, are forever advancing their own capabilities. In the process the region's technological capability itself is revitalized by the ongoing, self-organizing activities of its inhabitants. It can be a virtuous circle. Regional technological capabilities spawn entrepreneurial firms, which upgrade regional technological capabilities, which spawn more entrepreneurial firms.

Specialized and cumulative regional technological capabilities lie behind the competitive advantage of 'low-tech', high-income industrial districts common to the 'third Italy'. Such districts have developed a competitive advantage in design capabilities that have fostered industrial leadership in a range of design-led or 'fashion industries'. But beneath such design capabilities is a unique mastery of a range of technologies derived from a craft heritage combined with specialist engineering skills.

Massachusetts is remarkable in terms of an extraordinary depth and continuity of technological innovation capabilities. It is part of a region that has been on the cutting edge of new technology development since industry began in America. The processes of technological capability development and diffusion, however, are obscured by the linear sequence conceptualization of innovation initiated by basic research (Figure 4.1).

This is doubly so in Massachusetts because of the region's renowned research universities. The region's university research laboratories have an unrivaled record as a generator of techno-entrepreneurs and business spin-offs. But the headlines generated by individual success stories obscure the region's unique technological capabilities cumulatively and collectively embedded in its production system. The continuity of technological capabilities is deeply intertwined with the region's extraordinary innovation record and critical to understanding the region's economic growth and productivity level.

The region's production capabilities are largely hidden from view. They do not fit standard stereotypes. If the production system that defines the regional competitive advantage of the American mid-west is mass production, the production system that defines the competitive advantage of New England could be called precision equipment manufacturing. Two features of the region's production system stand out: unique history of technological leadership and unique production capabilities in precision machines and complex products.

Precision Machining

Precision machining and engineering is an example of a continuity and change in specialized regional technology capability. New England's distinctive production system and technological heritage began with the American System of Manufacturers, a term used by the British to capture the uniqueness of American industry in the mid-1800s. The American System of Manufacturers, based on the production principle of interchangeability, opened a production/technological trajectory of ever-greater machining precision which, in turn, fostered applications in ever-wider product domains and at ever-smaller device sizes. In fact, industrial history has followed a technological 'law' of diminishing size. The historical trajectory has been sustained and deepened by a series of technological transitions. It is not an accident that these technology transitions have often occurred first in a region rich in precision machining capability.

The law of diminishing size is illustrated in Figure 5.2. Industrial technological history can be divided into a predominately mechanical

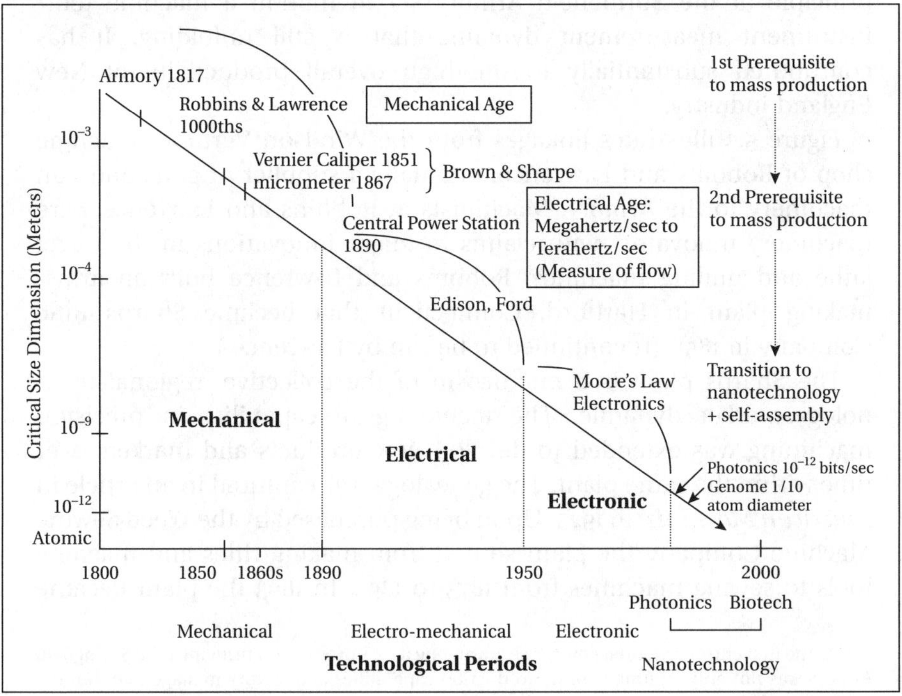

Fig. 5.2. The law of diminishing sizes

period spanning the nineteenth century giving way to an electro-mechanical period beginning at the turn of the last century and to an electronics period in the last half of the twentieth century. We are presently in the early stages of an opto-electronic or photonic-mechanical period. In each period mechanical technologies advanced and combined with electrical, electronic, information, and opto-electronic technologies. New England has sustained the capability to design and produce ever more refined mechanical devices feeding into machines, tooling, instruments, devices, and equipment. The genealogy of precision machining begins in the mechanical age and the principle of interchangeability.

1. *Mechanical Period*

The idea of interchangeability was widely known amongst leading engineers in Europe in the eighteenth century. It only became a principle of production when it was institutionalized in the form of the American System of Manufacturers or Armory Practices. The prime entrepreneurial firm was the Springfield Armory.[9] Application of the principle at the Springfield Armory set in motion a machine tool/instrument measurement dynamic that is still unfolding. It has contributed substantially to the high overall productivity of New England industry.

Figure 5.3 illustrates linkages from the Windsor, Vermont machine shop of Robbins and Lawrence, originally a supplier of guns and gun machinery to the Armory. Machinists at Robbins and Lawrence were machinery innovators with claims to major innovations in the turret lathe and milling machines. Robbins and Lawrence built an arms-making plant in Hartford, Connecticut that became Sharps Rifle Company in 1851. (It continued to be run by Lawrence.)

The Sharps plant is a microcosm of the collective, regional technology/market dynamic. The technological capability in precision machining was extended to develop new products and markets over time within the same plant. The genealogy was captured in an article in *American Machinist* in 1923. Upon being purchased by the Weed Sewing Machine Company the plant shifted from making rifles and machine tools to sewing machines from 1875 to 1893. In 1893 the plant became

[9] As the first entrepreneurial enterprise advancing a new production principle, the Springfield Armory was not only an innovator in production capabilities and factory management but the leader in defining a new set of skills and training workers. In these ways the Armory was a developmental firm, an inadvertent but powerful industrial policy vehicle.

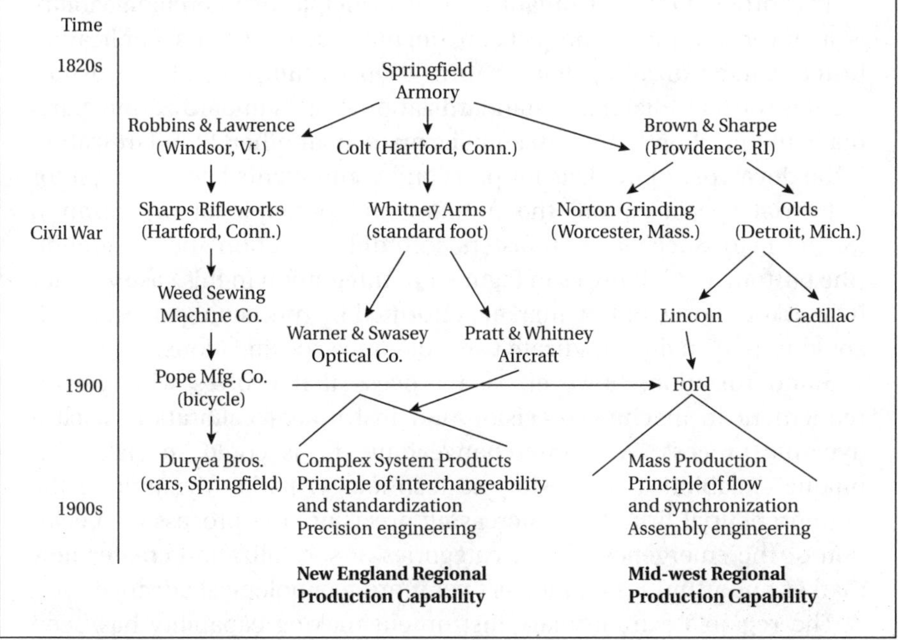

Fig. 5.3. Genealogy of two regional production systems

the Pope Manufacturing Company, the producer of Columbia Bicycles and Pope-Hartford Automobiles until it was purchased by Pratt & Whitney Company in 1914 (Hubbard 1923: fig. 2; M. Smith 1995). The regional competitive advantage in precision machining was developed over hundreds if not thousands of technology/market dynamics endogenous to the region's entrepreneurial firms.

The state of the technology/market dynamic in the nineteenth century is indicated by the refinement of machining tolerances. The machines that Robbins and Lawrence supplied to the Armory worked to thousands of an inch. But by mid-century, the standard was increasing to ten thousands. Brown and Sharpe, a Rhode Island machine shop, brought out a Vernier caliper gauge in 1851 and a micrometer gauge in 1867 (Roe 1916: 210–11). A micrometer is a millionth of a meter. Micrometers are used to measure machines working to tolerances of ten and hundred thousands. The claim is not that Brown and Sharpe were the first to develop such accurate measuring devices but that they were producing instruments and developing factory methods to realize their technological potential at the same time. The region's production capabilities were being advanced in the process.

The production and organizational principle of interchangeability is a never completed project, an ongoing challenge. Its application fosters standardization that, in turn, diffuses the principle. Measurement is the handmaiden of standardization. With standardization, parts made in one shop fit into assemblies made in another. Standardization is the developer of markets for parts and components and a catalyst for industrial specialization, the fundamental principle of organization (Stigler 1951). Specialization fosters both differentiation and integration (the bottom and left boxes in Figure 3.1). Integration in this case was not by markets alone, but by markets informed by precision gauges, which could impersonally adjudicate over tolerance specifications.

Standardization, however, is a process that evolves with greater refinement in machine precision and instrument calibration, itself a dynamic process. With interchangeability firms could specialize on unique capabilities and foster the technology/market dynamic of the entrepreneurial firm. With increasing precision, the process of speciation or the emergence of new categories of specialization creates new market opportunities and fosters yet more technological advance.

The region's extraordinary instrument-making capability has been an important contributor to a regional dynamic between instrument making and strength in science research (Billington 1983; Kline 1985; N. Rosenberg 1992; Wicks 1999). Sometimes, feedback effects have triggered new industries.

Astronomy, for example, depends upon instruments, and precision instruments have been a New England specialty since the region became the world leader in precision machining. Russell Porter, who worked at the Jones and Lamson machine shop[10] in Springfield, Vermont in the 1920s, designed the Hale Telescope on Mount Palomar, the world's biggest scientific instrument (Wicks 1999). The machine shop's owner, James Hartness, drew upon Porter's knowledge of optics to devise more precise measures of screw threads but saw the opportunities in lens grinding for instrument making. Sixteen machinists in the shop were members of the Springfield Telescope Makers in 1921. Most built their own telescopes, which required accuracy to the millionth of an inch. These capabilities and skills contributed to the emergence of an optical cluster in Sturbridge, Massachusetts led by companies

[10] Jones, Lamson & Co. was established in 1869 as a direct descendant of Robbins and Lawrence (Roe 1916: fig. 37). Robbins and Lawrence was awarded a medal at the Crystal Palace Exhibition in London in 1851. The British Government contracted with Robbins and Lawrence in 1854 for 150 machine tools to set up the Enfield Armory in north London (American Precision Museum, Windsor, Vermont).

such as American Optical Company.[11] They also contributed to advances in the science of astronomy and, eventually, the marriage of optics and electronics and the development of electron microscopes.

2. *Electro-Mechanical Period*

General Electric, founded in 1892, combined electrical and mechanical technologies. MIT simultaneously developed and advanced an electrical engineering curriculum and methodology that fostered both the advance and diffusion of emerging electrical-mechanical processes. The unit of measurement, a hertz, measured the flow of electricity in cycles per second. This opened up a new machine/instrument dynamic in pursuit of ever higher hertz. Precision engineering advanced in the form of the electrical devices required to modulate the flow of electricity.

Techno-diversification in Massachusetts electricity technology companies fostered new sub-sectors such as electrical switching devices at AT&T in North Andover and x-ray medical devices at Diano Corporation. Honeywell, established in 1927, became an equally important entrepreneurial firm which, combined with GE, were progenitors of New England computer firms such as Prime Computer and Apollo Computer (Hekman 1980; Rosegrant and Lampe 1992).

The measurements in the electrical period, in cycles per second, have an interesting feature in common with the principle of flow, the principle that guided Henry Ford and the emergence of mass production. It is possible that the concept of cycle time in electricity measurement was the inspiration for the concept of equal cycle times in manufacture and assembly of cars, the basis of the principle of flow. As noted in Chapter 2, Ford was an electrical engineer and many of his proudest achievements were in turbine electricity generation at his River Rouge facility.[12]

A yet more striking example comes later in the form of application to the central processing unit of the microprocessor. Descriptions of the role of the central processing unit are like reading Charles Sorensen, Ford's chief engineer (1957; see Chapter 2 above). Both use the language of synchronization and the metaphor of the metronome for synchronizing assembly, in one case material, in the other data. In this sense, the principle of flow, and its synchronization corollary, is now

[11] Wicks writes that three major machine shop spin-offs from Jones and Lamson in Springfield, Vermont continue to operate today in the same town under the ownership of Goldman Financial Group of Boston (1999: 75).

[12] I am grateful for Steve Miliaras for pointing this out to me.

constitutive of the architecture of the chip, as well as plant construction in high-volume manufacturing.

3. *Electronics Period*

Electronics was added to precision machining to generate entirely new regional growth dynamics in post–World War II New England, which are examined below. Computer companies and electronics firms like Raytheon drove the Massachusetts Miracle years. Calculations in bits per second became the next phase in the measure of precision and the target for a renewed machine/instrument dynamic. DEC was not the first, but it became the largest in a line of computer companies.

However, it can be said that Route 128 missed the succeeding generation of high impact applications in semiconductors and the PC industry. This time the machine/instrument dynamic that led the way was located in Silicon Valley. Known as Moore's Law, Intel processor speeds in calculations per second doubled every eighteen months reaching 1.7 billion calculations per second in 1999.[13] This has required an increase in the capacity of computer chips from negligible in 1971 to 14 million transistors in 1998. Micro machines are today etching wires that interconnect transistors as fine as 0.18 microns. A micron is one millionth of a meter (0.39 times 10^{-4} inch). Robbins and Lawrence, the pacesetters in their day, were measuring in roughly one-third the diameter of a human hair, the wires in a chip are one-five hundredth. The insulating layers, however, may be only 4 or 5 atoms thick.

It was not the first time New England missed a major application of a technology that it had pioneered. As noted above, the development of America's car industry relied heavily on the precision machining capabilities of New England but came to be centered in the midwest. Similarly, microprocessors and personal computers, the high-volume equivalents to the auto industry came to be centered in Silicon Valley.

[13] In the words of Robert Lucky (1999): 'Moore's Law is an incredible phenomenon. Why has it worked so well? After all, it is not a true natural law in the sense that the laws of physics are, nor is it a logical axiom that has been derived mathematically from basic principles. It is merely an observation of progress but one that has been an accurate predictor for 35 years. In spite of the fact that this law is the most important technological and economic phenomenon of our time, there is no accepted explanation for its validity.' Moore's Law is a technological roadmap and an example of a regulated or 'instituted process' that enables self-organization and mutual adjustment amongst numerous freely acting agents. It is more akin to an 'invisible hand' than a directed process. It has been an element in a highly successful industrial policy to revitalize the American semiconductor industry.

Why? The simple answer is that New England's competitive advantage has never been in volume production. The latter is anchored in the principle of flow, a production principle that has never thrived in New England and which is linked to different business models and engineering methodologies.

But, Route 128 did not go into terminal decline. Once again, the region has become a leader in the seemingly never-ending race for more precise manufacturing capabilities.

4. *Nanotechnology Period*

At the millennium the electronics industry faces a threat: the end of Moore's Law. After nearly thirty-five years, the number of transistors placed on a chip has surpassed 10 million and could reach 100 million. This translates into a manufacturing process in which the critical device dimensions have been scaled down from 25 micrometers in 1960 to 0.25 micrometers by the mid-1990s. For Moore's Law to continue to operate, the 2020s can project terascale integration or trillion transistor chips. This, in turn, involves scaling down critical device sizes to 0.025 micrometer or 25 nanometers.[14]

The electronics age is giving way to the opto-electronics or photonics age with yet more precision machining being designed. The measuring unit has become bits of information per second that can be transported on a single fibre. Switches are moving information bits in units of terahertz or 10^{12} bits of information per second. The unit of size measurement is a nanometer that equals one-billionth or 10^{-9} meters.[15] This is atomic resolution and remarkably microscopes capturing this dimension and nano-manufacturing devices are once again being applied in ever new applications. As in the first machine tool age, all products are being redefined in ways to take advantage of the new possibilities offered by information technology.

Nature manufactures at the nanometer scale. But nature does not build by scaling down but by 'self-assembly'. The information that shapes a cell is encoded in the atomic or molecular structure. Molecules

[14] The problem is that the microchip manufacturing process is already highly complex and unforgiving. The challenge is captured in a Semiconductor Research Association document: 'the prospect of no manufacturable technology for fabricating devices with components of sub-50 nm dimension' (Announcement for SRC/NASA Ames Workshop on 'Self-Assembly for Nanoelectronics', NASA Ames Research Center, 17–19 Nov. 1999).

[15] Ten gigabits/second or 10 billion bits achieved by Marlborough based Nexabit Networks (acquired by Lucent Technology in 1999; *Boston Globe*, 11 Nov. 1999) is reported to be three times faster than rivals Cisco and Nortel.

arrange themselves into specific organs. Similar self-assembly processes have been developed by chemists to fabricate polymers (plastic materials) by inducing molecules to link into long chains when triggered by the application of electricity, heat, or light. Precision engineering, in this context, means understanding and controlling self-assembly processes by which designs build themselves. In biotech production, such as the manufacture of synthetic DNA tissue, the size specifications shrink to one-tenth of atomic diameter. This is the size dimension at which nature constructs. It can only be explored with the tools made possible by information technology; at the same time it represents a distinctive information paradigm, information encoded in genes. These levels of precision are required for Moore's Law to be sustained. It means, however, the invention of entirely new manufacturing processes that mimic nature's own processes.

Each new technology involves a shift in the order of magnitude with which engineering objects are measured. At the same time it does not eliminate the lower order engineering tasks, but simply calls for systems integration capabilities.

Complex Products

New England's competitive advantage does not lie in mass production of consumer goods. New England has a regional competitive advantage in the manufacture of *industrial* machines, equipment, and instruments.[16] Industrial and commercial machinery (including computers), and electronic and electrical equipment (including telecommunication exchanges and switches, electricity transformers, chip-making machines, air traffic control systems, electro-medical devices) account for close to half of the region's exports. The share goes up to 75 percent by adding in instruments, engineering chemicals, and transportation equipment (primarily aircraft engines and parts) (Little 1993: 9). Some refer to these as the high-tech industries. They are equally representative of the precision equipment industry, which utilizes the

[16] In contrast, the American mid-west developed a regional technological capability and competitive advantage in mass production. In both cases the regional technological capability can be expressed in a wide range of final product areas. But, at the same time, regional technology capability is itself an expression of the cumulative dynamics of a region's production system.

region's production capabilities in precision machining and technology integration. The manufacture of precision equipment including instruments, machines, and tools, is a critical input into *complex system products.*

Complex system products tend to emerge and stay in New England. New England's competitive advantage in complex products springs from several factors.

First, as noted, Massachusetts has long enjoyed a world-class precision instruments and precision equipment making capability made up by hundreds if not thousands of firms collectively designing and making a range of products from jet engines to printing machines to telecommunication switching equipment to semiconductor making equipment. The heritage of specialist machine shops, tooling companies, instrument makers, equipment manufacturers, and injection molders collectively, constitute a flexible, open system supplier base.[17] After a slow start, this supplier base has embraced information technology in the form of computer aided design to compress the time to market for new product development (Forrant 1998). The Internet has been a similar tool hastening the transition to process integration of the supply chain (the *kanban* system).

Second, the region has a long heritage in core industrial technologies. For example, innovation in turbine technology dates back to the early days of the Lowell textile mills in the mid-1800s.[18] As in the case of many complex products, aircraft engine making represents a product concept initiated elsewhere but turned into a production capability in New England.[19] Pratt & Whitney and GE often capture 80 percent market

[17] The largest manufacturing sectors in greater Boston in the mid-1990s in employment are instruments (35,000), industrial machinery (23,000), printing and publishing (22,000), electrical equipment (21,000), and fabricated metals (11,000) (Terkla 1998: 15).

[18] Turbine technology was originally developed in New England as part of the system of canals and locks built to power the Lowell textile mills. James B. Francis, designer of the system of locks and canals that powered the Lowell textile mills, was an innovator in water turbine technology.

[19] Precision machining is equally encoded in the aircraft engine technology. The Pratt and Whitney Machine Tool Company was established as an arms maker in 1860. Both Pratt and Whitney had been employees of the Samuel Colt Armory which itself had links to Eli Whitney a controversial figure in the development of interchangeability. Frederick Rentschler, former president of Wright Aero, was looking for a site to develop air-cooled, radial engines for the US Navy. He went to Hartford and leased the rights to use the Pratt and Whitney name and located in empty space in Pratt and Whitney's machine shops. His design concepts were translated into a functioning engine and within three years the Pratt and Whitney Aircraft Company was an enormous success. Pratt and Whitney went on to produce close to half the total aircraft engine horsepower produced in America during World War II. GE developed the jet engine in Lynn, Massachusetts (see Almeida 1999).

Box 5.1. Jet engine technology fields map[a]

1. Other
2. Ramjets and rockets
3. Aeronautics
4. Casings
5. Tip clearance control systems
6. Rotors and stators
7. Airfoils
8. Combustors
9. Exhaust nozzles
10. Fuel systems
11. Gears and mechanisms
12. Lubrication
13. Couplings and seals
14. Control systems
15. Miscellaneous electronic systems
16. Fluid handling systems
17. Measuring and testing technologies
18. Materials and materials manufacturing
19. Coating and chemical processes and apparatus
20. Metallurgical processes
21. Metallurgical apparatus
22. Electrical machinery
23. Electrochemical machinery
24. Optics: systems and elements

[a] Based on US patent statistics.

Source: Prencipe (1998). Used by permission.

share of new orders for large commercial jet engines worldwide (Almeida 1999: 3).[20]

Third, the region has an industrial heritage not only in precision machining technologies but also in combining and recombining technologies to improve old or develop new products. For example, Andre

[20] Jet engine production is not in principle different from car engine production, but it inevitably requires more stringent testing of technological modification in any part on the performance of the whole, including the aircraft, under all types of conditions. In this, jet engine production is not intrinsically different from microprocessor production. But if jet engines were produced to the yield rates of the best chip-making fabs in the world, the airline industry would not be feasible. The combination of rigorous performance standards and interactive feedback

Prencipe has constructed a technology map of the jet engine based on patent statistics (1998). As shown in Box 5.1, he identifies twenty-four technical fields. The diversity is remarkable, including aeronautics, ramjets and rockets, airfoils, optic systems, electrochemical machinery, metallurgical apparatus and processes, measuring and testing technologies, fluid handling systems, control systems, fuel systems, exhaust nozzles, coating and chemical processes and apparatus, and materials and materials manufacturing.[21]

The precision equipment and machine and tooling industry have been critical to the resurgence of Route 128. Emerging entrepreneurial firms can develop new products, integrate technologies, and enter or open markets by partnering with companies for complementary technical and machining capabilities. It has meant that emerging enterprises have not been forced into head-to-head competition with regions that have developed unique capabilities in volume production required, for example, in consumer electronics. New England manufacturers cannot access local capabilities in high-volume, complex production activities. Furthermore, unlike Silicon Valley, Massachusetts has no Intels, Apples, Hewlett Packards, or other standard setting companies with household names. In the resurgence only EMC has made the Fortune 500 list.

This heritage, however, is not enough to explain why Massachusetts became home to the world's first high-tech industrial district.[22] For this we must examine the region's new technology development capabilities. Here the role of government research funding has played a critical role.

Research Labs and New Technologies

New generic technologies developed in Massachusetts in the middle decades of the twentieth century include microwave technologies, the digital computer, guidance systems, and the Internet. The federal government funded basic research for all four under defense-related

effects presents stern engineering challenges of an order of magnitude higher than both car and microprocessor production.

[21] An aircraft engine involves extremely precise tolerances which, in turn, has fostered sustained technological advances in lightweight materials, super alloys, and parts fabrication. These are all part of the collective entrepreneurial firm and market opportunity dynamic which underlies the development of regional competitive advantage.

[22] Perhaps high tech can be defined in terms of minimal critical size dimension.

budgets.[23] The first three were developed in nonprofit research laboratories administratively linked to MIT namely, the Radiation Laboratory, Lincoln Laboratory, the Instrumentation Laboratory (now Draper Labs). The fourth, packet switches, the key Internet technology, was developed (not invented) at Bolt Beranek and Newman (BB&N, a private research company founded by three MIT professors).[24]

Each nonprofit lab (and BB&N) pursued and drove a technology trajectory much like the world's most successful technology-driven firms. Furthermore, each has had a similar precipitating effect on regional growth dynamics (Figure 3.1). Each has specialized on a generic technology out of which new product applications have unfolded and new enterprises have been created. Thus, the labs have played the role of entrepreneurial firms in new firm creation. In the process they have built up unique regional technological capabilities. There is reason to believe that researchers from these laboratories, more so than faculty members in academic departments, have been the greatest source of techno-entrepreneurs that have led the new firm creation process in Massachusetts.

The region's capability in manufacturing complex products combined with research capabilities to foster new opportunities for technology-driven firms. A prime example is microwave technology associated with the early development of radar in England. A team of British scientists brought a single small magnetron (the microwave generating tube at the core of the machine) to the United States in 1940. The development of the microwave technology industry in Massachusetts involved both a federally funded research lab and the production capabilities of a partnering company. Raytheon developed

[23] Silicon Valley, in contrast, has relied more heavily on corporate labs for new firm and industry creation. For example, the personal computer and ethernet, or local area networks, industries can be traced to Xerox PARC and the hard disk drive and relational database industries to IBM's San Jose research center.

[24] BB&N was awarded the contract to develop 'packet switches' or 'interface message processors' in 1969. The idea (including the term) of packet switches, the fundamental concept leading to the Internet and other data networks, originated with Donald Davis, a computer scientist employed at the UK's National Physical Laboratory. (Paul Baran, at RAND Corporation, independently came up with the same idea but as a way to restructure AT&T's telephone system.) The idea was to chop messages into small packages, shove them onto the network, and let them find their own way to their destination by the easiest way route available. This meant long distance communication did not need to maintain a single connection along numerous telephone lines, through different exchanges, and run by different companies. It transformed the economics of communications. Instead of a long distance telephone call to send data, you called the networks nearest node, a local Internet service provider. BB&N pushed the concept another step by devising a technology to interconnect host computers of different manufacture and design to enable communication across computers (T. Hughes 1998; Abbate 1999).

lock step with MIT's Radiation Laboratory, set up in 1940 to coordinate microwave research. Britain could not produce enough machines. The reason, however, was not simply a lack of machinists during wartime. Raytheon engineers came up with a 'novel way to boost production . . . by assembling them out of laminated sheets instead of carving them laboriously out of solid blocks' (Rosegrant and Lampe 1992: 84). Instead of the predicted limit of 100 magnetrons per day, Raytheon's engineers' technique was producing 2,000 a day. Raytheon's production capability spurred the development of the technology.

In five years a new industry had sprung up around Route 128 converting Raytheon from a small vacuum tube producer into the region's largest defense contractor.[25] Raytheon's employment increased from 1,400 to 16,000 between 1941 and 1945 (Rosegrant and Lampe 1992: 85). The Radiation Lab, employing 4,000 at its peak, went on to develop over 150 systems 'that applied the versatile microwave technology to a dizzying array of applications' (84).

Regional growth ensued because of the existence of both the technological capability and the high-tech and manufacturing skill pools in the region. The greater Boston area may have been the only place that the capabilities and skills existed to ramp up a new industry this rapidly. This is an early example of the protean character of a region's collective enterprises to shed and take on labor as technologies advance and applications diversify. Later, with the development of the open systems business model, it will become a basis of regional competitive advantage in technology management.

The Radiation Laboratory built on the region's technological heritage and gave it a major boost. It is representative of a cluster of non-profit research laboratories that, collectively, have fostered technology trajectories that are still unfolding. Another leading example, the Instrumentation Lab at MIT, a World War II contemporary of the Radiation Laboratory, designed electromechanical control techniques to dramatically boost the accuracy of Navy anti-aircraft weapons. After the war, the Instrumentation Lab advanced its technology to provide guidance systems for long-range bombers, missiles, and Apollo moon missions.

[25] Raytheon is a case of industry/academia collaboration anchored in close personal relationships involving firm, university, and government. Laurence Marshall, a Raytheon co-founder and Vannevar Bush, electrical engineering professor and later president of MIT and the first national science advisor, were undergraduate roommates at Tuft University at the turn of the century. Otto Scott, author of a company history of Raytheon states that the collaboration between Raytheon and MIT researchers 'extended the firm's position to a unique scientific and engineering promontory beyond the usual commercial enterprise' (cited in Rosegrant and Lampe 1992: 68).

It became the Charles Stark Draper Laboratory Incorporated, an independent, nonprofit R&D company in 1973.[26] It, too, has fostered spinoffs. Rosegrant and Lampe estimate that fifty-five companies had spun off from the Instrumentation/Draper Laboratory by the 1980s.

When the Radiation Laboratory went out of business, its technology capabilities and staff morphed into the Air Force Cambridge Radiation Lab in 1947 with a staff of 1,100 and into Lincoln Laboratory, an MIT administered government laboratory, created in 1951. Located next to Hanscom Air Force Base on Route 128, Lincoln Labs' mission was to develop a radar- and computer-based air defense system following the Soviet Union's detonation of an atomic device in 1949. An air defense system involved the integration of technologies underlying missiles, radar networks, gunfire control, guidance systems, and high-speed digital computers (T. Hughes 1998: 17). Computer development was central to the project as computers were dubbed the 'brains' of an automated air defense system officially named the Semiautomatic Ground Environment (SAGE). This system became the first successful effort to 'apply computers to large-scale problems of real-time control as distinct from calculation and information processing' (Edwards 1996: 16; cited in T. Hughes 1998: 28).

Thus, Lincoln Labs, a 'non-academic' research center of the federal government operated by MIT, became a national center for electronics research, specializing in information processing and real-time control systems.[27] They built directly on the radar technologies developed at the Radiation Lab that provided the basis for the electronic circuits in the control units of the digital computer (T. Hughes 1998: 33). A major technological advance at Lincoln Labs was the development of magnetic flux core memory by Jay Forrester, the bottleneck technology holding back computer development. It has continued to specialize in radar, communications, digital processing, optic research, and advanced electronics for over half a century.

While more than fifty companies can be traced to Lincoln Labs, the best known is DEC, the first minicomputer company. Here, as in the case of the Springfield Armory in the last century, technologies and skills

[26] The Instrumentation Lab's budget reached nearly one-quarter of MIT's total budget in 1969. Its commitment to seeing designs through to products meant it was directly involved with America's major defense contractors. The militaristic purpose of its activities were weighed against the practical education opportunities it offered students in the late 1960s leading to the change in name and movement off campus (Rosegrant and Lampe 1992: 99).

[27] The annual budget of Lincoln Laboratory was $365 million in 1999 (David Mehegan, *Boston Globe Magazine*, 31 Dec. 1999).

developed in government 'labs' created opportunities for teams to reassemble as entrepreneurial firms and pursue variants of the generic technology. During the Miracle years, the minicomputer firms developed voracious appetites for labor. DEC, Data General, Prime Computer, and Wang Laboratories directly employed upwards of 200,000 people by the mid-1980s.

Hanscom Air Force Base became the late twentieth-century functional equivalent to the Springfield Armory of the first half of the nineteenth century. But whereas the Armory developed and implemented the principle of interchangeability, Hanscom developed and implemented the principle of systems integration.

Hanscom is no ordinary air force base. It is home of the Electronics Systems Center (ESC) the US Air Force's site for C^4I management. C^4I is a defense industry acronym that stands for command, control, communications, computers, and intelligence.[28] The ESC's role is concept development and systems integrator. It has managed nearly 200 C^4I systems.[29] It has contributed immeasurably to the region's unique capability and skill base in systems integration.

The SAGE project was perhaps as demanding of systems engineering as the Armory had been of machine designers and builders. In 1958, MITRE Corporation, a nonprofit organization, was established to focus on systems integration. It became the systems engineer for SAGE.[30] It, too, is co-located with Hanscom Air Force Base.

SAGE was but the first in a series of complex product systems developed for the military. In the 1970s ESC developed the Airborne Warning and Control System (AWACS) to detect low-flying aircraft. This required integrating radar technology, air-to-ground high-speed communications, computer technology, and software. In the 1990s it developed Joint Surveillance Target Attack Radar System (JSTARS) which has the

[28] Frank Stathas helped with the research on Hanscom and the Electronics Systems Center.

[29] The ESC is a systems acquirer and integrator. The design and manufacture of equipment are undertaken by civilian contractors. In its systems acquisition mission, to paraphrase its mission statement, the 'ESC serves as manager; determining the eventual user's operational needs, defining systems to best meet those needs, soliciting proposals from industry, selecting contractors to build the product, monitoring the contractor's progress, and eventually testing the equipment to ensure it meets the user's requirements' (<www.hanscom.af.mil/ESC>).

[30] MIT resisted Lincoln Laboratory's expansion to systems integration activities for SAGE for fear it would heighten pressures against MIT's deeper involvement in the industry side of the military-industrial complex. In fact, the MIT administration had earlier opposed Lincoln Laboratory's moves into computer programming and computer manufacture, fearing it was moving into competition with industry. In fact, Lincoln Laboratory and MITRE Corporation together created a huge labor pool in software and systems engineering that fed directly into the region's industrial sector enabling its rapid ramp-up in systems integration activities.

capability to detect, identify, track, target, and strike ground movements in virtually any weather.

At any one time the ESC may be managing a dozen or more C4I programs.[31] The ESC's biggest contracts go to the nonprofit research laboratories such as Lincoln Labs, the MITRE Corporation, and Carnegie Mellon and to the major defense contractors such as Raytheon, Grumman Aerospace, Boeing, Loral, Rockwell, and Marconi. But the ESC also manages dozens of contracts even in the $1 million to $3 million range. In fact, Hanscom draws upon over 2,000 small business firms that specialize in software development, telecommunications, radar, satellite communication, space technology, electronic sensors, and information management. Many are in the Route 128 area.

The rapidly evolving character of software–hardware complicates the systems integration challenge facing the ESC. A new generation comes on line every eighteen months. At the same time new C4I systems can take from three to ten years from concept to delivery. The ESC must, therefore, plan for pre-planned technology upgrades. It must anticipate, access, and adapt the latest technologies and diffuse new standards and innovations back to industry.

Developments in systems integration methodologies have complemented the region's technological heritage. Systems integration is the great facilitator of the integration and reintegration of diverse technologies for purposes of rapid new product development and innovation. The development of a regional capability to integrate information technology into the design, production, and constitution of the product has been a source of competitive advantage. It has leveraged the region's precision equipment and machine shop heritage into a regional capability to combine and recombine technologies in pursuit of new product applications.

The combination of systems integration and the region's unique production capability heritage in precision equipment may not have been planned, but it has been an opportunity seized.[32] But without a complementary skill formation program, the technological advance may not have been converted into regional economic growth.

[31] In 1996 the ESC was the lead manager for fifteen national C4I programs which totaled $8.1 billion.

[32] In recent years the organizational innovations associated with product-led competition in industry have fed back to inform the system integrator's role in C4I systems. For example, concurrent engineering, integrated product teams, TQM, self-directed teams, and continuous improvement are all means of harnessing feedback effects.

SKILL FORMATION

Skill formation is a complex process. It is often a by-product of more immediate goals. As we have seen, for example, the region's original development of a machinist labor force was a consequence of government investment in the production of arms. The Springfield Armory was no ordinary armory. It was also a pioneer in the development of the world's first machine tool industry based on the principle of interchangeability.

The institutional links between technical skill formation and industrial growth have varied. In the early nineteenth century, the formal and informal practices of machinists in government armories and machine shops formed an invisible college of knowledge creation and diffusion (see Chapter 4).[33] This invisible college was also a nurturing environment for the emergence of engineering and its eventual acceptance as an academic discipline. The growth of new industries in Massachusetts throughout the twentieth century involved the mutual development of engineering departments, teaching curricula, and technical research, on the one hand, and technology-driven enterprises, on the other.

This interactive relationship between technology-advancing enterprises and specialized curriculum in technology-oriented universities has a long history in Massachusetts. This has not changed. Nevertheless, the history can be broken into two periods. The first begins with the establishment of MIT as a land grant college in 1861. The second period dates from World War II to the present. The relationship was profoundly altered when the federal government escalated funding for research during and following World War II.

[33] 'Armory practice', the term used to describe the application of the principle of interchangeability, involved developing machinists with skills in machine making and work methods (Best 1990; Hounshell 1984). It was said of Henry Leland that he 'made micrometers and machine tools, automobiles and aero-engines, but above all he built men' (Hendry 1973: 83; Brown 1999: 10). Leland, apprenticed at the Crompton loom works in Worcester, Massachusetts and at the Springfield Armory, was further educated in precision machining at Brown & Sharpe in Providence, Rhode Island. Brown & Sharpe, a maker of instruments and tools that won prizes around the world, also designed small and affordable calipers that brought high standards of accuracy to everyday work in the machine shop. Leland was a carrier of Armory Practice to the mid-west where he became a founder of Cadillac and in 1907 opened the Cadillac School of Applied Mechanics. Cadillac was the first American company to win the Royal Automobile Club's Dewar Trophy for contribution to automobile construction and engineering and the first car to win its Standardization Test. During World War I, after a tour of England's aircraft plants, Leland established a plant to build 'Lincoln' aircraft engines. The plant was later converted to car engine production and sold to Ford (Brown 1999).

Engineering Methodologies and Entrepreneurial Firms

The Massachusetts Institute of Technology is not the only technology-oriented university in the greater Boston region. Others with engineering programs include Northeastern University, Boston University, Worcester Polytechnic Institute, Lowell Institute of Technology (now University of Massachusetts Lowell), and Wentworth Institute. But MIT sets the standard. No other institution anywhere has played a more central role in producing techno-entrepreneurs and shaping new industries over a span of more than a century.[34] According to an MIT/BankBoston study,[35] MIT graduates have started 4,000 companies nationwide and 1,065 in Massachusetts; the latter account for 25 percent of sales of all manufacturing firms and 33 percent of all software sales in the state.[36] But there is more to the story.

The process of mutual development between technology-driven companies and technology-oriented universities goes back a long way with MIT. A land grant institution, MIT was chartered as an 'industrial institution designed for the advancement of the industrial arts and sciences and practical education in the Commonwealth' in 1861. An MIT education meant an interaction of theory with experience in the laboratory and visits to machine shops, chemical plants, and electricity generation companies.[37] MIT represents a long struggle to elevate engineering, a profession that emerged from industry, to the highest echelons of academic respectability without sacrificing its close developmental links to industry. Its academic success is well known. But it has been a participant in the shaping of technology-driven industry in twentieth-century America. The telephone industry is an early example. Alexander Graham Bell invented and demonstrated the telephone using

[34] MIT's role in America's first high-tech industrial district inspired Frederick Terman, a dean of engineering at Stanford, to plant the seeds for a West Coast high-tech version. He persuaded administrators to establish the Stanford Industrial Park and two of his students, William Hewlett and David Packard to set up shop there. Another early occupant was Xerox's Palo Alto Research Center, the site of a series of innovations that came to constitute the personal computer (Cringely 1992). Sun Microsystems, Silicon Graphics, and Cisco Systems are but three other examples whose origins can all be traced to Stanford's classrooms.

[35] See 'MIT: The Impact of Innovation', web page at <http://web.mit.edu/newsoffice/founders>.

[36] According to *Mass High Tech*, the software industry of Massachusetts is driven by 'small firms founded by former executives who have cashed out before, or by recent graduates of the area's top engineering schools' (20–26 Sept. 1999, 17/38: 23).

[37] Richard Feynman, the Nobel Prize winning physicist had difficulties getting the accuracy he wanted in an MIT machine shop, but with the assistance of machinists could produce the desired results (Gleick 1993).

MIT's apparatus and laboratories in 1874. He was there at the invitation of Professor Charles Cross, who had established the first course in electrical engineering at MIT. In 1877 Bell Telephone Company was founded in Boston.

MIT's technical expertise has been a magnet for companies seeking to develop production processes in a wide variety of applications. Gillette, Boston's biggest industrial employer was the creation of a partnership between King Gillette, a traveling salesman for a bottle cap company and William Nickerson, an MIT trained chemist with knowledge of materials and manufacturing required to develop the machinery to produce low-cost, sharp blades. Founded in 1901, Gillette remains one of few Massachusetts high-volume manufacturing plants.

Important as examples of this type are, they do not capture the major impact of technology-oriented universities on industrial development. The greater impact is in establishing engineering methodologies and providing the technically educated labor force to create and operate research laboratories. These are critical inputs into a region and nation's stock of entrepreneurial firms. Here MIT's long history of involvement is unique.

The development of MIT's electrical engineering program was intertwined with the development of America's industrial laboratories in the electricity and electric power industries. The founding and early development of General Electric fits the pattern.[38] Before GE was formed by a merger of Thomson-Houston Company, owned by a group of Lynn, Massachusetts shoe manufacturers, and Thomas Edison's New Jersey operations, Edison had donated materials, machines, and dynamos to MIT for departmental instruction (Noble 1977: 137). Founder Elihu Thomson lectured to MIT's electrical engineering students at the invitation of Cross. GE conducted much of the early research in electricity and its Lynn and Schenectady plants were sites of work experience for generations of MIT engineers. In fact, Thomson served as acting president of MIT for three years beginning in 1920.

Landau and Rosenberg's account of the development of leading firms in America's chemical industry is a similar story (1992). Here, too, the discipline of chemical engineering and the growth of the chemical industry are part of a single process. The Research Laboratory of Applied Chemistry, established in 1908 at MIT, created the first vehicle for graduate studies in chemical engineering. The Laboratory sought research

[38] GE's Lynn, Massachusetts works became the site for the development of GE jet engines as well.

funding from industrial firms and practical experience for students. In 1916 the School of Chemical Engineering Practice was established at MIT and marked the world's first autonomous chemical engineering department.

Simultaneously, Exxon was creating an R&D capability in their new Development Department. Warren Lewis, a professor at MIT, and Robert Haslam, head of the Chemical Engineering Practice School, formed a research team of fifteen MIT staffers and graduates at Baton Rouge. Six of these individuals rose to 'positions of preeminence in petroleum and chemicals'. Landau and Rosenberg continue: 'Much of what took place in modern petroleum processing until the Second World War originated in Baton Rouge, and it was basically the MIT group that was primarily responsible for it' (1992: 91).

In effect, MIT's chemical engineering department, under the leadership of Warren Lewis established a new paradigm of industry and university partnering. In the words of Landau and Rosenberg:

> Lewis . . . created a very different approach. . . . Instead of bringing industry to the campus . . . he in effect brought the campus to industry. Unlike the Practice School, which also did this, he helped solve a number of the major problems of the industry. In so doing, he focused the discipline of chemical engineering on an overall, systems approach to the design of continuous automated processing of a large variety of products, first in petroleum refining but then, later, in chemicals. These developments provided the essential technological ingredients for the growth of the world petroleum industry. (1992: 91)

Specialist engineering consulting firms diffused the new chemical engineering methodology. Arthur D. Little, an MIT student, co-founded the world's first consulting firm in Boston in 1886 called Griffin & Little, Chemical Engineers. ADL, incorporated in 1909, not only convinced the chemistry profession of the value of industrial research but led the chemical industry in the embrace of industrial research.[39] Edwin Webster and Charles Stone, early graduates of MIT's engineering department, submitted a joint thesis and later institutionalized their collaboration as Stone and Webster, Inc. As an architectural engineering consulting firm, Stone and Webster played a similar role to ADL in the electric power industry.

On the financial side, MIT played a role in founding the venture capital industry. The first formal venture capital firm, American Research and Development Corporation (AR&D), was established in Boston in

[39] In the half century to 1946, the chemical industry accounted for more than 25% of new industrial laboratory discoveries (Rosegrant and Lampe 1992: 49).

1946 to spur the creation of new companies. AR&D brought to life an earlier plan of MIT President Karl Taylor Compton who, along with two other MIT professors, was on the advisory board (Roberts 1991: 33–4).

Research Laboratories and New Skills

The same industry/university dynamic that fostered entrepreneurial enterprises and advanced MIT's research capabilities and technical expertise in the first half of the century continued in the post-war period. But there was a major difference. As noted above, in the aftermath of World War II the federal government became the major source of funds for basic research in America. MIT's demonstrated research capabilities in partnering with corporate laboratories of over half a century better positioned the institution to seize the new funding opportunities than any other university in America. The means was to create a range of academic and nonprofit research laboratories. Government funding agencies turned to Massachusetts because the region offered research capabilities, entrepreneurial firms, and technical skills that could be rapidly mobilized to pursue new high-tech initiatives.

Laboratories and companies in Massachusetts are particularly successful at generating fundable research proposals (success at generating research funding is analogous to seizing market opportunities by entrepreneurial firms).[40] At the end of the century Massachusetts led the country in federal research dollars in academic and nonprofit research institutions per capita (MTC 1999: 46).[41]

Funding for basic research and technical skill formation are opposite sides of the same coin. Much of the federal funding goes into universities and teaching hospitals in the form of pay for student researchers and thereby feeds directly into advancing the regional skill base. People

[40] Federal R&D expenditures in academic and nonprofit research institutions in Massachusetts, per capita, was twice that of California, the second highest state, in 1997 (MTC 1999: 46). The ratio was three times for US Department of Health R&D expenditures, per capita, between Massachusetts and New York, the second highest state in 1997 (47).

[41] Massachusetts companies are the runaway winners of Small Business Innovation Research (SBIR) Awards granted by the Small Business Administration. SBIR are competitive grants to entrepreneurs to do 'proof of concept' research to establish technical merit and feasibility. The dollar value of SBIR awards per 100,000 people to Massachusetts companies in 1997 was over twice that of Colorado and three times that of California, the second and third highest states (MTC 1999: 34).

who have been and are being educated in science and engineering conduct the research and, in the process, advance the region's research capabilities.

The operational process of fulfilling contracts at Lincoln Laboratory, for example, necessarily has involved the employment and further education of thousands of electrical engineers. At the same time, the process involves the creation of new technological possibilities. Not surprisingly, teams of individuals who worked together in technology development have created new firms. Many are graduates of MIT, but they are also graduates of the region's nonprofit research laboratories.

From an economic growth perspective, the formation of a labor pool in the new skills associated with emerging technologies is particularly beneficial. Besides electrical engineers, software skills have been critically important in all high-tech industries. The skill formation challenge confronted by the SAGE project is captured by Thomas Hughes 'they realized that they had to train thousands of programmers at a time when their total numbered in the hundreds' (1998: 57). Hughes adds that by 1959, more than 800 people were working on software for SAGE.

The numbers did not diminish over time. The SAGE and post-SAGE projects have had a huge appetite for software skills. Software requirements expand as automated systems proliferate and increase in sophistication. All such systems are subject to 'minor' programming flaws that can shut down whole systems. Not surprisingly, Route 128 is a leader in developing computer-aided software engineering tools, user interface design tools, advanced software design methodologies, and software testing tools (National Critical Technologies Panel 1991: 55). Thus, SAGE and later C^4I projects have played a developmental role in creating a large pool of software and systems engineering talent that feed back into the entire manufacturing base of the region, much like the machinist and machine tool industry did in the last century.

The investment in basic research in New England is an important theme in understanding the capacity of New England to counter the forces of decline by renewing its technological capabilities. Advancing technological capabilities involves continuity and change. Sustained growth over long periods of time is about managing technological change and technology platform shifts. The skill dimensions of negotiating these transitions are easy to underestimate or ignore altogether. New England has benefited from educational adjustment processes that have fostered technological change by advancing the supply of skills in sync with emerging technologies. The region has been fortuitous in the case of the skills developed at the government-funded laboratories.

Manpower Development Planning

A remarkable feature of the Miracle years (1978 to 1986/7) was the responsiveness of the education system to the skill needs of the rapidly growing firms. As shown in Figure 5.4, the number of BA degrees in electrical engineering conferred by Massachusetts' universities and colleges increased from around 700 in 1982 to nearly 1,700 in 1988. The expansion in a region's 'production' of engineers is a costly process (also potentially highly productive). A ballpark cost estimate follows.

An expansion in graduates by 1,000 requires an increase of 4,000 students in four-year electrical engineering degree programs which, in turn, requires an expansion in faculty positions of roughly 270 (given a 15 to 1 student to faculty ratio) in electrical engineering plus a corresponding investment in facilities. Assuming an annual salary of $60,000 in the 1980s this translates to over $16 million in annual salary costs. A rule of thumb is that salaries in engineering and applied science must be matched by a 1:1 in costs for teaching and staff assistants, disposable materials, and bricks and mortar. This doubles the faculty salary cost to over $30 million annually to fund the expansion of 1,000 engineering graduates.

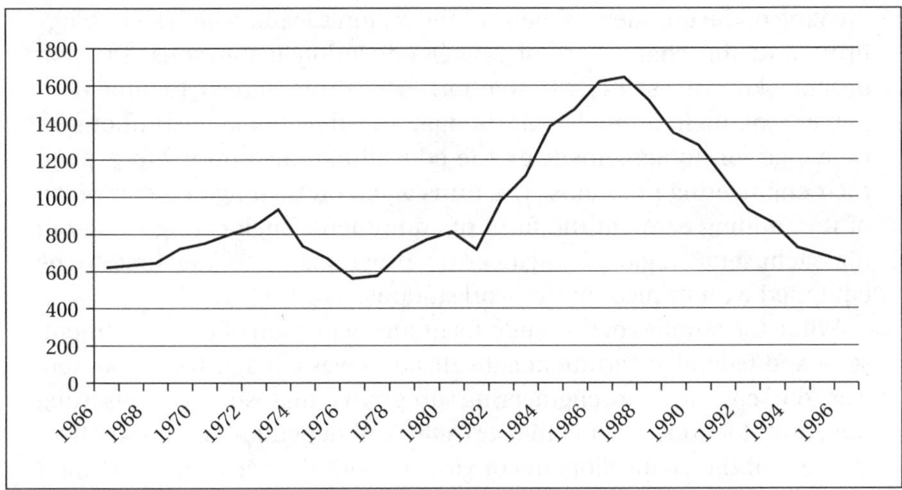

Fig. 5.4. Electrical engineering graduates in Massachusetts

Source: Data supplied by John Hoy, President, New England Board of Higher Education

To expand the number of college engineering students by 4,000 (1,000 graduates) will require an increase in the number of high school students by roughly 8,000. This translates to 270 new high school teachers in sciences and mathematics. At a student to faculty ratio of 30 to 1 and a 1980s average annual salary of $50,000, the total annual salary costs would have added to $13.5 million. If we assume a facilities and non-teaching staff cost of half, then the annual cost for high school education to expand the number of engineering graduates by 1,000 per year was $20 million in the 1980s.

The ballpark estimate, then, for a stepwise increase of 1,000 engineering graduates was $50 million annually in the 1980s. While this number is a small fraction of the increased output in the state, it was a big number for the educational institutions that expanded their engineering programs.

Only government has both the funds and legitimacy to make educational restructuring and investments on the scale involved. Nevertheless, the state government was not the leader but a third partner in the implementation of an informal manpower development plan. The rapidly growing, technology-driven firms and the engineering deans were the active partners in designing and implementing the expansion.

Technology-driven firms had resources but lacked skill labor; local universities had students but lacked resources. To address the mismatch, the Massachusetts High Technology Council sponsored a meeting of the founders of many of the region's leading high technology firms and the chancellors of higher education institutions. In what became known as the '2% solution', the firms agreed to provide 2 percent of their annual R&D budget to educational institutions in exchange for an agreement by the educational institutions to expand their engineering programs. The firms acted on their agreement. Much of the funding came in the form of equipment. Engineering faculty in Massachusetts' regional engineering programs were the first to be equipped with minicomputer workstations.

While the families of the students funded a portion of the investment, state and federal government subsidization was a major factor. So, too, was the cost to non-engineering programs that suffered offsetting budget reductions. In this the '2% solution' depended upon the effectiveness of the chancellors in convincing both the legislature and their university communities that engineering education had high priority.

As a manpower planning exercise, the limited number of firms that drove the economy during the Miracle years simplified the coordination of demand and supply of skilled labor. The result was a step increase in both engineering graduates and the technical skill base of the region. Technology-driven firms, educational institutions, and government funding partnered to provide the skill base required to fuel the growth and development of America's first high-tech regional concentration. Against the costs are benefits not only to the students involved and hiring firms but also to the region's economy. The knowledge-intensive industries established a competitive advantage that generated regional income growth and enhanced tax revenues.

In fact, the region has been harvesting the products of these earlier investments in technical education in both education institutions and within technology-driven enterprises during the Resurgence. The sharp drop-off in electrical engineering graduates that accompanied the crash of 1986 to 1992 has not turned around. The development of the Resurgence period technologies has relied heavily on skill formation investments by the educational system and human resource programs of companies enacted during and preceding the Miracle years. It has also relied on immigration for skills.

The Massachusetts labor force benefits from roughly 15,000 immigrants per year. The portion of recent foreign immigrant population to Massachusetts in 'highly skilled management, professional, and technical occupations' is estimated to be 33 percent. (According to the 1990 census, 28 percent of the immigrant workforce in the state had a bachelor's degree or higher (MTC 1998)). In-migration has taken up much of the slack from the shortfall of engineering graduates of colleges and universities in the state. The total pool of foreign born and, in most cases, educated technical pool has accumulated to a sizeable fraction of the total.

Furthermore, the figure suggests another source of increased technical labor supply in Massachusetts: graduates who remain in Massachusetts. Of the production of 6,000 graduates per year, a higher percentage stays in the state. The trend in net migration (domestic and international) over the Resurgence has shifted from minus 60,000 in 1991 to plus a few thousand. If this trend line continues and the international in-migration stays constant at roughly 5,000 per year, Massachusetts goes some distance to responding to the needs.[42]

[42] Figures on international and domestic migration, Massachusetts 1991–1998 (MTC 1999: 41).

CONCLUSION

Massachusetts has been fortunate. At mid-century the economic outlook for the region was bleak. Textiles and the shoe industry still employed 25 percent of the region's manufacturing workers in 1948 (Browne and Sass 2000: 201). Textile employment fell by 100,000 between 1948 and 1954, to 40 percent of its 1948 level. Shoemaking fared little better. Over the decade of the 1940s, the region's per capita income dropped by roughly 20 percent relative to the national average (202). Yet by the end of the century, Massachusetts' economy had been transformed and the region once again was high income by US standards. Why the turnaround?

The competitive advantage in Massachusetts is as much about technological continuity as change. While textiles and shoes were the biggest employers, there was more to the economy. The region's historic technological capabilities in precision machining, complex products and systems, and science/engineering education positioned it well for the minicomputer and defense industries that grew rapidly during the Massachusetts Miracle. Successful firms tapped the research base of the region's universities and laboratories to develop new technologies and grow rapidly.

In contrast, one can argue the return to economic growth in Massachusetts is a consequence of government-funded research centers at MIT. MIT-associated research laboratories have not only spun off companies, a large number of these companies have become entrepreneurial firms capable of driving their technology/market dynamics and, in the process, they have fostered the regional growth dynamics captured in Figure 3.1. Collectively, they have reinforced the region's competitive advantage in complex product systems and thereby driven growth.

Certainly defense spending and the region's research laboratories have played major roles. But economic growth is more complex than government funding of research centers even at universities as successful as MIT's in spinning off companies. Many universities have first-rate research centers (Carnegie Mellon and Johns Hopkins) and some even had success at spinning off firms and some enjoy a high rate of new firm creation (Cambridge University). But few are associated with the development of entrepreneurial firms and regional growth dynamics like those linked to MIT. If the explanation of Massachusetts' success is in something unique about research capability, one must explain the sharp decline in Massachusetts' growth between 1985 and 1992, when the region lost one-third of its manufacturing jobs. And one must explain the success of MIT in attracting so much federal research funding. Is it to do with, for example, politics, historical accident, or does it come back to the region's technological heritage in precision machining and complex products?[43]

However one lines up on these issues, the attribution of cause and effect does not accurately characterize the mutual adjustment processes that constitute the region's Productivity Triad, namely, the business model, the production capabilities, and skill formation. The interactive processes are critical to the productivity-led growth process.

Basic research will have growth effects *somewhere.* The region's unique research capabilities could lead to economic growth, but the location would depend upon where there were firms able to seize the opportunities. This is exemplified by the CNC machine tools. As noted, they were developed at MIT but served to advance the productivity, not of local industry, but of Japanese industry. The links to regional growth depended upon a business model with flexible production capabilities. Japanese companies that had earlier developed agile manufacturing methods and continuous improvement work organization were well positioned to use the new technology not simply as a way to reduce costs but to enhance flexibility.

Massachusetts, too, has production capabilities that have long benefited from basic research conducted elsewhere. As noted, the existence of the region's production capabilities is what enabled it to seize the opportunity of the invention of radar in mid-century and 'packet switches' late in the century. But to turn the prototypes into growth in output and rapidly growing firms, it required regional production flexibility. This involves industrial (inter-firm) processes of product chain disintegration and reintegration to realign the region's production capabilities and labor force around the new opportunities (left-hand rectangle in Figure 3.1).

This means that capabilities in basic research and production are not enough. To fully tap the region's innovation capabilities and use them

[43] In fact, this specific industrial heritage turned out to be an ideal infrastructure for information technology. New England's heritage of complex product systems turned from a disadvantage in the age of consumer electronics and incremental innovation to an advantage in the age of information technology and disruptive innovation. Consequently, the region has been a major beneficiary of the information technology revolution.

to drive growth, the business model had to be equal to the competition. The vertically integrated, hierarchical model that informed the leading firms of the Massachusetts Miracle did not foster techno-diversification but reinforced the region's historic tendency to domination by big firms and few sectors.

The downturn of 1985 to 1992 facilitated not only the realignment but also the transition to an open systems business model, a transition that has enhanced the region's technology management capabilities. Firms that went out of business had been organized according to vertically integrated, top-down, functionally departmentalized business model were poorly equipped to meet the new competitive challenge based on rapid new product development, endogenous technology management, and regional innovation. Their exit freed resources to be deployed in firms adopting the focus and network business model. In the process, the regional model of business and industrial organization was redefined to capture more fully the innovation and growth potential of systems integration and the associated decentralization and diffusion of design. The timing of the downturn is explained by a variant of Schumpeterian creative destruction working at the level of regional production system.

Silicon Valley was the first to apply the principle of systems integration at both the technological and business model level and thereby institutionalize a new model of technology management. The irony is that system integration has long existed in New England but as an engineering skill and technological capability, not as a unifying principle of production and business organization. But systems engineering and system integration as a technological capability were largely confined to closed system architecture.

Silicon Valley, as a New Competition, forced a wave of Schumpeterian 'creative destruction' across New England businesses. The severity of the industrial decline that ended the Miracle years had two effects: widespread business failure involving companies organized according to the dictates of vertical integration and the release of a huge labor pool of people educated and trained in system integration skills. The new business model depended upon a supply of skilled labor. Without this pool the regional growth dynamics illustrated in Figure 3.1 could not have driven sustained economic growth. It would have been choked by technical skill shortages.

The skills in the labor force and the technological capabilities that Massachusetts' enterprises had built over generations did not go away. They resurfaced in new firms, new products, and new applications. But most importantly they eased the transition to a new, open systems business model, a model more appropriate to exploit the opportunities offered by systems integration at the technological level.

The new, open systems business model advances two performance standards which are critical to competitive advantage in New England, rapid new product development and disruptive innovation (as distinct from incremental innovation). The region's machine shops facilitated the rapid diffusion of systems integration. The job shop heritage complemented a major dimension of systems integration, namely the capability to redesign the whole to take advantage of design changes in component parts or modules. The region's custom design heritage in machines and tooling was reinvigorated. Design was again important. But it was now integral to the region's business model.

The open systems business model made possible the full set of regional growth dynamics captured in the regional growth dynamics model. Now firm and inter-firm technology development teams could be formed and reformed in pursuit of new opportunities emerging as a by-product of the techno-diversification process. It was an ideal fit for Massachusetts.[44] It has reinvented manufacturing in the region.[45]

The techno-diversification of Route 128 is itself a consequence of the conversion of systems integration from a technological into a business and industrial organizational capability. The conversion can be understood in terms of the diffusion of the new model of technology management, the establishment of a complementary business model capable of driving the new principle, and an advanced, diverse, flexible, and targeted skill base.

The pace of organization transition to variants of the leadership/design dynamic such as high-performance work systems over this

[44] A company engaged in the manufacture of complex systems products enjoyed the advantage of the flexibility of a job shop but lacked the efficiency of flow systems. But the mass production systems are not designed to pursue the technology capability/market opportunity dynamic with the same degree of flexibility for incorporating disruptive technological change as the 'open systems' business model. In this sense, New England perhaps has gone further than Silicon Valley in establishing a complex systems product business model as distinct from flexible mass production (lean production). By the integration of software and hardware, job shops that were hopelessly organized according to the dictates of world-class manufacturing found a new business model by which they could pursue a strategy of rapid new product development based on technological systems integration.

[45] The new business model, one of regional innovation, is simultaneously a technology management capability for rapid new product development. It is driven by competition over the rapid development of new product concepts which, in turn, thrives on the dip-down model of innovation. This business system pulls in, and integrates, basic research into the manufacturing processes.

period was remarkable.[46] According to a recent report, the proportion of employees in firms in the United States that 'made some use of self-managed teams increased from 28 percent in 1987 to 68 percent in 1995' (Appelbaum et al. 2000: 9).[47] New England companies were not followers in this transition. Anecdotal evidence is plentiful.[48] In early 1990, seven Boston-area companies formed the Center for Quality Management to work together in TQM (total quality management).[49] It became a model for rapid application and diffusion of continuous improvement work organization.

In a sense the resurgence has been about the reinvention of a regional industrial system to fully exploit the opportunities inherent in the emergence of a new technology. Like Ford's use of electricity to redesign the manufacturing plant to apply the principle of flow, New England has, in effect, used information technology to redesign the region's industrial capability to apply the principle of systems integration. But ironically, complex product systems are in many ways a better production platform for technology management of disruptive innovation than is that of mass production.

The question now is, can the region's focus and network business model and corollary techno-diversity sustain growth, and foster technological and organizational disintegration and reintegration without severe downturns. If it can, it means that the region has replaced a blunt reallocation instrument (economic downturn) with a sophisticated instrument (open system networks). This does not mean the end of the forces of industrial decline in the region including the uncertainty of technology platform shifts, but it suggests that policies that enhance a region's technology management capabilities may be more effective than the blunt instruments of traditional macroeconomic policy-making. One of those is manpower development planning.

[46] An HPWS is 'a plant that has adopted a cluster of practices that provides workers with the incentives, the skills, and, above all, the opportunity to participate in decisions and improve the plant's performance' (Appelbaum et al. 2000: 9).

[47] 'Workers in an HPWS experience greater autonomy over their job tasks and methods of work and have higher levels of communication about work matters with other workers, managers, experts (e.g., engineers, accountants, maintenance and repair personnel), and, in some instances, with vendors or customers' (Appelbaum et al. 2000: 7).

[48] See Forrant and Flynn (1998); Best (1994); Best, Forrant, and Martucci (1995); and Tilly and Handel 1998).

[49] The Center identified 135 kinds of diffusion channels (Shiba, Graham, and Walden 1993). See Forrant and Flynn (1998) for a case study of making the transition to an HPWS.

CHAPTER

6

Cluster Dynamics in Malaysian Electronics

CHALLENGE: GROWTH WITH LOW VALUE ADDED

Malaysia's electronics industry is puzzling.[1] It accounts for one-half of Malaysia's total exports and employs one-quarter of the manufacturing labor force.[2] The annual rate of growth of manufacturing exports during 1970 to 1995 was over 25 percent per year and electronics accounts for two-thirds of manufacturing exports. Over the same 1970 to 1995 period, agriculture's share of exports dropped from nearly 75 percent to 13 percent and manufacture's share increased from 11 percent to 80 percent.

Indeed, the specialization in electronics is much higher than in most OECD countries, which gives Malaysia a strong foundation in the most innovative sectors in modern industry. The puzzle is why is Malaysia's per capita income so low given its apparent industrial structure? Before

[1] This chapter is a product of a study of the Malaysian electronics industry conducted by the United Nations Industrial Development Organization for the Economic Planning Unit of the Prime Minister's Department, Malaysia, sponsored by the United Nations Development Programme, Malaysia, and co-authored with Professor Rajah Rasiah. Giovanna Ceglie and Frederic Richard were the UNIDO officers in charge. Many of the observations on Penang are based on personal interviews conducted by the author in Mar. 1997 and Sept. 1998 arranged and accompanied by some combination of Lim Pao Li and Anna Ong of DCT Consultancy and Lim Kah Hooi of TEC Centre. Without the considerable respect all three enjoy in both private and public sectors, it would have been impossible to arrange the interviews with virtually the Who's Who of Penang electronics, starting with the Chief Minister, Dr Koh Tsu Koon.

[2] The electronics sector usually combines electronics and electrical products, but electronics make up over 90% of the total output and employment (MITI 1996: 52–4).

the Asian crisis, Malaysian per capita income was roughly $4,000, one-sixth that of Singapore.

The competitive advantage of Malaysian electronics has shifted from low-wage, labor-intensive manufacturing activities organized by foreign-based multinational companies (MNCs) to low-cost, rapid ramp-up, high-volume, increasingly automated manufacturing activities with special capabilities in assembly, testing, and packaging of semiconductors and hard disk drives. Nevertheless, the Malaysian electronics industry has reached a critical impasse: it is caught between lower wage rivals that are imitating Malaysia's present production capabilities and higher performance rivals with superior production and innovation capabilities (Best 1997*a*). Raising per capita income depends upon developing higher value adding production activities. The question is how.

The poor value added performance of Malaysian electronics is not lost on the government. Recognizing the problem, the Ministry of International Trade and Industry and the Economic Planning Unit of the Prime Minister's Office have developed a cluster-based strategy.

INDUSTRIAL POLICY

The *Second Industrial Master Plan: 1996–2005* (IMP2), prepared by the Ministry of International Trade and Industry, shares the assessment that sustained growth demands that the Malaysian electronics industry must make a transition 'to more automated operations involving high technology and knowledge-driven processes'. It will not be simple: 'this internationally-linked group which has been driven by rapid changes in technology, product development and innovation, changing consumer preferences and a short product life cycle, faces a number of challenges' (MITI 1996: 63).

The Economic Planning Unit's *Seventh Malaysian Plan* marks a subtle shift from reliance on foreign enterprises, as distinct from foreign direct investment, as the source of technology: 'The primary source of technology will continue to be foreign enterprises' (EPU 1996: 2). The application of the cluster-based approach, however, emphatically marks a new direction.

The IMP2 . . . focuses on the cluster-based industrial development approach [to] improve on the existing industrial foundation of the manufacturing sector. **It will further strengthen industrial linkages both in terms of depth and breadth**

> **at all levels of the value chain.** . . . [The] cluster-based *Manufacturing* + + strategy . . . involves two basic thrusts: the move along the value chain to increase value-added at either end of the chain . . . [and] the shift of the entire value chain to a higher level thereby increasing value-added at every point along the value chain. (EPU 1996: 30–1, bold in the original)

The *Seventh Malaysian Plan*, as well, stressed the role of government incentives to stimulate private sector involvement in the 'cluster-based manufacturing + +' strategy. A series of governmental technology policy related measures were introduced. The take-up rate, however, has been disappointing and science and technology indicators have not shown the desired advance (Best and Rasiah, forthcoming). In short, the pace of adoption and diffusion of technology has stayed stubbornly low in Malaysian electronics. The easy answer to the question of why the limited take-up of such programs is that Malaysian enterprises lack the technology management capabilities to make the transition to a higher value added industrial foundation.

The question is, will the cluster-based strategy drive the transition? The strategy depends upon the existence, or not, of linkages between clusters and transitions to higher value added activities and value chains. The task of theory is to explain development processes that lead to higher value added economic systems. The capabilities and innovation perspective addresses these linkages in terms of the three domains that constitute the Productivity Triad (see Figure 1.1).

The term 'cluster dynamics' signifies the extension of the term 'cluster' to account for the range of dynamic processes that underlie regional capability development. Capability development is the mediating variable between clusters and the value adding capacities of a region's manufacturing enterprises. The question becomes, do the capabilities exist within the Malaysian electronics industry to achieve the goal of the 'cluster-based, manufacturing + + strategy'?

An answer to this question involves an audit of the business organization, production systems, and skill formation systems within each electronics cluster within Malaysia. In fact, the Malaysian electronics industry is a composite of three regional clusters of roughly the same size in employment, namely, Penang, the Klang Valley, and Johor. Penang has the largest concentration with roughly 90,000 employed, followed by the Klang Valley with about 85,000 and Johor with nearly 80,000 (MITI 1996: 38).

The electronics clusters in each of the three regions have similarities and marked differences. All three clusters are variants of the Singapore model, in that foreign-based multinational corporations (MNCs) drive them. But this similarity obscures profound differences amongst the regions. The Johor region is part of a cross-region electronics cluster which does generate high value added but not high per capita incomes within Johor. Both the Singapore/Johor and Penang clusters will be explored to draw implications for industrial policy.

THE SINGAPORE/JOHOR REGION

Singapore's Productivity Triad

The electronics industry of Southeast Asia began in Singapore following an investment mission to the United States in 1967 to establish Singapore as an offshore manufacturing platform (Chia Siow Yue 2000: 12). In the same year Texas Instruments set up a semiconductor assembly plant to assemble and test simple integrated circuits for re-export to the United States. Following the American influx, MNCs from Europe and Japan followed. Reflecting national specialization, American MNCs tended to invest in electronic components (semiconductor and disk drive assembly) and industrial electronics (computer and telecommunications) and Japanese MNCs primarily in consumer electronics and electrical products.

Singaporeans benefit from a highly responsive education system. It has enabled local operating units to successively pull in higher value adding production activities from the home bases of MNCs.

Chia Siow Yue, director of the Institute of Southeast Asia Studies in Singapore points out that

> since the 1960s, the educational system has been continually restructured—with emphasis on technical and vocational education below tertiary level to provide a growing pool of skilled workers and technicians; and rapid expansion of engineering, business and computer education at tertiary level. Forty percent of the graduates from polytechnics and universities are trained in engineering and technical areas. The proportion of an age cohort enrolled in polytechnics and universities is targeted to reach 60% by the year 2000. Formal education is supplemented by training in specialized industrial training institutes to produce qualified craftsmen and technicians. The establishment of the Skills Development Fund provides upgrading training for those already employed. (2000: 2–3)

Singapore's skill formation program has been integrated with its policies to foreign-based MNCs. A dynamic entrepreneurial base is critical for acquiring technologies and exploiting market opportunities. But the development of locally produced high-value activities demands more. Singapore industrial policymakers recognized first, the crucial role of entrepreneurial firms and that entrepreneurial firms can be local, joint ventures, and foreign subsidiaries; second, that indigenous entrepreneurial capability was insufficient; and third, that entrepreneurial firms are both learning firms and have voracious appetites for engineering capabilities.

The heavy reliance on MNCs was a means of focusing on building manufacturing and technology management capabilities that matched with emerging market opportunities. The development strategy was based on synchronizing skill formation with the progression of firms along the production capability spectrum (Box 2.2). With the development of design capabilities, locally based firms (or subsidiaries) take a big step to becoming entrepreneurial firms. The strategy was not based on leapfrogging technologies but on step by step advances in production capabilities that facilitate the development of technology management capabilities and movement in the PS 3, 4 and PS 5 direction in Figure 2.1.[3]

Technology management capabilities, alone, do not explain the uniqueness of Singapore's electronics cluster and its high per capita income. But they have contributed to the extension of Singapore's competitive advantage from manufacturing to the delivery of low-cost, high-quality engineering services to 'packaging and integration' capabilities. The latter underpin Singapore's emergence as a regional headquarters for supplying manufacturing services.

The transformation did not stop with a re-division of activities within MNCs. Singapore's competitive advantage and business model are undergoing a transformation. Singapore's electronics industry was strategically converted from a labor-intensive manufacturing operations platform for vertically integrated MNCs to a horizontally integrated manufacturing-services cluster with ever increasing development of manufacturing/complementary service activities such as engineering-intensive product redesign and process automation and

[3] Mike Hobday presents a case study of Wearnes Hollingsworth Group, a Singaporean-owned, entrepreneurial firm. Wearnes began as a sub-contractor of connectors and progressed to OEM, ODM, and OBM in personal computers and added software and R&D capabilities to basic manufacturing skills in electromechanics and precision engineering. Hobday notes that: 'In the early 1990s, Wearnes still saw its main technological strengths in high quality engineering applied to electromechanical and electronic interfacing tasks, in connector manufacture, chip packaging, plastic molding and electroplating, rather than software or R&D' (1995*a*: 1183).

complementary business services associated with regional coordination, procurement, development, and integration activities.

The expression 'packager and integrator' comes from Enright, Scott, and Dodwell (1997). It captures the idea that Hong Kong or, by extension, Singapore firms are not mere coordinators of regional activities but 'instigators and initiators' of economic activity, match demand and supply on local, regional, and global levels. Such firms (or networked groups of firms) embody a complex of activities that enable them to add value

> through their knowledge of source and destination markets, through their familiarity with production capabilities of literally thousands of factories scattered throughout Asia, through advanced capabilities in logistics, and through expertise in managing subcontractors. Rather than a 'middleman', the Hong Kong [substitute Singapore] firm becomes a complete business partner for the customer, coordinating and putting together, 'packaging and integrating' a range of activities often beyond the capabilities of the customer . . .
>
> They provide a complete headquarters for management, financing, technology, design, prototyping, quality control, marketing, and distribution service between dispersed assembly plants on the one hand, and retail buyers on the other. (55)

The cluster that captures all of the firms involved in 'packager and integrator' activities breaks down any manufacturing/services dichotomy; more, it transcends the metaphor of value chain with that of value network. The idea of a value chain is derived from a linear, assembly line context; the idea of value network captures the idea of real-time coordination and design integration across activities.

The left-hand box in the regional growth dynamics figure captures the capability of a region to quickly form value networks (Figure 3.1). The network integrator in the dynamics paradigm is a functional equivalent to the roles of the auctioneer and/or the middle manager in equilibrium economics. The network integration capability operates at the cluster level much as systems integration capability operates at the enterprise level. In both cases each unit is flexible and design-responsive and the whole is subject to redesign to address new challenges. Whereas systems integration depends upon technical interface rules, network integration depends upon trusted social interactions. Proximity is important to both; thus the metropolitan advantage.

The extent and type of specialization in the top box of the cluster dynamic circular flow in a dynamic metropolitan cluster contains a whole range of service-type activities. In the case of Singapore many of these are elements of a manufacturing/services cluster. Singapore cannot be faulted for having ignored the role of 'low-technology' supplier firms to a flexible 'high-technology' cluster. Singapore's skill formation system has supplied a steady stream of skilled labor to maintain a regional small and medium-sized enterprise (SME) supply base composed of machine tooling, metalworking, plastic processing, die and mold making, instrument making, and related specialist inputs into manufacturing.

Growth and high value added in Singapore come from the development of cluster dynamics involving mutually reinforcing entrepreneurial firms, developing unique capabilities, spin-offs, and start-ups that are facilitated by skill formation and infrastructure, and a proliferation of specialist firms that can horizontally combine and recombine to rapidly carry out projects.

Singapore's electronics industry, from this perspective, has successfully negotiated two transitions: internal to MNCs from labor-intensive to automation and from automation to integrated manufacturing, and from vertically integrated MNCs to a dynamic cluster. In the mid-1990s, the electronics industry remains Singapore's most important manufacturing industry, accounting for 36 percent of manufacturing, value added, 25 percent of the manufacturing workforce, and contributing 12 percent of the island's gross domestic product (Pang Eng Fong 1995: 122–3). The foreign equity share of Singapore's electronics industry was 88 percent in 1992. All of these numbers are similar for Malaysian electronics. But the similarities stop here.

The Value Added Gap

The value added and per capita income differentials between Singapore and Malaysian electronics are large and persistent. For comparison, Penang represents the most advanced of Malaysia's three electronics regions and is roughly two-thirds as large in people employed (Penang has roughly 87,000 employed in electronics in contrast to 127,000 in Singapore). But Penang electronics generates under 4 billion ringgit (just over US $1 billion) to Singapore's S$13.20 billion (US $8 billion) which translates to US $12,000 in value added per person in Penang versus US $63,000 in Singapore. This multiple of five is less than the multiple of per capita income between Singapore and Malaysia of over six in 1997 (US $26,475 to US $4,320; exchange rate of US $1 = RM 2.81; EPU 1998 and Chia Siow Yue 2000: 1). This divide persists even within a single cluster. The political divide mirrors a skill formation divide that, in turn, segments labor within the cluster.

Electronics firms in Singapore faced a limited labor supply from the beginning. Given the early focus on labor-intensive assembly activities, increased wages created pressures on profit margins. Increasingly, lower value added manufacturing operation activities were relocated to low-wage neighbor states. Thus, high wages in Singapore meant the wholesale migration of factories into the adjoining region of Malaysia.[4] Singapore risked losing its manufacturing base and fears of industrial hollowing out were expressed.

However, even though Johor was converted into an electronics region that employs nearly 80,000, the region's per capita income has not converged with that of Singapore. This has been so even though Malaysia's labor surplus was converted into a labor shortage with over 20 percent of the labor force composed of foreign labor by the late 1990s. In 1997 wages were one-quarter and property prices were less than one-fifth those of Singapore (Sin-Ming Shaw 1997: 64).

What appeared as de-industrialization was simply factory relocation. The MNCs did not relocate their whole operations to lower wage, labor surplus regions in the region. Instead they maintained non-labor-intensive manufacturing and service-related activities in Singapore and relocated merely the labor-intensive activities offshore. The know-how and value added from engineering-intensive activities were not transferred even though the manufacturing operations take place in factories located in Malaysia (and in some cases conducted by Malaysian engineers working for MNCs with regional headquarters in Singapore).

The Singapore operations focused increasingly on more engineering-intensive activities, including automation, product redesign, design for manufacture, and logistics functions associated with regional procurement including complementary business, logistics, procurement, and financial services. For example, the division for product development projects focuses industrial design, upstream engineering and downstream activities in Singapore and repetitive manufacturing primarily in Malaysia followed by Thailand, Indonesia, and China (Tang 1996: 231). Much of the resulting manufacturing activities in the Johor region of Malaysia are third and fourth tier, unskilled, labor-intensive operations in consumer electronics-related industries. The problem is that while Malaysia has considerable production capabilities in electronics, it lacks

[4] In the early 1980s over 50% of the foreign direct investment by Singapore-based manufacturers went to Malaysia (Pang 1995: 117).

effective integration of the three elements of the Productivity Triad. Consequently, distinctive capabilities, a major source of high value added activities, are relatively underdeveloped. We turn next to the most promising electronics region within Malaysia.

PENANG

Penang, one of thirteen states of Malaysia, was suffering in the late 1960s. Its historic trading role virtually disappeared with the political turmoil and national realignments, and unemployment reached nearly 15 percent (Koh Tsu Koon 1995: 2). In 1969 the state government established the Penang Development Corporation to 'undertake and promote socio-economic development of Penang' (PDC 1994: 4). The PDC developed programs in industrialization, urbanization, urban renewal, tourism promotion, and human resource development. In the next twenty-five years Penang's manufacturing share in GDP increased from 13 to 50 percent (Koh Tsu Koon 1995: 2–3). Today its world-class, high-volume production capabilities in electronics are known around the world. Nevertheless, the capabilities that have fostered electronics growth in the past may not do so in the future. We look first at the basis of Penang's regional competitive advantage today.

Production Capabilities

The Penang region specialized first in assembly followed by the packaging and testing of semiconductors. High-volume production capabilities in electronic components were developed which spread to hard disk drives and, more recently, to myriad elements of the PC supply chain (DCT 1998).[5]

The region has world-class manufacturing capabilities in mass production (PS 2 levels in Table 2.1 and Box 2.2) including JIT and TQM systems with a number of examples of flexible mass production (PS 3). These production practices enable participating companies to achieve world-class performance standards in cost, quality, and time (not in

[5] DCT Consultancy Services, a wholly-owned subsidiary of Penang Development Corporation has identified dozens of specialist parts and components along the production chain that are produced in Penang and the companies involved (DCT 1998).

time-to-market for new product development or innovation). Further, the range of companies, services, and division of labor in Penang (virtually all of the activities required to rapidly set up and ramp up high-volume production on a JIT basis) are co-located.

While many of these parts and components are elements in global production networks which are coordinated at the headquarters of MNCs and do not cross-penetrate, recent years have witnessed a transition to a regional supply base with a growing degree of local horizontal integration. This has been accompanied by the emergence of a locally owned supplier base with increasing capabilities in technology management.

A number of studies attest to the superior technology management and supply base capabilities of the Penang region amongst the three regional concentrations of electronics and electrical products in Malaysia. For example, in a study of technology absorption and diffusion amongst local supporting firms in the electronics industry, Suresh Narayanan provides evidence of a large gap between Penang and Klang Valley. He makes the following summary statement:

> In terms of our transfer framework, while all firms in both areas have passed the first stage of transfer (adoption), progress in the second stage of absorption is markedly different between supporting firms in Penang relative to those in Klang Valley. While more than half the firms in Penang have moved to the third and fourth steps of technology absorption (repair/modification skills), the majority of Klang Valley is still at the first stage of absorption. (1997: 22)

The higher level of technology diffusion in Penang is linked to a much higher proportion of local outsourcing by local firms. Narayanan finds that while local supporting firms in Penang sourced 46 percent of their inputs locally, the figure was under 13 percent for Klang Valley firms (1997: 23). In a detailed study of the linkages between seven electronics companies and nine indigenous machine tool firms in Penang, Rasiah (1994) found that the latter fostered the growth of second and third tier suppliers. Narayanan summarizes Rasiah's findings:

> The first-tier vendors (those who had the first links with the electronics sector firms) have, in time, chosen to specialize in certain functions, and passed on some of their previous tasks to second-tier machine tool firms whom they now nurture. These second-tier firms have gone on to spawn their own third-tier subcontracting firms, giving them simply tasks likes parts fabrications which are no longer profitable for the former. In this way, not only has the number of machine tool firms increased but there has been a greater degree of special-

ization among them. These findings suggest a wider diffusion of technology through the agency of first-tier firms to smaller firms servicing them. The findings of this study have been corroborated by other observers as well (for example Lim 1992 [*sic*]; Teh 1989). (1997: 25)

Not surprisingly, MNCs continue to locate in Penang because it offers them a powerful production platform. The region offers capabilities for state-of-the-art manufacturing and rapid ramp-up to high performance standards to market-led or design-led companies from anywhere in the world.

An example is Xircom, a fast-growing telecommunications company that 'started the mobile computing revolution' with small, inexpensive adapters that make it possible for notebook PC users to access their corporate networks. The Xircom adapter turns notebooks into desktop PCs in terms of connectivity to local area networks but without sacrificing the mobility of the notebook. Xircom's products are made in Penang only. The local managing director was chosen because of his networks in Penang. He was able to build a management team; assemble the operations personnel; identify, set up, and equip a plant; and get it running to high performance in a time span that may be the fastest in the world. Making the plant operational has involved ongoing interaction with Automated Technology, a process automation supplier literally across the street. Automated Technology personnel work inside Xircom's plant.

Thus, Penang is a manufacturing production success story. Why, then, the low value added? The short answer is that Penang's electronics cluster is stuck in an increasingly low value added Productivity Triad. The challenge for the region is to make the transition to a production system in which design and manufacturing are integrated and to a cluster dynamics that fosters regional innovation capabilities. Of the three domains in the Productivity Triad, production is the strength. Cluster dynamics and skill formation are the weak links. We will explore each before turning to the role of government as a change agent for making transitions.

Cluster Dynamics: The Critical Impasse

Regional specialization in rapid ramp-up of high-volume manufacturing capability is a basis for competitive advantage. Nevertheless, entrepreneurial firms drive cluster dynamics and cluster dynamics foster capability development and innovation. The first challenge is to create and nurture entrepreneurial firms, local and foreign-owned.

The Malaysian electronics industry has a small base of small and medium-sized enterprises by international comparison. Since the establishment of the first semiconductor plant in Penang in 1972, the industry has grown to over 850 companies. Taiwan electronics, which has an industry with roughly the same number of total employees, consists of over 3,300 firms (Dahlman 1993: 257).

Nevertheless, Penang is developing entrepreneurial firm creation processes. By Malaysian standards, the new firm generation process in Penang is impressive. The period 1989 to 1993 stands out as a time when the number of electronics supplier firms in Penang increased threefold from roughly 150 to 450 (Rasiah 1995). Not all of these are entrepreneurial firms. But Penang is home to an impressive list of Malaysian-owned entrepreneurial firms in the electronics cluster.[6] These are firms that have achieved double-digit growth rates and have steadily upgraded their production and technological capabilities. In the process of upgrading their capabilities, they have opened new markets which, in turn, have focused further their distinctive capability development.

The development of supplier firms in metalworking, machining and tooling, and plastics is critical to maintaining the competitive advantage of electronics in Penang. While the number of Malaysian-owned entrepreneurial firms (firms with design and new product development capabilities) in electronics is limited, there are outstanding examples including Eng Technology Holdings, UNICO Technology, and Globetronics.

Eng holds 8 percent market share in the worldwide disk drive actuator (a precision component) market; its customers are the who's who of the world disk drive and semiconductor industry. Started in 1974 providing jigs and fixturing, it graduated to precision die sets and tooling supplied to the rapidly growing electronics industry. Today Eng consists of four main subsidiaries employing 350 people, but it also is involved in a series of joint ventures in Penang, the Philippines, and Hong Kong in order to supply actuators on a JIT basis (Lim Kah Hooi 1997; Rasiah 1998 and 2000).

[6] Leading examples include BCM, UNICO, Eng Technology, Micro-Carbide Engineering, PK Electronics, Bakti, LKT Group, Aman Hamzah Plastik, Carsem, and Globetronics.

Intel Cooperative established UNICO in 1992; the first product was the assembly of motherboards for Intel Penang (P. Lim 1991; Lim Kah Hooi 1997). Several Intel managers were seconded in the start-up. Management has rapidly integrated upstream from a printed circuit board assembler to an OEM (original equipment manufacturer) and ODM (original design manufacturer) box product manufacturer through alliances with companies in Canada and Europe. In 1996 UNICO signed four joint venture agreements to manufacture PC workstations, Pentium notebook computers, modems, CD ROM drives, and digital enhanced cordless telephones. UNICO seeks to become a US $1 billion company by 2002.

Globetronics, incorporated in 1990, was founded by two local techno-entrepreneurs who left Intel Penang to do contract manufacturing.[7] In the words of Lim Kah Hooi (1997): 'At that time Intel was transferring new products at a fast pace from its corporate headquarters and Intel Penang was looking for a fast way of building up its capacity. As such Intel Penang decided to transfer out the older products together with the entire set of equipment to Globetronics'. Globetronics has formed joint ventures with Sumitomo Metal Electronics Devices of Japan to supply the semi-conductor industry with ceramic substrates, PCB assembly, leadframe plating, and burn-in services. The company's goal is to become a turnkey contract manufacturer to the semiconductor industry.

The emergence of Altera, the region's first design studio, signals a new, critically important development in Penang's transition. The skills needed for 'front-end' operations like chip design, systems integration, applications engineering are in short supply in Penang and what does exist is bottled up in the R&D facilities of a handful of MNCs. Altera is breaking the mold; it founders are former Intel employees.

These companies represent individual success stories that reveal both the strengths and weaknesses of Penang. The strength is that many of the elements for making a transition to a more advanced Productivity Triad exist; the weakness is that the transition demands not merely examples but diffusion processes. Without a critical mass of firms pursuing a focus and network business model, the networks remain thin and the internal/external dynamic that drives regional capability development and innovation has limited force.

[7] The Malaysian Technology Development Corporation holds 30% of Globetronics shares.

The Systems Integration Challenge

At present, the dynamics of technological differentiation, integration, and variation are extremely limited in Penang (bottom, left-hand, and top box activities in Figure 3.1). Consequently, technological diversity is limited and technological speciation (the creation of new industrial sub-sectors) is non-existent. This is mainly because the electronics MNCs do 'product proliferation' rather than product design and new product development in Penang.[8] But this is changing.

Making the transition to a Productivity Triad which will support not only manufacturing but product development and technology management capabilities (PS 4 and 5 in Table 2.1) will require the development of a critical mass of entrepreneurial firms with systems integration capabilities. Penang is fortunate in having leading models operating within the region.

Intel and Motorola's design centers are a microcosm of the kinds of design capabilities that must become regional for Penang to make the transition from a region with many elements of a static electronics cluster to a cluster dynamics made up of a regionally networked system of enterprises. Both design centers have carefully conceived programs for developing design capabilities. As shown in Figure 6.1, design capabilities in these cases involves the disciplines of mechanical engineering, electrical engineering, and software engineering and expertise in media and communications, industrial design, and manufacturing.[9] Nineteen different software tools are involved; a regional design center needs to support training in each tool.

Intel's Penang Design Center, established in 1980, has 250 people and has progressed through three stages. First, they engaged in the design and redesign of mature products, for example the Intel 286 microprocessor, to improve optimization, yield rates, and robustness. At the

[8] Martin Bell and Mike Hobday conducted a survey of engineering, technical support, R&D, and recent innovations in twenty leading electronics companies in Malaysia. Their data show 'substantial technical support for production and near-term technological needs' and '[A] great deal of innovative activity is carried out, not only in changes to products and processes but also in the design and application of organizational changes' (1995: 47). But add that 'In no cases was long-term or basic research (e.g. into new materials or advanced software engineering) undertaken locally. . . . In a few cases some research related to product design and process developments was carried out by the largest firms' (1995: 47).

[9] The Penang Design Center seeks to develop state-of-the-art design and manufacturing capabilities to transform product concepts into viable products. Advances in software, and modularization, have driven down the design cycle time. The chip design process has five phases: product definition, functional design, logic design, circuit design, and layout design.

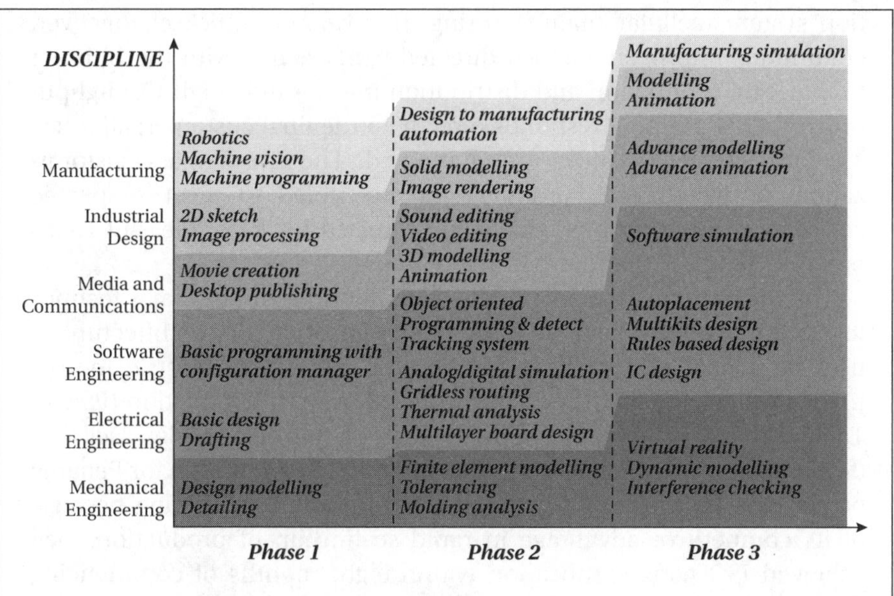

Fig. 6.1. Design capabilities and skills integration

Source: Penang Design Center

same time they developed the capability to design chips which led, in 1992–4 to the second stage: product proliferation. During this period the first patent was awarded. Stage three has involved the Penang Design Center in original design for commodity or embedded applications and for PC central processing units (CPU) and chip sets. A second patent was awarded for intellectual property from their work in a new 8 bit CPU for embedded microprocessor applications, four other patents are pending. The mission of the design center is 'to deliver compelling products faster than our competitors'.

Motorola is a similar story (Ngoh 1994). The R&D center started with four engineers and has nearly 120 today. Motorola Penang enjoys the design leadership in Asia for the CT2 cordless telephone. The center does new product design, product–process interfacing, and advanced manufacturing processing.

Dell Computer is a manufacturing leader that could drive open systems integration and capability partnering in the region. Dell's Asian headquarters are in Penang. Dell is an example of the opportunity that the Internet has created to build a mass customization business model. Dell's 'produce to order' business model combines the Toyota production system (cellular manufacturing, JIT, *kanban*, quick changeover, continuous improvement, self-directed work teams) with the Internet to integrate production and distribution into a single high-throughput process. Dell's factory responds directly to the final customer; all intermediary distribution links are eliminated. The era of mass customization, in which each product was assembled to meet a specific customer's specifications, has been promised for a decade, but Dell's organization plus the Internet made it possible.

The implications are potentially as profound as other major technological innovations, such as Ford's redesign of factory architecture to use the arrival of fractional horsepower, unit drive electric motors to achieve, for the first time, synchronized or mass production (PS 2 in Table 2.1). To achieve the opportunities of the new model, Dell has developed ramp-up capabilities that are the exception even for Penang; or perhaps Dell located its regional headquarters in Penang because of its competitive advantage in rapid scaling up of production. Dell achieved ISO 9002 certification within eight months of commencing production, the legal minimum timeframe.

Furthermore, Dell pursues a simultaneous launch strategy. This means that the products made in Penang are first-generation products, the same products made in Dell's home office plants. This increases the challenge and opportunities for local suppliers to Dell to be on the cutting edge of new product and technological developments.

Intel, Motorola, and, potentially, Dell are exceptional in the commitment to local innovation and opportunities they offer for driving cluster dynamics. They are developmental firms within the Penang context which are enhancing the skill base of the region (technical and managerial skills), a prerequisite to making the transition to integrated manufacturing associated with PS 4 and PS 5 in Table 2.1. But most importantly, they are carriers of systems integration capabilities in both the technological and organizational dimensions.

What are needed are dozens of locally owned entrepreneurial firms such as Altera's, Eng's, UNICO's, and Globetronics. But for the diffusion process to generate cluster dynamics and growth, a regional skill formation process must match the demand for engineering and science skills with the requisite skills.

Skill Formation and the Gap

The most crucial shortfall is in the skill formation required to foster entrepreneurial firms and industrial innovation. There are no shortcuts: innovation in electronics is engineering-intensive. Penang's limited innovation-related skills, given the considerable manufacturing capabilities, illustrates the limits of an electronics infrastructure that does not include strong skill formation capabilities in areas such as electrical, mechanical, and software engineering as well as computer science, systems analysis, and information technology generally.

The importance of skill development in the process cannot be overemphasized. As one Penang CEO put it, 'If the changes outside the organization are happening faster than the changes inside, then the end is near' (Lim Kah Hooi 1997: 4).

The problem is understood in Penang. Koh Tsu Koon, the Chief Minister of Penang, indicates the numbers involved, if not the scale of investment in higher education required to address the challenge:

> It is estimated that there are now about 12,000 scientists and engineers with a Bachelor of Science degree or equivalent working in Penang. This works out to a ratio of 10,000 scientists and engineers per million population, which is lower than that of over 25,000 per million population in Singapore and Hong Kong. We must therefore aim to reach the ratio of 25,000 by year 2002. . . . With Penang's population expected to reach 1.4 million people, we would need at least 35,000 scientists and engineers by then, which means that we must produce and recruit some 23,000 scientists and engineers within the next eight years, or about 3,000 per year. This is a very tall order indeed. (1995: 12)

With a ratio of 10,000 scientists and engineers per million population, Penang more than quadruples the Malaysian national figure of 2,300 per million. This means that Penang will likely have to grow its own engineers and scientists. While individual firms can poach engineers from one another and can harvest the existing crop of students, the region as a whole must plant new seeds in the form of an expanding flow of students entering into engineering and information technology programs.

Industry and state government has a history in Penang of responsive collaboration in skill formation at the technical skill level. Each year the Penang Skills Development Center offers courses to over 8,000 students (PSDC 1998). The collaboration has contributed to the targeting of curriculum and upgrading of shopfloor skills appropriate to high-volume manufacturing production.[10] In recent years the PSDC has moved into information technology with a series of pilot projects that, if scaled up, could make a big contribution to upgrading the IT capabilities of the manufacturing labor force.

Why the lack of a similar program at the engineering education levels? Faced with a skill shortage of manufacturing and technician skills in earlier years, industry and regional government combined to create the Penang Skill Development Center to expand skills.

The main answer is that, the world over, even big companies do not have the time horizon to engage in skill formation investments for engineers or computer scientists. It was a matter of months between the time the concept of the PSDC was established in May 1989 and courses were underway; within months companies were enjoying the benefits of training programs.

The first reason, then is time scale: it takes not months but years for the training of engineers and software developers. The second reason is that the qualifications for teachers are much higher. In the case of technician and manufacturing skills, companies themselves run related training programs and could quickly upgrade the quality of teaching staff.

Therefore, the bottleneck constraint in engineering skill formation is qualified teachers. It takes four years to increase the output of new engineers or scientists at the Bachelor of Science degree level even if the supply of qualified university entrants is available. To increase the flow by 3,000 per year means 12,000 students in a four-year program and, with a student to teacher ratio of 15:1, 800 additional faculty with the appropriate engineering and science qualifications. This is a tall order indeed.

Given the shortage of engineers and scientists in Penang, finding over 800 faculty with the requisite capabilities and experience will be difficult. The major pool of candidates would likely be from within the MNC companies and Malaysians working overseas. To attract faculty will require considerable attention to quality of life issues. But it would also involve considerable attention to a curriculum appropriate to building on the strengths and strategic opportunities for Malaysian electronics.

The benefits from building up university education programs in engineering are not only in skill formation of engineers. As noted in Chapters 4 and 5, the development of both the Route 128 and Silicon Valley electronics clusters involved the simultaneous development of

[10] Lim Kah Hooi documents the areas of strength and weakness (1997).

university departments, research institutes, and curricula, on the one hand, and rapidly growing entrepreneurial enterprises, on the other. This dynamic is the hothouse environment that has nurtured techno-entrepreneurs, important drivers of cluster dynamics. The best Asian model for the development of techno-entrepreneurs is Taiwan (Dolven 1998; Ernst 2000; Mathews 1997; Wade 1990).

To conclude, it appears that the Penang electronics industry is in the midst of a deeper transition in competitive advantage, the outlines of which are becoming clearer. The specifics will be worked out as capability development and cluster dynamics evolve. But unless all three elements of the Productivity Triad are in sync, the developmental processes may well be short of fuel in the form of human resources. This captures the challenge of making transitions to new *systems.* Without adequate graduates, new graduates cannot be produced. Nevertheless they must be. This is the case in Penang. A breakthrough to a new system will require the development of a change program in which companies, universities, and regional and national governments all participate.[11]

Cluster Governance

Penang is the most successful of the three electronics regions in Malaysia. Its technology management capabilities are more advanced than elsewhere. This is due in important part to effective 'management' of regional competitive advantage by Penang regional governmental authorities. Management here refers to instituting processes that foster capability development and, potentially, cluster dynamics.

Firms in all three regions operate within the same broad governmental policies, incentive systems, and 'national system of innovation'. Nevertheless, the relations between governmental agencies and enterprises are distinctly different in each region. Firms in the Klang Valley are locationally positioned to benefit most from central governmental services. Not only are the central governmental agencies located in the Klang Valley, but the region enjoys an extraordinary infrastructure

[11] The range of incentives that attracted MNCs to Penang were successful, but they are not appropriate for addressing the transition challenge. Incentives that mask economic fundamentals—incentives that if withdrawn, would not leave behind lasting economic activity in the region—must be avoided. Effective industrial policy is more about education policy and technology policy than about tax incentives.

which includes a range of advanced education institutions, the Malaysian Technology Park, the Multi-media Super Corridor, as well as close relationships with a host of governmental agencies with missions to implement the Industrial Master Plan II.[12]

The Johor and Penang regions are located at the extreme south and north parts of Malaysia. The Johor region has the least interaction with Malaysian government agencies and the least electronics-related infrastructural investments particularly in enterprise zones and industrial parks. This is due to the distinctive character of electronics development in Johor: electronics in the southern region is integral to a Singapore/Johor cluster with little direct linkages to the central and northern regions of Malaysia.

The Penang region, in contrast to the southern and central regions, does not have the proximity to either the central government agencies located in the Klang Valley or an advanced electronics industry located next door. It has benefited from national policies and infrastructural investments to a greater extent than Johor. But the most striking difference is the pivotal role played by regional level developmental agencies, particularly the coordination role of Penang Development Corporation (Rasiah 2000). Three features stand out from the capabilities and innovation perspective.

First, Penang regional policies have successfully converted multinational companies into developmental firms. Developmental firms are those that play a pivotal role in upgrading the technological capabilities and skill base of a regional cluster. They can be the agents of transformation growth or the transition to more advanced production systems (see Table 2.1). Examples include the Springfield Armory which applied and developed the principle of interchangeability and created a labor pool of skilled machinists (Table 2.1), Fairchild in Silicon Valley, and DEC along Route 128.[13] Developmental firms are critical to the skill formation process and thereby the suppliers of the critical resource to the new firm creation process.[14] In some cases developmental firms are

[12] A partial listing of industry assisting agencies includes Malaysian Industrial Development Authority (MIDA), Ministry of International Trade and Industry (MITI), Malaysian Science and Technology Information Centre (MASTIC) of the Ministry of Science, Technology and the Environment, Small and Medium Industries Development Corporation (SMIDEC), Malaysian Institute of Micro-Electronic Systems (MIMOS), Standards and Industrial Research Institute of Malaysia (SIRIM), and Malaysia Technology Development Corporation (MTDC).

[13] Contracts administered by Hanscom Air Force Base's Electronics Systems Center were pivotal to the emergence of 'development firms' such as DEC (see Ch. 5).

[14] DEC, as an employer of tens of thousands of technical staff, was a major contributor to the skill formation of the Route 128 area, skills which were critical to the transition to systems inte-

not examples of new business models, but facilitate their emergence by advancing the other two elements of the Productivity Triad: technological capabilities and skill formation.

The policy of the PDC was to seek out the world's most successful electronics firms. Penang electronics have advanced with the development of these companies. Lim (1991) describes in detail Intel's progressive moves from assembly to incremental change generating capabilities making it possible for headquarters to transfer technology to Penang and for the local plant to move to more complex higher value added activities.

Rasiah identified cases of human capital deepening in local divisions of MNCs fostering technology transfer, particularly via skilled personnel moving to local firms (Rasiah 1995: chs. 6–7). In Rasiah's words: 'Intel, AMD, National Semiconductor . . . and Motorola Malaysia reported that former personnel . . . had started up new firms, and have offered substantial technical support to local firms' (1998: 10). This is not surprising as these companies are developmental firms in the United States and have long spin-off histories. National Semiconductor's subsidiary plants in Penang, Dynacraft and Micro Components Technology, trained many of the region's key personnel in precision engineering and metalworking which now run successful local firms, including Rapid Synergy.

Besides UNICO and Globetronics, the CEOs of Sanmatech, Rodel, and Molex, and Altera (the region's first design studio) came from Intel.[15] Ex-Intel managers also played key roles in the development of Dell-Penang and AIC Semiconductor, which is locally owned. Two of Intel's design engineers left to help set up AMD's design center.

Spin-offs from Motorola are supplying MNCs with world-class production performance include Sanda Plastics, LBSB, Eastrade, and BCM Electronics. Micro Machining, a subsidiary of National Semiconductor, developed the skills of key people at Priority Plus (a local contract manufacturer) and Rapid Synergy (mold making and plastics products).

An example of how entrepreneurial firms can be created as part of a spin-off process is Motorola's supplier development program with BCM

gration and thereby sustaining innovation after DEC had gone into decline. A developmental firm is analogous to a 'franchise' athlete on a professional sports team; it is around such firms and individuals that regions and teams are built and thrive. Finally, a developmental firm can be government-owned, as in the case of the Springfield Armory (see Ch. 2).

[15] The information in this paragraph was supplied by Wong Siew Hai, Managing Director of Intel Malaysia and Anna Ong, DCT Consultants, in personal interviews.

Electronics. BCM sales have more than doubled every year and headcount has grown from 120 in 1994 to 1,500 in 2000. Over the same period their technical capabilities have advanced each year in line with a technology development plan.[16]

A five-year manufacturing know-how transfer and skill formation development program drove the five-year technology capability growth path. The manufacturing know-how transfer involves the following sequence:

- back end manufacturing of accessory products (1993–4)
- front end build of accessory products (surface mount technology transfer, skill transfer) (1995)
- materials procurement, stockroom and storage management (planning, buying, vendor interface, minibank) (1996)
- turnkey management (materials sourcing, materials procurement) (1997)

Engineering know-how passes through the following steps:

- materials quality engineering (failure analysis, vendor development, vendor process characterization) (1996)
- process/reverse engineering (internal process characterization, root cause analysis and design of experiments, statistical process control methods, product enhancement, prototyping, pilot manufacturing) (1997)
- research and development procurement (phone systems, radio frequency technologies) (1998)

Elements of this and similar supplier upgrading programs are developed and diffused at the Penang Skills Development Center. In this way the skill needs of entrepreneurial firms can be matched with the education curriculum development.

The second distinctive feature of the Penang Development Council is the integration of skill formation with technology advance and new firm creation policies. All three regions have skill development centers, but only Penang has a skills development center that is coordinated with the technology development activities of entrepreneurial firms and new firm creation processes.

[16] From doing manual assembly of cable connectors and belt clips in 1994, BCM's technical capability growth path has progressed to large pitch to fine pitch surface mount technology, from basic RF to digital and analog VHF/UHF RF, to systems integration.

Under the auspices of the PDC, the PSDC has played the role of integrating visible and invisible education and expanding the supply of technically trained workers in sync with the development of technology management capabilities of the region's enterprises. It has contributed to growth of the region because technology management and skill formation are opposite sides of the same coin.

But the skill development program in Penang has had a leveraged impact on growth because of the new firm creation process that has long been promoted by the PDC. All three electronics regions in Malaysia have production units that are elements in foreign-owned global production networks. But in most cases the build-up of local skills and capabilities remains bottled up within the MNCs. The success of Penang has been about turning such skills and capabilities into inputs for the new firm creation process. This is the starting point for a 'horizontal' or cluster dynamics internal to the region.

Regional agencies such as the PDC and the PSDC have an advantage over national agencies in fostering regional growth dynamics. The Malaysian Industrial Development Authority, for example, administers a vendor development program at the national level. But the focus is not region-specific. The Motorola and BCM example implies that a supplier development program should focus not on filling product gaps but on capability development. While some aspects of capability development are national, others may be regional.

A third governance-related factor has contributed to the relative success of Penang. The three electronics regions represent two different industrial policy perspectives. The first perspective is the capital accumulation model derived from conventional growth theory; the second is the capability development model in which productivity is governed by capabilities. It is as if the capability perspective guided the Penang authorities.

The two models can be termed integrative and departmentalized, or global versus local optimization. As noted, the central cluster enjoys an incomparable range of governmental agencies with industrial policy related missions. The fault is not in the effort of officials. What differs is the degree of integration of governmental agencies with each other and the degree of synchronization of the governmental agencies as a whole with the specific technological and organizational development of each region's entrepreneurial firms.

The industrial policy methodology in the central and southern clusters reflects the traditional instruments and goals, means and ends approach of public economy economics (Musgrave 1959). This approach is to design separate instruments for each goal: match instruments and goals. The implicit assumption is that each goal and instrument can be separated out and addressed individually.

This approach is to design separate instruments for each policy goal. The implicit assumption is that each goal and instrument can be treated independently. There is no governmental body with the responsibility and authority to integrate policy instruments that impact on skill development, business organization, and technology management in either the central or southern clusters.

In the northern cluster, the PDC plays the integrative role most successfully. As a result, the region enjoys advanced organizational capabilities to address issues requiring collective action. The PDC and its agencies have a demonstrated capability to address issues of collective concern and to develop responses (Rasiah 2000). The success at collective action removed the fears of sharing information that is common to business and facilitated the development of an open system in which companies share concerns and institute processes to act on them.[17]

The active role industry leaders play in the PDC provides a social context for fostering networking capabilities and, in turn, open systems business models. It is as if the PDC was established to 'manage the commons'. In this case the 'commons' is a regional Productivity Triad. Commons cannot be managed by individual actions alone but must have a basis for identifying the common good and developing institutional means to achieve them. The internal/external dynamic is an example: it requires an open system in which firms have the trust to network for complementary capabilities. The open system, in turn, fosters capability specialization and the new firm creation process as well as the diffusion of design.

The PDC offers a model for the division of functions between central and regional government with respect to industrial policy. The central government has developed the vision and set the strategy framework but the most effective policies have been designed, developed, and implemented at the regional level. Policy instruments should reflect the real situation of firms and that depends upon the regional system in which they operate and its specific challenges and opportunities. The task for central government is to provide leadership and to set goals but

[17] Not only each firm, i.e. A, B, C, and D, but the inter-firm links represented by ab, ac, ad, bc, bd, abc, abd, acd, bcd, abcd can also be 'managed'. Thus, the white spots in the industrial 'cluster' chart are no longer ignored. This is an application of Deming's 'theory of the system' to inter-firm relations (1982).

within a governance structure that decentralizes and regionalizes policymaking. Policymakers that are participants in social, business, and education networks at the regional level are better positioned to design, integrate, and enact policies. Monitoring of the effectiveness of regional policymaking has two major roles: to learn for purposes of redesigning and improving policy and to provide examples of success stories both to other regions and the national policymaking framework.

SUMMARY

Malaysia is an electronics industry success story. The industry has grown at double-digit rates for three decades. But it has been growth in output not in value added.

The output growth of electronics in the region surrounding Penang has been particularly impressive. Penang's institutional, physical, and skill formation infrastructures orchestrated by the Penang Development Corporation were highly successful in guiding the transition to a high-volume manufacturing cluster.

But even in Penang the level of value added is small, although Penang has attracted many of the world's leading electronics companies and built an electronics cluster.[18] The low value added is reflected in a low per capita income level given the advanced level of production capabilities. Why high growth and low value added?

The answer can be explained in terms of the domains of the Productivity Triad. Malaysian electronics growth has been a consequence of establishing high throughput manufacturing plants (PS 2 and 3 in Table 2.1). But output has grown in quantity not in value terms. As a follower in the establishment of high-volume production systems, Malaysia has faced declining prices. This problem will be exacerbated as new high-volume producers come on line.

On the business organization side, the Malaysian electronics Productivity Triad lacks entrepreneurial firms with the capacity to develop distinctive capabilities that command higher returns. Therefore technology capabilities have not been driving growth of firms or regions. Furthermore, without entrepreneurial firms and open systems

[18] Lim Kah Hooi (1997) suggests a drop in electronics value added from 31.4% in 1985 to 19.4% in 1994.

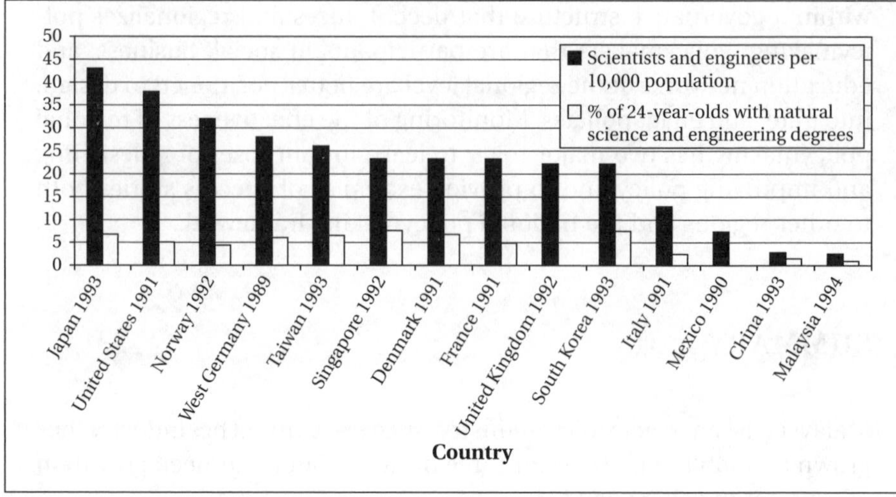

Fig. 6.2. International comparison of science and engineer graduates

Note: The year refers to the column with the number of scientists and engineers engaged in R&D per 10,000 population. The United Kingdom figure is not included, as it was not comparable. The second column refers to the number of 24-year-olds with natural science and engineering degrees. The years vary.

Source: National Science Board 1996: 3–25, appendix table 2.1; 1998: table 3–19

business organization the cluster dynamic processes do not foster greater capability specialization.

With respect to skill formation and innovation, Malaysia lacks engineering and science graduates. Figure 6.2 captures the challenge. Malaysia needs a tenfold increase in the science and engineering graduates as a proportion of the population to achieve the same levels as Singapore, South Korea, and Taiwan.

Competitive advantage can change. Each region's competitive advantage is established in a process of competition across regions, many of which may be developing more advanced production and enterprise capabilities. The more regions that seek to occupy the same product space, the lower the value added to each region as prices are driven down.

This, in turn, reflects a worrying reality: high-volume manufacturing capability is increasingly becoming like a commodity. With the build-up in volume-production capabilities throughout East Asia, manufacturing plants are in excess supply. China's emerging capabilities in this area will only intensify the tendency of mass production manufacturing to be commodified.

In contrast, the 'packaging and integration' activities, that link global demand with production, and 'service and technology' enhanced manufacturing capabilities are relatively scarce and command higher returns.[19] The problem is that Malaysian electronics clusters lack the 'packaging and integration' capabilities relative to Singapore and both the product development and technology management capabilities of Taiwan; instead, as a manufacturing center without product development capabilities it is squeezed by regions with similar capabilities throughout East Asia. Worse, as a follower, Malaysian electronics clusters have an uphill struggle in pushing up value added as highest value added accrues to the pioneers in making the transition to a more advanced Productivity Triad. The advantage to a follower is that the path to higher value added is more clearly mapped. The challenge is to proliferate and accumulate the technology and market dynamics of entrepreneurial firms. It is this process which will foster a distinctive technology capability trajectory and competitive advantage in each region.

The Penang Development Corporation has been an exemplary intermediary organization in identifying and acting on collective needs and facilitating local enterprises to seize development opportunities created by the presence of MNCs. A transition to a more advanced Productivity Triad is called for and will require a coordination role to synchronize skill development with emerging cluster dynamics and technology capability development. The 'tall order' of a gap in engineering and science education referred to by the Chief Minister will require institution building which will, in turn, require a large commitment of government funding, local political leadership, and industry/education institution partnering to develop the skills required to make the transition.

The opportunity is to build on all three region's production platforms. Each has branches of foreign-owned and operated entrepreneurial firms. Many of the large American and Japanese companies invest sizeable amounts, individually and collectively, in shopfloor skills. An audit of the quantity and quality of 'invisible college' graduates from these programs would reveal a considerable regional asset or 'social capital'. These skills represent sizeable regional assets that have been accumulated over the three decades of rapid growth.

[19] Cary Kimmel, a Xerox executive, reports that a Xerox survey of suppliers in East Asia conducted over 1987–9 revealed the following: 'companies that provide S&T [factors related to service and technology] experienced a growth rate of over 400 percent during the three-year period compared with only 30 percent for the more traditional contract manufacturing companies. It is of more than passing interest that the greatest growth was experienced by those companies located in countries with well-defined national policies that encouraged the growth of S&T capabilities' (1993: 158).

The emerging cluster dynamics, particularly in Penang, offer a regional capability in new product development as well as production which takes time to develop, is not easily imitated, and is problematic in high-wage regions. It offers a competitive advantage platform upon which Malaysia can advance to higher technology management capabilities.

CHAPTER

7

The Case of Northern Ireland

The Northern Ireland Department of Education conducted a survey of the 225 students who qualified in electrical/electronic higher education courses in the academic year 1996/7. Only 25 percent were working as electrical and electronics engineers *within Northern Ireland*.[1] This statistic is like an economic thermometer measuring the health of the patient. Engineering/science graduates are the high-energy fuel that propels high industrial growth rates. Unable to absorb advanced technological skills, it is not surprising that the Northern Ireland economy suffers from low productivity, lack of innovation, and slow growth. It is like a patient suffering from diabetes, unable to absorb glucose.

The problem is not lack of government funding of industry. Enterprises are highly subsidized. In fact, regional assistance to Northern Ireland manufacturing enterprises regularly funds between one-third and one-half of net capital spending.[2] But large subsidies have not been catalysts for innovation, capability development, skill formation, technology management, or regional growth dynamics.

The challenge for policymakers is to assist a transition to a higher performance economy. Productivity growth comes from advances in production capabilities, including technology and skills. A tenet of the capabilities and innovation perspective is that step changes in productivity involve *synchronized* advances in business organization, production capabilities, and skill formation. These three elements form the Productivity Triad represented in Figure 1.1.

[1] Department of Education of Northern Ireland, cited in *Sector Working Group on Electronics Final Report* (1998: 13), <http://www.Strategy2010.com>.

[2] Regional assistance as a percentage of net capital expenditures for manufacturing in England, by contrast, has declined from 3% to 1% between 1988 and 1995 (NIEC 1999: 18).

Skill formation goes hand-in-hand with the advance of a region's entrepreneurial firms. Upgrading skills, for example, will not translate into regional growth unless the skills are shaped and reshaped as part of a mutual adjustment process with a region's production capabilities and entrepreneurial firms. As enterprises develop capabilities for new product development, technology management, technology transition, innovation, and networking, for example, they employ or access engineering/science skills and integrate them into their production operations. The failure to absorb three-quarters of the region's technically educated graduates suggests that, at present, a regional competitive advantage is not being developed in knowledge-intensive activities, at least on any scale. It is a reflection of the lack of capability development in Northern Ireland business enterprises.

Skill upgrading, production capability advance, and enterprise growth are mutually interactive in technology-led growth experiences.[3] The task is to identify the fundamental obstacles to, and opportunities for, rapid growth. Each of the three elements of the Productivity Triad is examined in the context of Northern Ireland. We start with the business model.

BUSINESS MODEL

The agent of technological change is the business enterprise. If the technically educated graduate is the high-energy fuel for growth, the engine is the entrepreneurial firm. The lack of demand for engineering/science graduates by business enterprises in Northern Ireland is a manifestation of the deep source of poor economic performance in the region: its business model. Northern Ireland lacks entrepreneurial firms.

Entrepreneurial firms negotiate the integration of technology into production and thereby enhance the productivity of labor and capital by the development of production capabilities. Three technology-progressive features of entrepreneurial firms have been distinguished. First, entrepreneurial firms are the agents of the technology capability and market opportunity dynamic. They develop and host unique

[3] At the level of the firm, this means to move, for example, to multi-product flow (JIT or agile production): a company must simultaneously replace batch with flow production principles, supervisor with team-centered work organization, and educate workers and managers in problem-solving practices and their new roles. At the level of the region, it means that to jump to higher productivity change has to be coordinated at the level of business organization, technology management, and educational system.

regional technological capabilities. Second, entrepreneurial firms are the initiators of cluster growth dynamics that, in turn, foster a range of technology-advancing processes. Third, entrepreneurial firms pioneer systemic advances in production capabilities, one of which is technology management.

Technology management capabilities at the enterprise and regional levels can be powerful levers for growth. Technology management institutionalizes processes by which a firm and region can leverage the world's technology pool on an ongoing basis. The term 'technology management' captures the capability aspect of technology; technology is embedded in production capabilities.

The business model that prevails in Northern Ireland cannot be characterized as entrepreneurial. One indicator is innovation. Innovation is low by international comparison, particularly for countries with similar levels of advanced engineering and science skills. A recent Confederation of British Industry survey of innovation expenditures found Northern Ireland to have the lowest reported levels in the United Kingdom. Northern Ireland manufacturers reported spending 2.5 percent of turnover on innovation compared to 12.2 percent for Wales (the highest region) and 6.8 percent for all cases (CBI 1998*a*: exhibit 37). Unfortunately, the results of the CBI survey 'paint a disappointing picture of innovation in the UK' (CBI 1998*b*: 4), which suggests that by global benchmarks, Northern Ireland suffers a sizeable innovation gap.

A second indicator is productivity. Here, too, Northern Ireland is low by comparison with the United Kingdom, which, in turn, suffers a gap of 20–40 percent with leading European economies and the United States (DTI 1998: chart 3.11). In a matched plant comparison conducted in the late 1980s, Hitchens, Wagner, and Birnie (1991) found that productivity levels in Northern Irish plants were roughly half that of West German counterpart plants. There is little evidence of a reduction in the productivity gap over the decade of the 1990s by either academic studies or industry reports. The Northern Ireland Growth Challenge states:

> the failure by firms to innovate with new products and move on to higher value-added activities has led to limited/no up-grading of their sources of advantage. The result has been a relatively low-wage, lower value-added private sector economy, which faces the continuous threat of job losses through competition with the lower-cost emerging economies. (1995:9)

Fortunately, however, entrepreneurial firms can be found in Northern Ireland. They are beacons of light showing the way to a high growth future.

Entrepreneurial Firms

The starting point for considering growth dynamics in Northern Ireland is the entrepreneurial firm. Productivity growth is about increasing the rate and number of technology capability and market opportunity cycles that constitute and motivate entrepreneurial firms.

What are the criteria for an entrepreneurial firm?

- driven by a technology/market dynamic[4]
- growing at a rapid rate (10+ percent per year)
- unique capability
- collectively entrepreneurial: balances top-down and bottom-up initiatives
- high-performance work systems.

Have entrepreneurial firms existed in Northern Ireland's history? The region does have an illustrious industrial history beginning with linen and followed by shipbuilding and machine making (O'Grada 1994; Bardon and Burnett 1996). Northern Ireland's business history includes the likes of Harry Ferguson, the tractor maker, J. B. Dunlop, founder of the tire company, and Edward Harland and Gustav Wolff, whose company has built 1,700 ships (including the Titanic) over a span of 140 years. Thus, the region has had entrepreneurs and successful industrial enterprises. And it has enjoyed growth, particularly during the heyday of the shipbuilding, linen, and rope-making industries. But growth was resource-led rather than productivity-led. Growth was generated by mobilizing labor and capital into enterprises in which product, process, technology, and skill changed slowly, if at all. The linen industry, an extreme case, was a low-wage, high-employment industry with a high dependence on child labor (Bardon and Burnett 1996: 66; O'Grada 1994).

Consequently, the region has been slow to make the technological and sectoral transitions of the industrial leaders in other parts of the world (see Figure 2.1). It has suffered from concentration on non-

[4] The technology/market dynamic is a shorthand way of expressing the production capability/market opportunity dynamic described in Ch. 3. The idea is that as firms pursue new technological possibilities they build capabilities (such as research teams) which, with each success, become excess capacity looking for new outlets; at the same time, innovations redefine the market and create new market opportunities where these firms have an initial advantage. The successful completion of a single cycle precipitates a new one.

dynamic clusters that have tended to stifle the emergence of new technologies, enterprises, and industries.[5]

This is changing. While an audit of entrepreneurial firms in Northern Ireland does not exist, examples do.[6] A short survey follows.

Boxmore

Boxmore is an entrepreneurial firm.[7] Its 25 percent annual growth rate over a decade and a half is supported by a technology capability/market opportunity dynamic that is driven by alliances with the world's most successful pharmaceutical companies. These companies find the customers, Boxmore supplies the packaging services. To realize the market opportunity, Boxmore has developed rapid production capability responses which often involves innovation of two types, seeking new technological combinations in materials, printing and packaging, and 'dip-down' innovation involving partnerships with Northern Ireland university research centers. When Harold Innes, CEO, purchased Boxmore in 1983, it made fibre boxes, a mature product, for agricultural processors. To meet productive opportunities, Boxmore combined an ever-greater mix of technologies including printing; PET plastics to make bottles; fluorine gas to make inert, impact-resistant barriers to contain products that previously needed glass containers. At the same time, they were continuously upgrading the packaging materials to meet the needs of the world's market leaders in healthcare products. High-volume needs were met by supplying only customers that wanted multi-site support around the world. They have diversified their customer base into the agri-chemicals divisions of the same pharmaceutical parent companies, and into beverages (including Guinness and Coca-Cola).

The strategy is to build network alliances with market leaders to supply packaging needs with innovative products. These market leaders provide incentives and ideas for product and service innovations in packaging. Recently, Boxmore bought the in-house packaging operations for Glaxo. Over the years, Boxmore has bought a range of small, family-owned companies in Northern Ireland to implement new

[5] Checkland (1981) uses the upas tree metaphor to describe the stifling effects that concentration on limited technologies had on Glasgow. See techno-diversification section below.

[6] The number of firms in Northern Ireland that could be classified as fast cycle time competitors (PS 4 in Table 2.1) is limited. No obvious locally owned candidates could be found. Some MNCs fit the bill.

[7] Boxmore employed about 1,400 people and had a stock market valuation of £120 million in mid-1999.

technology combinations. Boxmore invests at twice the rate of its competitors.

Early on, Boxmore invested in IT (information technology) to improve customer feedback, MIS (management information systems), plant and process performance, and CAD (computer-aided design), and for benchmarking purposes including tracking patent developments. Modernization and innovation have brought Boxmore into ongoing partnerships with both Queen's University Belfast and the University of Ulster in using software for packaging and bottle design, and innovations in polymers and barrier technology.[8] These relationships enable Boxmore to pursue a pro-active innovation strategy rather than respond to the innovations of competitors. Success depends upon many factors, including good engineering and production people and managers with the ability to work with the world's best run health technology companies. Boxmore supplies a limited number of customers in Northern Ireland who benefit from the diffusion of best practices from Boxmore's sophisticated global customers.

Boxmore's success has meant that it enjoys 80–90 percent market share in the health technology packaging 'cluster' for Northern Ireland. Of the many lessons to be learned from Boxmore, one is that Northern Ireland is not large enough to support an entirely regional growth dynamic. Entrepreneurial firms are likely to be highly networked for complementary capabilities with firms in other regions.

Randox

Randox is a locally owned, knowledge-intensive entrepreneurial firm. The only UK manufacturer of clinical chemistry diagnostic reagents, Randox is also one of the world's fastest-growing diagnostic companies exporting to 120 countries. The company employs over 80 research staff and is unique in its systems integration capabilities. Figure 7.1 shows the range of scientific and engineering disciples that this small company requires to meet international R&D standards. Randox demonstrates the meaning of technology integration teams.

Research is focused on developing new diagnostic products and new technologies. For example, Randox has invested £7 million in the development of a 'revolutionary diagnostic testing system which utilizes

[8] Graphics design for advanced materials, for example, involves three-dimensional imprinting enabled by software advances. For this reason, Boxmore has to hire IT people. As part of health technology companies, Boxmore must keep abreast of developments in environmental technologies including recyclable and biodegradable plastics.

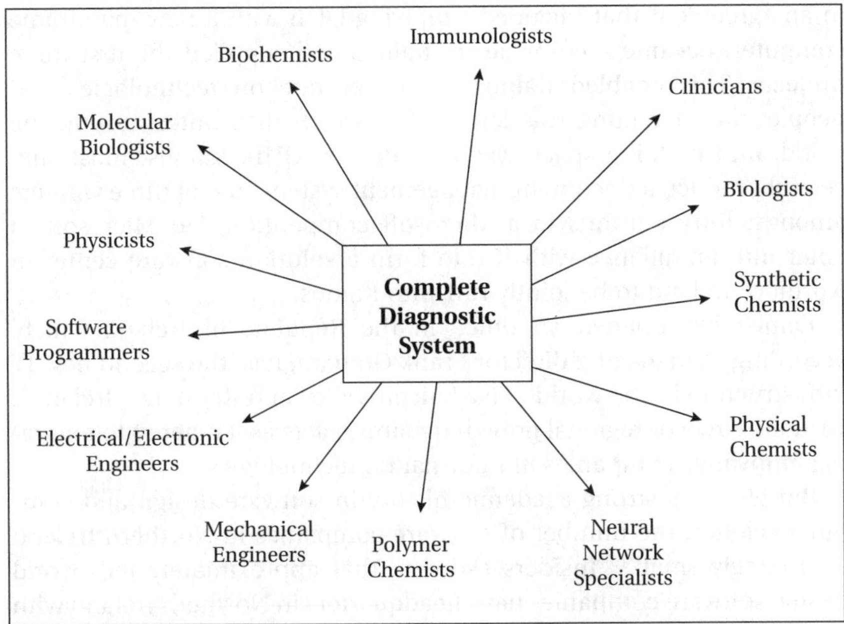

Fig. 7.1. Multi-disciplinary R&D group

biochip array technology enabling very high laboratory workloads to be carried out on one instrument' (IRTU n.d.: 35). Dr Peter Fitzgerald, the founder and managing director, is a chemistry graduate of Queen's University Belfast, and Randox's unique technological capabilities have been developed in networking arrangements with university laboratories. For example, the Northern Ireland Semiconductor Research Center fabricates the unique integrated circuits that are co-designed with Randox. The Center has a versatile research laboratory, rather than a dedicated chip plant, and has done leading research in direct silicon wafer bonding technology.

Kainos

Kainos, a software design company with proprietary programs, has grown at 25 percent per year for over a decade and employs 200 people. Half owned by QUBIS Ltd (a high-technology holding company of Queen's University Belfast (QUB)) and half by ICL/Fujitsu, Kainos is the largest of eighteen spin-off companies from QUB.[9] In the beginning ICL,

[9] For a description of QUBIS Ltd, set up by Queen's University in 1985, and the fifteen enterprises it has fostered, see Cartin (1996, 1998).

in an agreement that included supplying QUB with a new mainframe computer, became a co-owner of Kainos and supplied the first three projects. This enabled Kainos to concentrate on technologies and people; the marketing was left to ICL, which distributes around the world, and building space was provided by QUB. Kainos' most successful product, a document management system, one of three winners amongst forty entrants in a Microsoft competition, led Microsoft to enter into an alliance with ICL to form a solution software center in Northern Ireland to be jointly run with Kainos.

Kainos has opened an office in the Republic of Ireland which, according to managing director Frank Graham, has 'the second best IT infrastructure in the world'. Like Silicon Valley and Route 128, Ireland's virtuous circle of regional growth dynamics acts as a magnet to emerging innovative companies in information technologies.

But given its strong academic history in software design and computer science, the number of software companies in Northern Ireland is strikingly small.[10] Insiders estimate that approximately ten 'world facing' software companies have headquarters in Northern Ireland with another seventy software companies that are 'Ulster facing' in their marketing orientation.

The skill base cannot explain the lack of entrepreneurial firms in software. Webforia, a software start-up company with headquarters in Redmond, Washington State, located in Northern Ireland because of the 'hard development software' team that it could put together, which Brian Cassidy, a co-founder (and educated in Northern Ireland), claims would rival any team anywhere.

Seagate

Seagate has developed a local R&D capability to upgrade the disk drive chip-making processes in Northern Ireland that could evolve into new product development capability. The Seagate Corporation has fully developed systems integration capabilities and follows a similar strategy to Intel of integrating R&D and manufacturing.

Seagate illustrates the difference between MNCs that bring employment and those that transplant capabilities with the potential to trigger local growth dynamics. Since coming to Springtown, Seagate has built

[10] Professor Tony Hoare, now of Oxford University, is widely considered to be one of the three or four top intellects in the history of UK computer software design (McLean and Rowland 1985). He taught and researched at QUB in the early years of his career and left his imprint in software design capability and well-trained students.

up a strong R&D capability in conjunction with a Research Consortium in advanced materials involving four research laboratories at QUB and the University of Ulster. Seagate's Springtown R&D Center now employs thirty people but has plans to expand to 100 in the next few years. But Seagate is not simply harvesting science and engineering graduates, it is planting seeds for advanced skills. For example, Seagate sponsors four research graduate students for each academic year. A range of university lecturers from various related disciplines (physics, electronics, computing, chemistry, and engineering) and twelve sponsored students have visited Seagate's labs in Minneapolis. Dr Aric Menon, Vice President of Seagate Research, is an Honorary Professor at both universities. The research in advanced materials in general and in magnetic recording specifically will form a skill base important to many industries. QUB is now offering a master's course in materials science that aims to meet the needs of Bombardier-Shorts, Harland & Wolff, and AVX as well.

Seagate illustrates the industry/university partnering that constitutes the regional innovation model developed in high-tech regions. These partnerships are crucial for shaping the skill formation process and linking innovation to regional growth. They underlie the industry/university dynamic in which specific and advanced technological knowledge are simultaneously created and expressed in both unique company capabilities and the university curricula. These provide a basis for regional diffusion of advanced skills.

Nortel

Nortel is a Canadian based, world leader in fiber-optic switching and transmission systems equipment R&D. This means that Nortel is on the cutting edge of the transition to nanotechnology captured in Figure 5.2. The Monkstown manufacturing facility is co-located with Nortel's Northern Ireland Telecommunications Engineering Center (NITEC). NITEC employs over 300 people (a tenfold increase from 1988), mostly graduates, in the province's largest R&D facility. NITEC has built up a substantial capability in product development and technological innovation for optical network products, including digital processing, multiplexing equipment, and telecommunication network management. Nortel was a pioneer in systems integration and design modularization in the telecommunications industry, with specialized technological knowledge in integrating product systems with country-specific communication protocols.

Nortel has always been closely involved with tertiary education in Northern Ireland. Academic staff at the Digital Signal Processing Laboratories (DSiP), for example, do research on the rapid design of integrated circuits for telecommunications, multi-media, and broadcasting applications which bridges the fundamental research activities of the electronics engineering at Queen's University with research applications at Nortel. Product technicians with skills in testing and diagnosis are also critical to the facility; they tend to be graduates of colleges of further education. Nortel hires software people which it trains in hardware, as well as the other way around.

Nortel maintains a substantial product development center in Northern Ireland because of the capabilities that have been built since its takeover of Standard Telephone and Cable's facilities in the mid-1980s. Its Montreal facilities are less well placed for working closely on product development and transmission management systems with European customers. This includes network design, network installation, and pre-installation testing. But Nortel has invested heavily in product design and development capabilities, including prototyping, design for manufacturing and rapid new product development in its Northern Ireland facility. Modular design, for software and hardware, is critical to driving down the development cycle from twenty-four to eighteen to twelve and increasingly to six months. The competitive advantage of the plant is not in manufacturing costs for standardized products. Contract manufacturers specialize in such facilities, which are highly footloose.[11]

Nortel has won the UK Quality Award (as well as BT Northern Ireland) and is making the transition to self-directed work teams. The next step in late 1998 was to move to multi-functional work teams. Many of its processes are benchmarked with 'best in class' internationally. The company is vision-led and emphasizes a 'town-hall' approach as the best method of communication. Top officials meet with employee groups of forty to fifty three times a year to elaborate the company's vision. Nortel has approximately 200 local suppliers, but forty enjoy roughly 80 percent of the business. BEMAC, a local supplier of sheet-metal products, is on Nortel's international approved vendor list.

[11] In the words of Alan Bowers, Nortel's Business Planning and Benchmarking Manager: 'Products with no technology involved can be lifted and moved tomorrow' (interview, 2 Dec. 1998).

Techno-diversification

The degree of techno-diversity in Northern Ireland's industry is limited. The industrial organization of Northern Ireland has been dominated by a combination of a few large, vertically integrated enterprises and small firms that supply the local market. Without entrepreneurial companies, techno-diversification has been limited; without techno-diversification and new firms, industrial speciation did not occur and the region became further locked into the traditional industries and skills; without new industries, skill formation was stalled, both in the formal and informal education systems. Consequently, the region does not have the inter-firm and extra-firm infrastructure for dynamic industrial districts of the 'third Italy' type. The growth dynamics of such districts depend heavily upon the decentralization and diffusion of design capabilities, high degrees of techno- and micro-diversity, and open systems for easy inter-firm networking.

From the growth dynamics perspective, a growth path dominated by a few firms has both a positive and negative side. The positive side is that such growth economizes on scarce managerial talent and gives powerful direction from top to bottom of a single enterprise. The negative side can be explained in terms of barriers to internal and regional growth dynamics from dominant enterprises organized in a top-down hierarchy.

G. S. Checkland has used the metaphor of the upas tree to capture the syndrome of decline in Glasgow, a syndrome which was built into the causes of its success:

> Conditions external to Britain were changing in an irrevocable way: her share of world trade and of shipbuilding was rapidly diminishing. Clydeside was thus confronted with creeping obsolescence on a massive scale. In regional terms, the old structural problem deriving from Victorian and Edwardian times was still there. The upas tree of heavy engineering had killed or discouraged the growth of other industries of a more modern kind beneath its massive and intertwined branches; now the upas tree itself, so long ailing, was decaying, its limbs falling away one by one. Not only had it been inimical to other growths, it had, by an inversion of its condition before 1914, brought about limitation of its own performance. (Checkland 1981: 48)

The legendary upas tree was believed to have the power to poison other growths for a radius of fifteen miles (Checkland 1981: p. i). For Checkland, the upas tree represented a few firms in a few industries and the associated skills that long dominated the economy and industrial policymaking in Glasgow. The unintentional side effect of an industrial policy to preserve firms can be to build barriers to the emergence of change agents, including new business models, techno-diversification, and industrial 'speciation'.

The upas tree effect can be particularly devastating at a time in which transformational growth offers the greatest opportunity. This is a time when maintaining a region's competitive advantage depends upon making a transition to new principles of production and organization.[12]

Networking

Open systems networking operates on only a limited scale in Northern Ireland. This, in turn, limits regional capabilities for new product development and innovation. Furthermore, the limited depth and breadth of networking capabilities increases the barriers to entry for specialist firms.

A number of world-class machining and tooling firms serve the multinational corporations, such as Moyola, which collectively offer the range of activities required for new product development capabilities. However, in contrast to regions with a critical mass of firms pursuing design-led strategies, the breadth of specialist companies in feeder industries is limited in Northern Ireland. If this heritage were to be run down further, the industrial future of Northern Ireland would be in question because of the mixture of formal, technical, and tacit skills in such firms.

Companies in the light industries such as clothing, metalworking, machining, and furniture face a dilemma that demands a collective response. The pattern in UK light industries has been one of sub-

[12] The decline can be explained in terms of the idea of a competitive system developed in Best (1990) as follows: the leading industries of Belfast, and Glasgow, were organized according to principles of production and organization that became obsolete with the emergence of a New Competition elsewhere. The new principles, mainly mass production and the organizational innovations associated with, first, the central office functionally departmentalized and, later, the multi-divisional form fostered an order-of-magnitude increase in performance standards. Managers in the Old Competition saw the problem in terms of wages and labor discipline; they sought lower wages and government subsidies. The problems, however, were organizational; a business model had emerged elsewhere that could achieve higher productivity and support higher wages. No amount of wage reductions or government subsidy could address the root of the problem. Industrial policy, too, became the management of decline, an ultimately hopeless task.

contractors to retailers who pursue economies of scale and enjoy considerable market power. On the one hand, such companies can partner with powerful retailers to reach large final goods markets. On the other hand, the extraordinary market power of UK retailers is an obstacle to the process of establishing design-led, open system models of industrial organization.

UK manufacturing firms, too often, do not specialize by capability or choose partners with complementary capabilities; instead, they seek to master a range of capabilities, ineffectively. Not surprisingly, the fragmented (non-networked) character of UK firms in these industries has left them ill-equipped to compete against networked groups of companies enjoying the industrial district model common in Western Europe. The micro-diversity in such industrial districts is a boon to new product development, new technological combinations, and technological diversification. UK companies, in contrast, are not design-led, have not pursued skill formation partnerships, and, not surprisingly, have not been receptive to the integration of software and hardware or information technology and production.

The aerospace industry, however, led by Bombardier-Shorts offers an example of an emerging open system model of industrial organization. Shorts, established as a balloon maker in 1901, received the first volume production order for airplanes from the Wright brothers in 1908. Shorts moved to Belfast from Bristol in 1937; it was nationalized in 1943, and privatized in 1989 when it was acquired by Bombardier, a Canadian snowmobile firm that has become a major supplier of rail passenger carriages and the third largest maker of civil aircraft (though a distant third behind the leaders).

Shorts today specializes in the manufacture of engine nacelles, the pod that holds jet engines, which it supplies to all jet engine manufacturers. It also specializes in the composite, carbon-fibre technology used in fuselage construction, and landing gear doors. As part of the Bombardier Group, past activities in missile air defense systems have been transferred to Thompson-CSF.

Aircraft and aeronautical design activities at Shorts illustrate how decentralization of design can accompany integration into global production networks. While Shorts is no longer responsible for design of whole airplanes, it has a unit of 400 design engineers who are integrated into Bombardier Group's design engineering capability. The Belfast group is involved in the overall concept stage and then takes responsibility for the design of the parts of the airplane which they manufacture, mainly fuselages and nacelles.

Shorts is developing two capabilities critical to its new role: a responsive, short cycle time supply base and six sigma quality system. Both these activities involve moving up the production capability spectrum to higher technology management capabilities and the diffusion of world-class manufacturing capabilities to a supplier base which, in turn, will create new opportunities both for suppliers and firms in other sectors that use the same supplier base.

Present networking partners include Moyola Precision Engineering, Langford Lodge Engineering, and Huddleston Engineering, which supply components and tooling; Project Design Engineers, which designs testing rigs, tools, and special purpose machinery; Mallaghan Engineering, which designs and manufactures aircraft ground handling systems; Denroy Plastics, which supplies injection molded components; Martin-Baker, a global market leader in ejection seats; B/E Aerospace (US), which designs and manufactures business class seats; RFD at Dunmurry, which designs and makes liferafts, lifejackets, and aircraft recovery systems; linen napkins, headrests, and towels are supplied by Ewart Liddell, Ulster Weavers, and Club Herdman; and Active Multi-Media, which designs web sites and searchable databases for executive jet services companies.

This system of alliances and partnerships is, however, the exception in Northern Ireland. Not surprisingly, given the limited sectoral and technical diversity, networking has been limited.[13] The size of the supplier base is also limited which, in turn, will limit growth potential, unless there is a diffusion of world-class practices to a much wider range of companies.

PRODUCTION CAPABILITIES

Links between production capabilities, including technology management, and industrial structure were examined in Chapter 2 and illustrated in Figure 2.1.

Northern Ireland industry is heavily biased towards the PS 1 and PS 2 poles in Figure 2.1.[14] Few firms in the PS 3, 4 pole deploy complex

[13] The North Ireland Growth Challenge's Engineering 'cluster team' has organized a group of eleven suppliers to the aerospace industry into an 'association' which could become a model.

[14] In the food processing industry, a number of companies that supply leading distributors such as Tesco and Sainsbury's are under pressure to introduce product extensions on a regular basis. These companies, however, are not growing rapidly. Instead, they face commodity market conditions and have limited unique capabilities. This means limited productivity.

production activities, particularly ones involving high-volume, mixed production processes.[15] A limited number are in the PS 5 segment of knowledge-intensive sectors. The implication from our previous discussions is clear: Northern Ireland's industrial future depends upon building capabilities to support production in the PS 5 direction. This is the region of systems integration, design integration, low-volume production activities that can build a competitive advantage in knowledge-intensive activities. This sector is critical to Northern Ireland's industrial future, given the region's small size and its technological heritage. But policies designed to enhance the 'knowledge-driven economy' must be grounded in what companies actually do and what capabilities they actually have, individually and as part of regional systems, and what capabilities they can develop.

The lack of sectoral change over time is a reflection of limited movement up the production capabilities spectrum. Company visits suggest that, while many plant managers are aware of aspects of world-class manufacturing practices, few have first-hand experience in observing such practices or have been involved in modernization programs.[16] Even plants that are supplying multinational companies rely upon outdated quality programs and plants that have not been reorganized according to processes instead of functions.

At present, the requisite capabilities for a knowledge-driven industrial system on a scale to drive a high rate of growth are lacking in Northern Ireland. The challenge is to develop such capabilities; without them, breakthrough innovation may occur in university research centers and new high-tech firms may well emerge in science parks, but they will not be part of a regional growth dynamics.[17] They will

[15] Desmonds, a supplier of 12.5 million garments a year for Marks and Spencer, has made the transition to PS 3. In the words of Dennis Desmond: 'In the old days, around 10 years ago, it took three to four weeks from the fabric coming in until a finished garment was dispatched. Now it takes three to four hours' (*Financial Times*, 21 Mar. 2000). In fact, Desmonds could well be an entrepreneurial firm. The company's Northern Ireland plant specializes in innovative fabrics in a short lead time production capability. While the industry was shrinking in Northern Ireland, Desmonds grew by 10% in 1999.

[16] This is changing. In 1998 the Industrial Development Board of Northern Ireland commissioned a pilot project using the 'theory of constraints' approach to management (process integration and bottleneck analysis) aimed at 'improving throughput, reducing work-in-progress and enhancing margins' and a training program organized at the University of Ulster at Jordanstown at which thirty companies attended. For other such examples, including benchmarking and strategic alliance initiatives, see Chief Executive's Report, Annual Report & Accounts 98 99, IDB Northern Ireland.

[17] The Cambridge Phenomenon (UK) suggests that science and technology parks around a world-class university can foster an industrial district of high-tech firms. But on the negative side, the Cambridge Phenomenon has not driven regional growth dynamics (see Fig. 3.1). Techno-diversification, inter-firm networking, and industrial speciation have been

be peripheral to the forces that shape the industrial future of the region.

Making such transitions is not easy.[18] The rapid pace of introduction of technologies in the success stories is a consequence of the prior or simultaneous development of a specific set of production capabilities. Rapid growth in recent times has meant regional diffusion of the capability for rapid absorption of technologies. This capability, however, is a consequence of applying the principle of multi-product flow (driving down cycle times) first in production and second in new product development. But making the transition to multi-product flow requires the development of corollary organizational capabilities (variously named *kaizen*, continuous improvement, high-performance work organization, total quality management, self-directed work teams, and plan-do-check-act). This means considerable investment in skill formation to achieve the requisite performance standards.[19]

An informal audit (based on a series of shopfloor tours) of production capabilities in Northern Ireland reveals a limited number of firms that have developed the principles of flow, multi-product flow, or systems integration. The contrast between foreign-based and local firms is evident in plant visits. Inward investment enterprises that compete on the basis of rapid new product development and disruptive innovation are enterprises that have developed technology management capabilities and which require advanced skills. Systems integrators like Nortel and Seagate are examples in Northern Ireland. Examples else-

limited. Cambridge, Mass. as part of Route 128/495, has been associated with both powerful regional growth dynamics and transformational growth to PS 5. The Republic of Ireland has used manpower planning in information technology to nurture a PS 5 pole regional dynamics in which multinational firms have played a significant role in generating local techno-diversity and inter-firm networks. For a description of the Irish software industry, see O'Gorman, O'Malley, and Mooney (1997).

[18] As noted, the transition to the open systems business model and associated entrepreneurial firm start-up system in 1990s United States was engendered by market pressure from the superior performance of the Japanese *kaisha*-led PS 4 production system. Firms were forced to restructure and downsize which, in turn, created opportunities to grow new enterprises organized according to the new principles of production and organization. At the same time, the transition to self-directed work teams increased the integrative skills, and therefore managerial skills, of the workforce. Here, downsizing pressures and multi-skilled, problem-solving workers combined to foster the emergence and growth of small firms. Public policy contributed as, across the country, states pursued policies that made it easier to start and grow new business enterprises. The MIT example is a case study of techno-entrepreneur creation in emerging technologies. Such unintended industrial policy helped Massachusetts considerably.

[19] Unfortunately, the issue of 'on the job' skill formation is not taken up in the vision statements. A 1978 household survey showed that two-thirds of the workforce had vocational or higher qualifications in Germany, against one-third in the UK. See National Economic and Social Council (1992: 123).

where include rapid cycle time assemblers like Dell and Toyota; fast new product development cycle time competitors like Motorola; and fast innovators like HP. These enterprises have strong internal pressures to build networking alliances to supply parts and components. Unfortunately, few such enterprises have been established in Northern Ireland.

High-performance work systems are virtually non-existent, with the exception of a number of software development firms such as Kainos and a select few foreign enterprises such as du Pont, Nortel, and Seagate. Some locally owned firms that supply transnational firms have begun the process of developing cellular manufacturing and self-directed work teams. The great majority, however, are organized in terms of batch production, high inventory systems, and Taylorist, supervisor-centered work organization. Product-led competition will not become part of the industrial landscape until a critical mass of firms emerge with the high throughput (or short cycle time) production capabilities to produce multiple products on the same line and a work organization with the capability to design quality into the production process.

High throughput (short cycle time) capability can be measured in terms of high inventory turns (sales divided by inventory), rapid response rates, and short delivery times. Desmonds is an example. The Northern Ireland apparel company has reduced throughput time (the time between the arrival of fabric to the dispatch of finished garment) from three to four weeks to three to four hours (*Financial Times*, 21 Mar. 2000).

The quality performance standard can be measured in defect rates or by international quality assessment exercises. Here, too, there are Northern Ireland success stories but too few to impact on growth. Northern Ireland has approximately 23,000 VAT registered firms. Over 80 percent of these have less than ten employees. Bob Barbour, Director and Chief Executive of the Northern Ireland Quality Center estimates that as much as 70 percent of these would not score more than 150 benchmarked against the 1,000 point score of the European Business Excellence framework. Perhaps 3 to 4 percent would score between 400 and 500 points and 25 percent would score somewhere in between. Only a few of the larger private sector organizations have scored over 600 points, which puts them among the best in Europe.[20] A comparative

[20] In order to improve this situation, the Northern Ireland Quality Center has developed a specially customized scheme for SMEs under the title, 'Pathways to Excellence', based on the European Business Excellence framework. Under the scheme, recognition is granted to firms when they reach three distinct phases of improvement. Finally, when a score of 400 has been achieved the company may apply for public recognition and the 'Mark of Excellence'. This puts

study of quality capabilities of small firms in Northern Ireland and Massachusetts by Nola Hewitt-Dundas (1997) suggests a substantial gap across four sectors.[21]

Short cycle time in *production* and quality capabilities, in turn, are a precondition for integrating design and manufacturing and becoming a short cycle time competitor in *new product development.* The success of Desmonds illustrates the point. Desmonds has not sought to maintain a competitive advantage in the production of commodity fabrics but in the 'manufacturing base to produce new, innovative fabrics' (*Financial Times,* 21 Mar. 2000: p. iii). Rapid new product development rests upon a production foundation of short cycle time and high quality performance.[22]

Upgrading technology management capability is the next step. Unfortunately, it is not considered a powerful resource for growth in most Northern Irish business enterprises (or policy documents). But technological advance is the most powerful driver of growth and technology management is a means of converting the world's vast pool of technological and scientific knowledge and experience into improving production capabilities and productivity.

The major reason for the lack of attention to technology management stems from the lack of high-performance work systems. Technology management depends upon such practices. Exhortation by policy-makers to firms to become more innovative cannot be acted upon by enterprises that lack technology management capability. Likewise, managers with an appreciation of technology still depend upon technology management capabilities to turn technology into a basis for

the organization on a database of excellent companies at a national and international level. Firms that are currently in the 400–500 score have a self-assessment capability to measure and track their performance continually against world-class standards. By June 1998, the Northern Ireland Quality Center had assisted fifteen companies up to the 400 point level. By the same time, 1,218 firms in Northern Ireland were ISO9000 registered. The current ISO standard equates to approximately 150–200 points against the European Business Excellence framework. These numbers and information are from an interview with Bob Barbour (10 June 1998) and an update by e-mail correspondence (30 Mar. 2000).

[21] Hewitt-Dundas's research included metal goods, mechanical engineering, electrical and electronic engineering, and food processing. One hundred percent of Massachusetts' small firms had developed quality control systems ('during production') in three of the four sectors and nearly 90% in the fourth. Measures of their Northern Ireland counterparts ranged from a low of 22% in mechanical engineering to a high of 67% in electrical and electronic engineering. Only 33% of metal goods and 40% of food processing firms in Northern Ireland incorporated quality control into the production process (1997: 198).

[22] The following quotation from Dennis Desmond is an example of how an entrepreneurial firm identifies a market opportunity and builds the production capability to respond: 'A retailer's biggest problem is availability. There is a need for manufacturers to develop a highly responsive system' (*Financial Times,* 21 Mar. 2000).

competitive advantage. The knowledge economy offers great opportunity, but it will not drive economic growth without attention to production capabilities.

SKILL FORMATION

Industry/Higher Education Innovation Dynamics

Northern Ireland's educational system offers a basis for competitive advantage with considerable potential. Few regions in the world of the size of Northern Ireland have the range of university-level disciplines in engineering and science-related areas, particularly in information technology.

Its university system can boast world-class research facilities in several areas. The Digital Signal Process Center, for example, at QUB has spun off a successful start-up business and works closely with Nortel at the cutting edge of a technology with a huge growth potential. Likewise, biomedical science at the University of Ulster, which includes research activities in biotechnology, human nutrition, cancer and aging, diabetes, radiation science, and vision science obtained the highest possible 5* in the 1996 Research Assessment Exercise, 'the highest ranking in terms of size and rating out of 68 UK universities in this highly competitive area' (McKenna 1998: 6).[23]

Shorts has a long and close 'partnering' relationship with higher education. While six units of Queen's University achieved a grade 5 for the 1996 Research Assessment Exercise, only the fifteen-person Mechanical, Aeronautical and Manufacturing Engineering Department achieved a 5*. The industrially funded Shorts Chair and its secondment of a senior Vice-President of Shorts to the department suggest a strong industry/university partnership in aerospace.

These examples, added to the entrepreneurial firms described above, attest to the existence of the science and engineering research base vital to developing a competitive advantage in knowledge-intensive capabilities in Northern Ireland. At the same time, however, of the more than twenty-five Northern Ireland Research and Development Centers,

[23] See McKenna, 'Outline proposal submitted to DED on establishing Science Parks in Northern Ireland, August 1998', by Prof. Gerry McKenna, Pro-Vice-Chancellor (Research), University of Ulster.

relatively few have active industry/university partnerships and a sizeable number do not have active student involvement.[24]

A notable exception is Queen's University Environmental Science and Technology Research Center (Questor). Its mission statement reads as follows:

> The QUESTOR Centre is an industry/university cooperative research centre carrying out fundamental and strategic, integrated, multidisciplinary scientific research in selected critical aspects of environmental science and technology. The research programmes seek to provide understanding aimed at finding cost-effective solutions to environmental problems allied to encouraging industrial endeavour and minimizing environmental impact.

The main focus of research is on techniques for effluent clean-up and clean technology. The range of projects, the active involvement of twenty-one companies, the opportunities for students, and the international links are all impressive. The member companies range from manufacturers of pharmaceuticals, chemicals, instruments, textiles, and beverages to suppliers of electricity and water. The Center is also an innovator in developing a methodology to facilitate environmental technology transfer to small and medium-sized firms. A major attraction to companies is the interdisciplinary character of the research that enables a company to network with expertise otherwise hidden away in disparate departments. Projects have involved faculty members from the following departments working together: agricultural chemistry, chemical engineering, chemistry, civil engineering, computer science, microbiology, and psychology. The Center has brought into the university state-of-the-art testing equipment, some of which does not exist in even the most well equipped industrial laboratories.

Questor is a model in terms of university responsiveness to companies designing research projects in a way that preserves a university's commitment to the openness and public nature of knowledge creation and diffusion.[25] This gives students the opportunity to work on projects that are industrially relevant, cutting edge, and publishable. For these reasons Questor has a mix of post-docs, Ph.D. candidates, and undergraduate students involved in industry funded, faculty supervised

24 See IRTU (n.d.), *Research and Development Capability in Northern Ireland*, Industrial Research and Technology Unit, for a directory and description of Northern Ireland research and development centers.

25 Questor, founded and run by Prof. Jim Swindall, is the first European industry–university cooperative environmental research center in Europe modeled along the lines of the US National Science Foundation's Industry–University Cooperative Research Center program; in fact, it is the only non-US center in the program (see IRTU n.d.).

research projects. In addition, the model enables researchers in companies to work and network with a broad community and advance the technology management capabilities of their companies. Finally, Questor is currently developing a program involving partnerships between companies and primary school teachers to address the lack of students opting for science and engineering courses.

Here Northern Ireland has a best practice model. Industrial policy funding which goes to companies to support industry/university cooperative research programs has a potentially huge upside: it addresses the lack of technology management and innovation capabilities in Northern Ireland industry. It has a very limited downside: capabilities are advanced even if the participating companies fail, and students are provided with opportunities that can only enhance their career opportunities.

The problem is that while the success stories of industry/university partnering have been market tested, they are not widely diffused.[26] The size of the IT programs at UU and QUB are particularly impressive and are a magnet for IT companies given the global shortage of skills in this area.[27] The opportunities for industrial policy are considerable.

The potential is equally great, and unmet, for collaboration in skill formation between companies, existing and emerging, and the colleges of further education. These colleges enjoy little guidance in manpower development planning. They are aware that their counterparts in the Republic of Ireland have played a major role in advancing the Productivity Triad of advanced technology management capability, new business models, and skill formation that have enabled sustained growth.

Skill Formation and Growth Dynamics: Lack of Manpower Planning

The domain of 'manpower' planning is strikingly omitted from government vision statements in Northern Ireland: high growth without

[26] For an excellent summary of university and industry collaboration in Northern Ireland, see Beatty (1997). Beatty is the director of the Northern Ireland Technology Center, Queen's University Belfast, which has many of the features of Questor in equally relevant technological areas, including factory automation, CAD, product design, rapid prototyping, and instrument calibration.

[27] See J. Hughes (n.d.) for a description of the size of educational program and infrastructure of IT in Northern Ireland. See also Software Industry Federation (1998). For the Republic of Ireland, see FAS (1998). Two other important documents are Irish Software Association (1998)

a complementary skill formation capability has never occurred in productivity-led growth.

The story of every successful rapid and sustained industrial growth experience is simultaneously an account of the pro-active and strategic institutional development of visible and invisible colleges of knowledge diffusion. Business enterprises harvest the crop of new graduates; educational institutions, funded largely by the government, plant and cultivate the crops. The challenge is to integrate the two into a single process that respects the common good features of education. This demands a supply of 'economic virtue' or 'social capital' in which the common good is politically negotiated. The skill formation system is immobile; it is a critical capability shaping a region's competitive advantage. Undermining the skill formation system is simultaneously reducing regional career opportunities and placing limits to growth.

The UK Department of Trade and Industry's *Competitiveness White Paper* notes that the large and growing global skills gap in information technology (IT) has 'one notable exception . . . Ireland, where the ICT industry—which on a per capita basis is the same size as the UK's—benefits from an annual output of Electronic Engineering graduates at three times the UK level' (DTI 1998: appendix, part 8). The Republic of Ireland has achieved the NIGC goal of 'fastest growing region in Western Europe' with manufacturing output increasing nearly five times that of Northern Ireland over the 1993–8 period (DED 1999: 58). In an excellent example of manpower planning by Chris Horn, a reference is made to the fact that over seventy studies on 'employment projections and skills needs have been carried out in recent years' (1998: 6). Horn argues that 'the skills issue is one of the most critical facing the economy'.

An example of manpower planning in a growth industry is reported in 'Building on Ireland's Skill Opportunities' (Horn 1998). Chris Horn, the chairman of the Expert Group on Future Skills Needs, writes that the high growth scenario will demand 8,300 annual technology graduates and lays out four strategies for achieving the goal. The current annual supply of technology graduates (1997–2003) is projected to be 5,400 in the Republic of Ireland of which 3,100 are degree-level professionals and 2,200 are diploma/certificate-level technicians (Horn 1998: 9).[28] In comparison, the supply of IT graduates from QUB and UU will average

and Horn (1998). Dr Chris Horn is Chairman/CEO of IONA Technologies Plc., and chair of the Expert Group on Future Skills Needs.

28 The 5,400 includes 'the Government's plan announced in March 1997 to substantially increase the numbers of engineering technicians (+750 new entrants annually) and computer professionals (+1000)' (Horn 1998: 9).

about 825 and from FE colleges about 1,000 over the 1997–2001 period, roughly one-quarter as many at the profession degree level and one-third in total (Software Industry Federation 1998: 9).

The high growth scenario is costly in the short term. For example, to increase the number of professional graduates by 400 would require 2,120 new degree places which, at a student to staff ratio of 21:1 would require 100 new teaching positions. But measured in lost growth opportunity, the failure to make the investment is the truly high-cost scenario.

Process Integration and Manpower Planning

Skill formation is a multi-activity process that can be subject to the process improvement methodologies that have been developed to enhance flow within firms and along the supply chain in world-class manufacturing. It means that all the activities required to convert a raw material into a final product must be linked in order to capture the interrelationships. Linking the activities into a single process focuses attention on the linkages along the supply chain. It is the first step in rethinking and redesigning the process to improve it.

While procedures have been developed for integrating processes which involve material flow along the supply chain, the development of skills has remained fragmented and the linkages unattended to. Skill formation is a process involving numerous activities that are rarely integrated into a single process. This lack of integration locks the demand and supply of skills into place; each reinforces the other as the supply of skilled labor matches the demand to preserve a steady state. But the lack of integration is a critical barrier to growth. Growth demands a lock-step increase in supply and demand for specialist skills. This requires redefining the institutional relationships by which supply and demand are coordinated.

Process integration of skill development is the domain of manpower planning techniques. But successful manpower planning depends upon process integration. Moving from a disintegrated pattern to an integrated process is about the development of supply chains for skills. Not surprisingly, the interrelationships are often ignored and usually obscured. Like the old model of manufacturing, functional departmentalization leads to shifting blame instead of improving flow. Advancing the rate of skill formation and defining the precise combination of generic and specialist skills requires process integration and simplification across activities involving employers, teachers at all levels, and education authorities. Without the bottom-up, close-to-the-road, tacit knowledge which can only be supplied by practitioners, the most sophisticated planning exercises will lack the inputs required to make them work. Thus, here again, the transition to high growth depends upon developing the organizational capabilities to embed advanced techniques.

The development of integrated manpower development programs can be an important source of regional competitive advantage. Skill pools and schools are local, immobile resources. Furthermore, graduates from regional colleges and technical schools around the world tend to remain in the region. The industrial development role of the regional college or university involves responsive collaboration with industry and government in skill formation appropriate to that region. The fact that investment in skills takes time and strong relationships that cut across educational institutions and business enterprises means that they cannot be easily replicated.

CONCLUSION: THE LACK OF GROWTH ENGINES

Northern Ireland suffers from poor performance in innovation and productivity. The immediate cause is the lack of an enterprise 'culture' often referred to as a BMW syndrome. But the deeper cause is the business model. The prevailing business model, with a number of outstanding counter examples, is not conducive to technological advance and innovation.

Northern Ireland lacks entrepreneurial firms. Few companies are organized for product-led competition. Many firms have been successful in a market niche and are important to the economy of Northern Ireland. The latter are important in many ways, but they are not engines of rapid growth anywhere in the world. Entrepreneurial firms, organized in terms of the technology/market dynamic, propel regional growth dynamics and transformational growth to a more advanced regional technology management capability.

Technology management is pivotal to the growth dynamics analysis. Leaders in industrial development have developed new models of technology management and high growth followers have developed regional capabilities to manage technology. Technology management at the firm level is about developing the organizational capability to manage the technology/market dynamic; technology management at the regional level means fostering the virtuous circle of regional growth dynamics. Both involve policies concerning technology transfer, adoption, adaptation, development, combination, diffusion, and diversification.

Fostering rapid growth in Northern Ireland will involve coordinated organizational change in each of the three domains, business model, production capabilities, and skill formation. The concept of the Productivity Triad (Figure 1.1) captures the systemic dimension of organizational change at enterprise and regional production levels. The three domains are not separable and additive components of growth but mutually interdependent sub-systems of a single, mutually adaptive developmental process. The concept of Productivity Triad offers a vision for achieving rapid growth in which industrial policy plays a major role.

The lack of entrepreneurial firms is to the capabilities and innovation perspective what the lack of a capital goods sector is to a capital accumulation model of growth. The lack of entrepreneurial firms is a serious obstacle to growth and should be the central challenge to industrial policy. But industrial policy in recent years unintentionally contributed to the problem. The emphasis on entrepreneurial firms as the source of growth, rather than capital accumulation, makes policies of subsidizing capital investment suspect.[29]

[29] This sentence paraphrases Richard Lipsey (1993) but substitutes entrepreneurial firm for innovation as the source of growth. From the capabilities and innovation perspective, innovation is an effect of the activities of entrepreneurial firms.

CHAPTER

8

Policy Implications

The capabilities and innovation perspective elucidates forces that drive regional growth and decline. Growth is pivotal to the achievement of many policy goals including employment, a budget for public goods, and a healthy environment. The task of this chapter is to search the perspective for policy implications.

THE PRODUCTIVITY TRIAD AND GROWTH ANOMALIES

The Productivity Triad of business model, production capabilities, and skill formation is a heuristic tool that focuses attention on the determinants of regional or national productivity growth. In the preceding chapters the Productivity Triad is applied to growth 'anomalies' or success stories that have proven stubborn to explanation by conventional growth perspectives. Three examples will be reviewed briefly.

The first example is the American productivity 'paradox' which refers to the slow growth of the American economy during the 1970s and 1980s period during which information technology was introduced widely. But from the capabilities and innovation perspective, the development of new capabilities, not the introduction of new resources or technologies, drives productivity growth. Information technology did not show up in the growth statistics as long as it functioned simply as a more efficient means of processing information. The boost in productivity awaited the information technology-induced effects on production and organizational capabilities. And exercises in capability development take time.

The productivity statistics did surge in the 1990s. The increase in productivity was a consequence of the introduction of systems integration, not as a one-off activity, but as an organizational capability with the power to drive competitive advantage. Information technology was a means to this transition. The analogy to Henry Ford illustrates the theme. Whereas Ford used electricity to rethink production according to the principle of flow, companies such as Intel have used information technology to rethink production according to the principle of systems integration. But whereas system integration for Ford was a one-off affair, the development of a systems integration capability is about instituting processes of continuous redesign.

Systems integration is a principle of both production and of organization. As a communication enabler across engineering and science disciplines, information technology has a unique capacity to facilitate process integration. The integration of software and hardware can be a powerful tool for continuous redesign and rapid new product development in many industries. As a facilitator of virtual imaging, information technology opened the doors to the world of nanotechnology and the organized pursuit of the law of diminishing size.

Systems integration also takes the form of the widespread diffusion of an open systems or focus and network business model. Focus refers to businesses that specialize in distinctive capabilities and partner for complementary capabilities; open systems refers to common standards which facilitate inter-firm networking and thereby a commercial infrastructure that enhances capability specialization. Further, open systems facilitate cluster dynamics in the form of ongoing technological differentiation, integration, and recombination across networked groups of firms. Systems integration in technology and business organization establishes a competitive advantage based on the decentralization and diffusion of design capabilities. The result is a production system which can drive rapid new product development and technological change. Productivity increases were a consequence of the development of these capabilities not innovations in information technology.

The second example is the case of the resurgence of growth in Boston's Route 128 after the severe downturn of 1986 to 1992. Here regional resurgence is explained in terms of a transition to a business model which revitalized production and technological capabilities that have long underpinned the region's competitive advantage. The region's heritage in precision machining and manufacturing complex product systems, and its leadership in technological innovation and skill formation were at risk due to a vertically integrated, hierarchical business model that kept innovation bottled up in a limited number of firms. The same production and skill formation capabilities, combined with an open systems business model turned out to be ideally suited to leadership in rapid technological change and new product development. The region's success in the 1990s can be attributed to the transition to a Productivity Triad in which systems integration operates at both the technological and organizational levels.

A third example is the rapid growth experiences described in terms of the East Asian 'miracle' (World Bank 1993). The East Asian 'miracle' is explained in terms of the development and diffusion of production systems anchored in the principle of flow. Sustained rapid output growth in the East Asian leaders was enabled by the extension of the principle of flow to multiple products and to new product development. Rapid productivity growth was linked to the development and diffusion of indigenous production capabilities in new product development and technology management. Regions and countries that have diffused these capabilities have enjoyed rapid growth and achieved transitions to high levels of output and income per capita.

The Productivity Triad also reveals the productivity growth limits of the transition to high-volume production systems. In the case of Malaysia, the limits to productivity advance, but not output growth, are explained in terms of the lack of investment in engineering, math, and science skills that are required to make the transition to local new product development and technology management capabilities. In the cases of Japan and South Korea, the limits to growth reside in a closed system variant of the entrepreneurial firm. The strength of the closed system business model for flexible mass production and incremental innovation has become a barrier to the 'horizontal' or cluster dynamic innovation processes of techno-differentiation, integration, and speciation.

Understanding the underlying principles and processes that drive growth does not make policymaking simple. But it does suggest that powerful growth drivers do exist and that policymakers can institute policies that support them. At least, policymaking can be designed in ways that do not thwart them inadvertently.

CAPABILITY DEVELOPMENT PROCESSES

The growth dynamics in the three domains of the Productivity Triad are listed in Box 8.1. The first is in the area of production capabilities. Here attention is focused on technology management and technology transition capabilities. We then turn to the cluster dynamic growth processes and focus on policies to foster entrepreneurial firms and networking capabilities. The third domain is knowledge creation and diffusion.

The three domains of the Productivity Triad can be distinguished for purposes of examining growth processes. However, industrial policy-making for any of the domains should be developed within the context of the integration of all three. In fact, a central task of industrial policy-making is coordination of governmental agencies to foster the mutual adjustment processes that constitute the Productivity Triad.

The links are particularly evident in regional government success stories. For example, local governments in the 'third Italy' mediate between the development of organizational capabilities of small firms and international market opportunities. Likewise, governmental

Box 8.1. Productivity Triad growth processes

- **Production capability development**
    - production capabilities
    - technology management
    - technology transitions
- **Cluster dynamics**
    - entrepreneurial firm
        - technology/market
        - top-down/bottom-up
    - networking
        - techno-diversification
        - capability integration
        - techno-speciation
- **Skill formation**
    - visible
    - invisible

agencies from the Springfield Armory in the early 1900s to the Penang Development Corporation in recent decades have acted as coordination agents across the three domains of the Productivity Triad. In all of these cases developmental agencies are fostering a capability development and market opportunity dynamic but at the level of the region. Thus, in the domain of governmental policymaking, as in production and business organization, capability development can be an ongoing 'managed' process.

Production Capabilities

The production capabilities spectrum shown in Box 2.2 offers criteria for locating a region's production plants in the global production order. The criteria are derived from the literature and the quality awards that emerged in the 1980s and 1990s to benchmark world-class manufacturing processes.[1]

The production capabilities spectrum identifies the specific production challenges to advancing a region's productivity at any point in time. These challenges can focus industrial policy initiatives. However, successful initiatives must address the challenges with organizational change methodologies that work at the enterprise level within the context of specific regions. A number of organizational change methodologies have been developed in recent years.[2]

Iawo Kobayashi's (1988) 20 keys methodology is an outstanding example. The 20 keys framework provides criteria for distinguishing amongst five levels where a plant scores in comparison to world-class standards across 20 dimensions.[3] It is a system for self-assessment that can be conducted by the workforce following a brief training program. Thus, the organizational change methodology is based on the principle of inclusion: those required to make a new system work are to be

[1] Representative examples that characterize world-class manufacturing include: Deming 1982; Ishikawa 1985; Womack, Jones, and Roos 1990; Imai 1986; Watson 1993; and quality award programs such as the Deming Prize, the Baldrige Award, and the Shingo Prize.

[2] Representative examples of change methodologies include: Goldratt and Cox 1984; Harmon and Peterson 1990; Japan Management Association 1987; Hayes and Wheelwright 1984; Kobayashi 1988; Reid 1990; Schonberger 1986; Sekine 1990; Shiba, Graham, and Walden 1993; Suzaki 1987; and Weisbord 1987.

[3] The author, with colleagues, has introduced Kobayashi's 20 keys program for self-assessment and production transition in groups of companies in Slovenia, Jamaica, Honduras and Moldova (Best 1993; Bizjak and Petrin 1996: ch. 2; Petrin 1995: 10; Best and Forrant 1994; Best 1992).

involved in designing and developing the new practices.[4] The five levels for each key offer criteria that can become operational goals to guide production improvement action plans and to evaluate workforce performance.

Examples of successful national policies to upgrade skills to advance production capabilities include the Training Within Industry program developed during World War II in America and the quality movement developed in Japan. Both of these programs targeted the skill formation process as a means of advancing national productivity.[5] Each is briefly examined under skill formation policies below.

Technology Management

Developing technology management capabilities to tap the world's pool of technology can be a powerful vehicle for rapid growth. A tenet of the capabilities and innovation perspective is that social organization must be in place in advance of or simultaneously with technology advances. Hence the stress on technology *management*.

The East Asian economies that have achieved high rates of growth have a critical mass of industrial enterprises with the capability to adopt, adapt, and diffuse technologies that originated in the most technologically advanced nations. Japan, South Korea, and Taiwan have developed the capability to develop new products and processes based on refining, fusing, and advancing generic technologies. These are the attributes of technology management.[6] Sustained high growth rates depend upon instituting technology management processes identified in Table 2.1 (column 7).

[4] See Forrant (1998) and Forrant and Flynn (1998) for a case study of the role of regional industrial policy agencies in enterprise transitions to more advanced manufacturing capabilities. See Shiba, Graham, and Walden (1993) for an organizational change methodology that involved a group of companies working together. Philip Shapira (1998) surveys the Manufacturing Extension Partnership joint initiative of federal and state governments in the United States to develop a national infrastructure to support 'the deployment of new technologies and improved business practices among small and mid-sized manufacturing enterprises' in the 1990s.

[5] Lessons from Japanese and American industrial modernization programs are discussed in Best and Forrant (1996*b*).

[6] Slow growth followers, on the other hand, lack the capabilities to tap the world's pool of technologies. This is not surprising. Successful technology management, like the establishment of price for Alfred Marshall, depends upon both blades of a pair of scissors; supply (production capabilities) must be matched by demand (market opportunities). While demand in price theory is mediated by income, demand in technology management is mediated by technological capabilities.

But technology management is not simply an appendage to production either in practice or theory. Firms and nations have learned the hard way that new technologies and technology management capabilities cannot be simply added onto production systems. This is because technology management possibilities are limited by and rooted in the principles that shape the production system. Put differently, upgrading technology management capabilities is an oft-stated goal; implementation, however, often involves making a transition to production systems and business models in which the desired technology management capabilities are built into the organizational architecture. This makes economic transition difficult. Understanding the organizational challenge and the implications for growth calls for a theory of industrial change derived from fundamental principles of production and organization.

Placing design at the center of economic development and change processes creates space for technology management capability as a target for both enterprise and governmental policymaking. Regional or national technology management capabilities are critical to understanding the organizational and systemic forces that shape productivity and growth challenges and opportunities.[7]

Two implications for an industrial policy of technology management stand out. The first is the availability of the worldwide technology pool as a cheap resource *for firms with technology management capabilities*. But unless firms have technology management capabilities the growth process will be stunted. This suggests why mission-driven business and production modernization agencies that teach and diffuse participatory management practices such as *kaizen*, small group activity, cellular manufacturing, and total quality management have been central to the development and diffusion of technology management in rapidly growing regions. At least the roadmap for advancing production capabilities is now clear. Technology management capabilities are refined as enterprises move up the production capability spectrum (Box 2.2). Today these linkages are matters of historical record. When examined and properly understood, they offer powerful growth levers at the enterprise and governmental levels.

A second implication is that the history of the evolution of models of technology management is also a high growth roadmap for technology

[7] By systemic forces I am referring to the inter-connectedness amongst the elements of the Productivity Triad. While business model, production capabilities, and skill formation all contribute to productivity, making the transition to a higher Productivity Triad involves a change program that works in each domain simultaneously.

followers. A history of changes in industrial leadership can be presented in terms of transitions to new models of technology management (a sequence of 'new competitions'). These transitions underlie the shifting composition of industries and products of Figure 2.1. Regions with a critical mass of firms that were pioneers in the emergence of new models enjoy jumps in productivity and growth. The implied policy roadmap is of a terrain that alternates between hills representing the transition to new principles of production and organization associated with higher levels of technology management, and plateaux where the new principles and capabilities are diffused across firms and industries. The speed of the vehicle, representing the rate of growth, inevitably slows for the transitions but, if the hills are climbed and the new principles established, the vehicle can again enjoy a long spell of steady speed (industrial growth) before a new hill is eventually encountered.

At each point along the way, growth for the technology followers occurs for as long as the ratio between wages and production capabilities is low compared to other countries. But the process of growth will advance wages until following nations make the transition to a new level of production capabilities and, enjoying a lower ratio between wages and production capabilities, undersell the market leaders.[8] Having achieved a new, higher level of production capabilities, a region or country enjoys growth as the new practices and technologies are diffused to old and new products, by old and new firms. However, in the process, wages rise and opportunities for further diffusion diminish and growth becomes threatened as imitating regions and nations in turn develop the requisite production capabilities to move into the same markets but with lower wages.

To sustain growth, enterprises in such regions must be making the transition to the next level of production capabilities. Once a critical mass of enterprises makes this transition, a new range of opportunities

[8] Kaname Akumatsu (1962), a Japanese proponent of a unique theory of industrial development, described a process common to development literature but added an interesting twist. Countries would move from imports to import substitution to exports as they learned from foreign technologies. He described the process in terms of three waves of flying geese for each product. Imports would be represented by the first gaggle of geese in flying formation: increase, peak, and fall off; production the second gaggle: increase, peak, and decline; and exports the third gaggle, again representing an inverted V pattern. He described these patterns as occurring first in 'crude' products and later in 'refined' products; in final goods and later capital goods. Where a country is at any point in time is determined by the balance of forces between the level of development and wage rates. Higher development leads to higher wages and a loss in exports of easier to produce goods. The idea of a production capabilities spectrum combines the principles of production and organization described in Ch. 2 with Akumatsu's notion of sectoral transitions.

opens up as the region or nation becomes competitive in more technically and organizationally advanced activities and products. Growth reasserts itself as the opportunities are taken up until, once again the ratio of the wage rate to the respective production capabilities rises above that of competitors. If a region or country successfully makes the transitions along the production capability spectrum, then growth capacity will continue to increase.[9]

Technology Transitions

Technological change is inherently uncertain. No one can predict with certainty which companies will become leaders and which technologies will set the standards. In fact, powerful companies can often be the least likely to read the future correctly. This has long been the case in telecommunications.

In 1876 Western Union Telegraph, the largest non-railroad corporation in the country, turned down an offer to the rights to telephone technology.[10] Its president, William Orton, dismissed the phone as a 'toy' and a 'scientific curiosity'. Three years later, Western Union signed an agreement with Bell Telephone to stay out of the telephone business to concentrate on its hugely profitable telegraph business (G. Smith 1996: 38). While Bell agreed to stay out of long distance telegraphy, rapid technological improvements turned Bell into a highly profitable company and, in 1896, when the 1879 agreement expired, the Bell System could not be challenged. Western Union was reduced to a minor role in the communications industry.

The disruptive effect of technology transitions on business enterprises cuts across all business sectors. In fact, Bell was equally

[9] The dynamic process described starts with production capabilities and moves to higher rates of investment, greater learning-by-doing, greater competitiveness, and sustained high growth. Savings follows from high profits. In this account, high growth generates savings; the conventional view attributes high growth to high savings but does not satisfactorily explain the sudden surges in savings. The capabilities and innovation perspective starts with the firm and thereby focuses explanation on organizational capabilities and competitiveness; the conventional view begins with the consumption and savings choice of individuals as the determinant of growth. Empirical evidence presented by Singh (1995) supports the production-oriented perspective.

[10] Ironically, Western Union's technology, built on Samuel F. B. Morse's invention, was digital, but analog technology would come to dominate telecommunications for the next hundred years. Only as a consequence of the microelectronics revolution would telecommunications return to digital technology (Lucky 1999).

dismissive of the transistor, invented in its own laboratories in the 1940s. Few, if anyone, foresaw the emergence of microelectronics and the semiconductor industry. William Schockley, inventor of the transistor, took his invention to Silicon Valley and started a new company out of which were created an unparalleled progeny of entrepreneurial firms in the information and communications industries (Saxenian 1994).

For policymakers, the issue is not with the success of individual firms or even specific technologies but the promotion of technological change. Here patterns are more predictable. The contours of technology trajectories that underlie patterns of economic growth follow a historic logic.

Moore's Law is an example of an unfolding technology trajectory.[11] It is also an extraordinary example of increasing returns linked to technological advance. But from a longer-term perspective, it is simply the speeding up of a long technological trajectory that began with application of the principle of interchangeability. As shown in Figure 5.2, Moore's Law represents a segment in a 200-year trajectory of shrinking critical size dimensions that has been sustained by technology transitions.

Figure 5.2 illustrates both the change and the continuity dimensions of technological change. But it also suggests that technology transitions are themselves, in part, a response to challenges. The challenge presented by the path of shrinking size dimensions has focused projects of engineers and scientists. Companies have identified new market opportunities in terms of the potential for new product development offered by yet smaller critical size dimensions. In the process, new firms and new industries have emerged to replace firms whose competitive advantage was anchored in technological capabilities that had driven previous technologies.

Companies may come and go and the prosperity of regions may rise and fall based on their capabilities to anticipate the opportunities and effects of technological change. But the parameters of the trajectory have been remarkably constant. They are not fixed by natural law, but they offer a target for both technological research and business and industrial policymaking. An established target is itself a coordinating

[11] In 1965 Gordon Moore, a founder of Intel Corporation, made the observation that the width of the wires and the sizes of the device structures in microelectronics circuitry were shrinking at an exponential rate. Every eighteen months, he predicted, the number of transistors that could be placed on a chip would double. Costs would decrease and productivity would double in tandem with each eighteen-month cycle. It has been an accurate predictor for thirty-five years. See Chs. 2 and 5 above.

force across the whole range of companies and activities required to achieve it.

The evolution of precision machining toward ever-smaller critical size was not lost on industrial leaders, including industrial policy-makers. Sematech, a joint industry–government research consortium, was formed in 1987 to improve chip-manufacturing capability in the United States. The government put up $100 million to match the same sum from an industry consortium. The idea was not to produce chips in a jointly owned facility but to develop technologies that could be distributed to members. Gordon Moore (1996: 172–3) describes Sematech's purpose:

> its founders organised a series of industry wide workshops to identify the technological advances required for U.S. semiconductor and supplier industries to catch up with Japanese industries. The outcome, in March 1988, was a timeline and the specifications for a sequence of technological generations that would lead to parity by 1994—a 'road map for semiconductor technology'. The timeline specifications required the demonstration of a 0.8 micron technology in SEMATECH's new wafer facility in 1989, with further advances to 0.5 micron technology in 1990, 0.35 micron technology in 1992, and 0.25 micron technology in 1994.

The goals for Sematech were set in terms of line-widths, the size of the smallest dimensions that a plant can produce. The Semiconductor Industry Association, founded in the 1970s, coordinated the activities of the Semiconductor Research Consortium, a sister organization established to organize and focus university research (Moore 1996: 170), and Sematech. These agencies 'provided a road map for 15 years, pointing out key technology needs and the times at which those technologies would be required to keep the semiconductor industry on the historic productivity curve of a 30% reduction in cost per function per year' (173).

The goals were achieved; no chip-making plants anywhere were able to work to smaller size dimensions. US market share in microchips were again internationally competitive (*Economist*, 2 Apr. 1994: 77). The predictability of Moore's 'law' was used to great effect in government policies in the United States to resurrect the semiconductor industry. In this sense, Moore's 'Law' is as much an industrial policy and business strategy as it is a scientific law. Together, industry and government turned the projected trajectory into a reality.

The example illustrates how industrial policy can foster technological and industrial leadership even in the most technologically advanced companies and regions. It also illustrates how technological 'laws' can guide policy.

Entrepreneurial Firms

Entrepreneurial firms create both products and capabilities. Perhaps the greatest challenge of industrial policy from the capabilities and innovation perspective is to institute processes of entrepreneurial firm creation and development. Various models exist.

The rapid growth experiences of Japan and South Korea were based on the growth of a few industry-dominating enterprises in each sector. The *kaisha* (and the South Korean variant or *chaebol*) is a model of entrepreneurial firm development that proved highly successful. They proved particularly successful at driving the rapid development and diffusion of the production capabilities associated with PS 2 and PS 3 (Table 2.1).[12]

The *kaisha* model, however, does not encourage an ongoing process of entrepreneurial firm creation and proliferation. For this we turn to the open systems business model and cluster dynamics. The entrepreneurial firm start-up system is particularly strong in the Silicon Valley and Route 128 high-tech regions in the United States and in the design-led and the fashion industries of the 'third Italy'.[13] Taiwan, Ireland, and Israel have all established variants, if on a smaller scale.

A business strategy of focus and network (focus on a distinctive capability and partner for complementary capabilities) can trigger the cluster dynamics illustrated in Figure 3.1. The open systems business model expands opportunities for yet more entrepreneurial firms which, in turn, deepens the networks of specialist and partnering enterprises.

A vibrant regional growth dynamic fosters an industrial ecology in which entrepreneurial firms emerge, grow, and die and, in the process, advance regional technological capabilities and productivity. Once the

[12] The relationships between the Japanese variant of the entrepreneurial firm and its industrial policy infrastructure are examined in chs. 5 and 6 of *The New Competition* (Best 1990).

[13] In a comparison of European with American high-tech regions, a recent McKinsey study found that compared with Silicon Valley and Route 128, where 73% and 69%, respectively, of all companies with sales of more than $50 million were established after 1985, the share of such companies is 17% in the Munich region, 20% in the Stuttgart region, 24% in Paris, 25% in the Dusseldorf region, and 31% in London (Kluge, Meffert, and Stein 2000: 100). See Cooke (1998) for a survey of enterprise support policies in 'dynamic' European regions.

inter-firm dynamics are underway, new firm creation is built into the process. Rapid growth and new firm creation feed on one another. Fast growing, technologically driven firms provide the managerial experience critical to its reproduction in yet new firms. Old, developmental firms provide feedstock to new firms much like fallen trees do for seedlings in the rain forest. The process enhances regional competitive advantage based on a unique blend of technological diversity and regional specialization.

The implications of open systems models of inter-firm organization for business cycles are profound. In a regime of vertically integrated enterprises, transitions to new technologies often involved large-scale enterprise bankruptcies and unemployment. The process of Schumpeterian creative destruction was part of a process of releasing resources from enterprises that were locked into old technologies. Enterprises that had built distinctive capabilities in one technology are rarely the drivers of emerging technologies (Christensen 1997). But they can often be the barriers to the emergence of new technologies. In extreme cases, big firms can create the 'upas tree effect' of poisoning a region's industrial ecology (see Chapter 7). By contrast, in a regime of specialist and partnering enterprises, the process of new firm creation built into vibrant open system business networks is one of pulling resources from less to more promising pursuits without regional business decline.

Regional governments are responsible for maintaining high levels of employment but in an open systems business model this does not translate into supporting individual firms. Rather, it calls for reducing barriers to new firm creation and technological change. The rationale for industrial policy in the capabilities and innovation perspective is to institute processes that foster capability development. The logic is that capability development is an ongoing process in part because production is simultaneously a process of new resource creation. Here the market is a source of opportunity to guide technology development. It is not defined independently of the capability development process.[14] Therefore the notion of an ideal allocation of resources is not a guide to industrial policymaking designed to foster growth. The contribution of resources to output is not pre-given, but dependent in part on how they are used in production.

For regions lacking such capability development and market opportunity growth dynamics, the policy challenge is to trigger the processes

[14] In contrast, both the free market and the protectionist perspectives presume a firm or market dichotomy.

by fostering entrepreneurial firms. This is a big challenge.[15] There is no recipe, but different new firm creation processes have been successful. The task is to *examine the existing process* to identify policy leverage points. Taiwan has created new entrepreneurial firms and new industries *via* state-funded science parks that have fostered such firms in the form of high-tech spin-offs.[16] The use of high-tech labs in the creation of Taiwan's semiconductor and computer industries has much in common with federally sponsored R&D labs in Massachusetts. Both involve technical skill formation, fostering techno-entrepreneurs, and high rates of new firm creation. But, more so than in Massachusetts, the new firm creation process in Taiwan was an element in an intentional and integrated industrial policy designed to advance regional competitive advantage (San Gee and Wen-jeng Kuo 1998).

Foreign direct investment can quick-start the process by introducing new principles of production and organization to a region. International firms may or may not be entrepreneurial firms. The challenge is to identify entrepreneurial firms with advanced technology management and networking capabilities and simultaneously to develop institutional means of fostering local application and diffusion of the constituent practices and skills. The combination of access to foreign sources of technology and complementary local capability development creates opportunities for local growth dynamics. Policymakers in the Irish Republic triggered local growth dynamics by attracting foreign direct investment with advanced technology management capabilities in combination with investment in technical education. Israel has used the in-migration of highly skilled personnel from abroad, particularly from the ex-Soviet Union countries in combination with public and private venture capital funds to develop a regional new firm creation capability.

Deregulation can be a powerful trigger for the creation of entrepreneurial firms. For example, British Telecommunications, uninten-

[15] Monopolies, however, are not bad per se. The critical distinction is not the number of firms in a market but business strategy and organization. Business strategies based on the pursuit of distinctive capabilities can be distinguished from those that seek strategic assets to limit competition. The latter are primarily rent seeking. Monopoly in the pursuit of distinctive technological capabilities can be consistent with fostering cluster dynamics; rent seeking by control of strategic assets is not. Policymakers cannot know whether a specific firm is pursuing a rent seeking or capability development strategy simply by counting the number of firms in a market. It demands an assessment of each enterprise's capability development characteristics.

[16] The Hsinchu Science-Based Industrial Park offers a range of incentives and services but also specifies minimal rates of R&D and proportion of workforce that are scientists and engineers. Taiwan has some 4,000 electronics firms, most of which started out as small firms. See Dolven 1998; Ernst 2000; and Mathews 1997.

tionally, had sired some 120 telecommunications start-ups within four years of the opening up of competition in 1991.[17] Some of these have become rivals, forcing BT to become more entrepreneurial.

But 'free market' policy is not enough. Regional growth dynamics require the creation and growth of new business enterprises, the development of new production capabilities, and an extra-firm infrastructure that supports rapid firm growth (Garnsey 1998). Establishing the constitutive processes requires technology capability development within firms and a complementary skill formation and regulatory environment.

Entrepreneurial firms can be fostered indirectly by advancing bottom-up managerial capabilities. The integration of doing and thinking, of conceiving and executing, of designing and doing in the organization of work is, at the same time, redefining work to include managerial activities.[18] For this reason, the decentralization and diffusion of design associated with high-performance work systems (HPWS) can foster new firm creation. In fact, the extent to which a firm has made the transition to a HPWS is one measure of its capability to do rapid new product development and therefore of entrepreneurial capability.[19] The quality movement has developed a range of indicators of the productive capabilities of enterprises that are, at the same time, a sequence of well-defined practices which must be integrated into production to advance productivity. The measurement system is simultaneously a means of identifying the tasks required for organizational change.

Much attention has been focused on financial markets as the enablers of entrepreneurial firms' emergence and development. Venture capital and stock markets are certainly facilitators of the high new firm creation rates in Silicon Valley and Route 128/495. But the value adding advances generated by the underlying technology capability and market opportunity dynamics, at both the enterprise and

[17] After an initial period of severe job losses, the introduction of new technologies by rapidly growing entrepreneurial firms is transforming the industry. Combined with the personal computer and Internet revolutions, the transition to photonic technologies has led to a proliferation of products, created vast market opportunities, and fostered vertical disintegration.

[18] Much attention has been given, rightfully, to the processes by which universities produce techno-entrepreneurs. However, 'invisible' college graduates create new firms as well. In both cases, an entrepreneur is one who sees a productive opportunity—either a market niche or a productive capability—and matches opportunity to capability by developing a team and forming a company.

[19] The pervasive diffusion of the new model of work organization in America in the 1990s documented by Appelbaum et al. (2000) may be linked to the high ratio of new to all firms documented by Kluge, Meffert, and Stein (2000). As already noted, the proportion of employees in firms that made some use of self-managed work teams increased from 28% in 1987 to 68% in 1995 (Appelbaum et al. 2000).

regional levels, must ultimately valorize the financial returns. Other regions including Taiwan and the 'third Italy' have created industrial ecologies with high new firm creation ratios without formal venture capital industries. The critical source of new entrepreneurial firms is other entrepreneurial firms and opportunities for new firm creation proliferate with open system models of industrial organization.

Open Systems Networking

Entrepreneurial firms drive increasing capability specialization and regional growth dynamics. The internal technology and market growth dynamic that defines the entrepreneurial firm initiates a range of inter-firm growth dynamics. Shown in Figure 3.1, these include techno-diversification; integration, dis-integration, and reintegration fostered by open networks; internal/external dynamics; and industrial speciation (and new industry creation). Open system networks foster increasing specialization in technological capability in tandem with a focus and network business model.[20]

Open systems are inter-firm networks in which the constituent firms can pursue technological capability development but still plug back into the overall system. Industry standards facilitate the process by which firms can partner in a production system. The more general the standards, the greater the potential to pull more firms and resources into the production system. Powerful individual firms can impose industry 'standards', but they risk turning open systems into closed systems of industrial organization in the process. Closed systems, in turn, hinder the new firm creation process with negative effects on the mobilization of resources, regional innovation, and technological change.

Industry associations and governmental agencies have a role to play in establishing standards that foster open systems and regional growth dynamics. Agreement on standard screw size, for example, was an early example of a standard that encouraged open systems during the time of the American System of Manufacturers (Roe 1916). Similarly, the Internet's open standards allow everyone to connect with everyone else and thereby develop network economies. Today's web applications,

[20] Three models of inter-firm coordination are atomistic price competition, closed networks as in the Japanese *keiretsu*, and open systems networks. Each model fosters a distinctive internal/external dynamic in the sense that internal firm and inter-firm organizations are interactive (see Lazerson and Lorenzoni 1999).

written in Java programming language, provide a common language and open systems across a massive assortment of hardware and software programs in the world's stock of personal computers.

The point of open systems is not simply that communication engenders increased specialization. Like the invention of electricity, it creates opportunities to develop new business models and advance production capabilities. Dell, for example, did not simply use the Internet to reduce distribution costs, but to link the customer to production scheduling and thereby integrate distribution and production in a business model that offered a step-wise increase in productivity and simplified scaling up for rapid growth.

The Internet also facilitates the use of advanced information technologies such as CAD/CAM/CAE for collaborative product development processing.[21] The open systems protocol of the Internet enables seamless integration of design information across virtually all computer systems and resource planning systems.[22] But for such product design tools to be effective, the various departments of the enterprise must be internally networked and aligned or process integrated. Otherwise, information technology gives rise to isolated islands of computerization in which information is proprietary and system integration is limited.[23]

Similarly, establishing a digital technology infrastructure can assist firms seeking to become entrepreneurial firms by facilitating a transition from business models organized in terms of value chains to ones organized around value networks. The value chain metaphor, derived from assembly line concepts, was suited to long product life cycles in which communication across functional departments was routine (designed for unchanging products and technologies). Digital technologies assist real-time coordination across functions in the form of value networks that blur departmental boundaries, reduce middle management functions, compress new product development cycle times, and assist communication across technology disciplines and communities. Robust value networks, within and across firms, increase

[21] CAD is computer aided design, CAM is computer aided manufacturing, and CAE is computer aided engineering.

[22] See 'Adaptec: Getting the slack out of cycle time', *Fortune*, 8 Nov. 1999, for an example of a 'value network' involving Internet facilitated partnering across multiple countries.

[23] Nanyang Polytechnic's Computer Integrated Manufacturing Center offers a range of manpower development and information technology partnering arrangements to Singaporean companies. Its website is <www.technocim.edu.sg>. This center was established as part of Singapore Economic Development Board's Report of the Committee on Singapore's Competitiveness (CSC). The vision, short-term recommendations, and long-term strategies are summarized at <www.sedb.com.sg/vision/vi_cs.html>.

the responsiveness and flexibility of groups of companies to market opportunities and technology change.

The concept of open systems can likewise be a means of reducing size-related barriers to knowledge creation, application, and diffusion. An example is the notebook computer consortium established by the Computer and Communications Laboratories of Taiwan's Industrial Technology Research Institute. Against the wishes of the bigger firms, the government allowed 46 firms to become consortium members with equal access to 'design specifications and prototypes, detailed technical reports for each stage of development, motherboard designs, mass production samples and training classes' (Ernst 2000). By 1994 Taiwan had become the world's largest producer of notebook PCs. The development model has focused on differentiated and design-intensive products from the beginning. Instead of a few firms developing a competitive advantage in high-volume production, the policy called for many specialist firms pursuing unique technological capabilities based on common, publicly available interface rules.

Industrial policy that focuses on the diffusion of design standards and other support services for technological advance, as distinct from subsidizing individual firms advances regional competitiveness. Companies compete as members of networked groups of companies and the diffusion of new practices and principles across networked groups is critical to making the transition to more advanced technology management capabilities. An example is JIT (just-in-time) production. JIT depends upon an inter-firm coordination of inputs and outputs which, in turn, puts pressure on suppliers to synchronize cycle times. This, in turn, creates pressures to move to cellular manufacturing and high-performance work systems.

Networking is relevant for growth at all levels of production capabilities or degrees of sectoral specialization. Regions with companies at any of the four poles of Figure 2.1 can benefit from networking capabilities to trigger the external/internal dynamics of design-led clusters.[24] In open systems, networking capabilities and capability specialization feed on each other to boost design and experimentation. In fact, just as the internal technology capability and market opportunity dynamic of the entre-

[24] While advancing production capabilities is the basis for industrial diversification, it does not require movement of the composition of industrial output in the PS 5 and PS 3, 4 directions as indicated by Figure 2.1. Instead, advances in technology management capabilities enabling rapid new product development can lead to growth and productivity advances in traditional, light-industry sectors such as furniture and footwear. But in every case, the business model of focus and network must be promulgated in line with the principle of increasing specialization.

preneurial firm fosters the decentralization of design, inter-firm *networking capabilities* foster the diffusion of design. In this way, open system networks are an infrastructure to enhance regional innovation.

As the networking capabilities of a region become more robust, that region takes on more the semblance of a collective entrepreneur. The collective entrepreneurial firm is a self-organizing change agent composed of networked groups of mutually adjusting enterprises.[25] It is a composite of networking firms that collectively administer the regional growth dynamic processes but without central direction. The open systems model of industrial organization enhances flexibility, reduces new product development time, and fosters innovation.

Many governments have initiated cluster research projects to identify the geographical concentration of industries and networks. Some have gone further and developed measures of regional innovation to identify cluster dynamics.[26]

Skill Formation

Skill formation, business model, and production system are the three elements of the Productivity Triad. This means that the productive capability of an economy can be viewed from any one of the three domains. It also means that making a transition to more advanced productivity triads involves mutual adjustment amongst all three domains.

Skill formation is a long-term process, including formal and informal sub-processes, embedded in partnering relationships across schools, firms, government, and the polity. Nurturing these relationships is as basic to the skill formation process as investing in the physical infrastructure is to supply chain management in the manufacturing process. But it takes more time and involves more stakeholders. The public policy challenge is to coordinate investments in skills, formal and informal, with advances in production and technology capabilities.

Enterprise or governmental policy initiatives to make the transition to more advanced models of technology management or technology

[25] The idea of the industrial district as a collective entrepreneur is applied to the 'third Italy' in Best 1990: 207–8.

[26] The Ministry of Economic Affairs in Slovenia introduced a policy to co-finance joint projects involving at least five companies in marketing, product development, technology improvements, and specialization in supply chains. The take-up rate has been high, as the Government has supported 130 projects mostly in technology development and marketing. See Petrin, Vitez, and Mesl (2000).

domains (see Figure 5.2) will be undone without the requisite skill base. As shown in Figure 4.4, regional growth processes are limited by the supply of engineering and scientific personnel available to staff rapidly growing firms. Mutual adjustments between technology advancing enterprises and skill formation institutions, internal and external to the enterprise, are integral to growth dynamics.

For example, applying the principle of interchangeability involves product engineering, just as applying the principle of flow means diffusion of process engineering skills. The development of both the Route 128 and Silicon Valley electronics clusters involved the simultaneous development of university departments, research institutes and curricula, on the one hand, and rapidly growing entrepreneurial enterprises, on the other. This dynamic nurtured techno-entrepreneurs, an important source of new firms, and mediated labor demand and supply with the requisite skills.

The links between innovation and skill formation elaborated in Chapters 4 and 5 underscore the role that skill formation can play in economic growth. Regions can build competitive advantage by anticipating technology transitions with skill formation programs. To build competitive advantage a region needs to be able to ramp up production and this requires a labor supply that meets the needs of rapidly growing companies.

Technological innovation is an ongoing process that can occur in many different places. Many corporate and government laboratories, and research universities have been the site of technological breakthroughs which have created the potential for product applications and enterprise growth. In other cases, however, such innovations do not lead to growth within the same region.

Two mutually interdependent processes are involved in converting technological innovations into regional competitive advantage and growth. Without both in place the potential of the innovations will not be realized in the form of product applications developed within a specific region.

The first is the integration of various activities that constitute the new product development process. As shown in Figures 4.2 and 4.3, this involves not only basic research but also developmental and applied research and the integration of all three with production. Put differently, upstream, downstream, and manufacturing engineering must all be in sync if the region is to develop a regional competitive advantage. Design integration across the research functions and amongst the requisite components is itself mediated by an emerging product concept. Some regions do only manufacturing, but they will not enjoy high value added or productivity. Other regions will do the R&D and upstream engineering activities but will likely suffer ultimate loss in competitive advantage if these activities are not integrated with production.

The second is the development of a corresponding skill formation system, or pipeline. An example is the development of electronics and the minicomputer industry in Massachusetts during the 'Miracle' years. The region could not have grown without the simultaneous expansion in electrical engineers from roughly 600 to 1,600. The education costs in terms of new engineering faculty and facilities was roughly $50 million annually. It was a small price to pay in the development of the first high-tech industrial district in electronics. While the productivity in terms of increased output cannot be isolated, the development of associated industries such as information technology contributed to the technological renewal of firms across a broad band of industrial sectors, boosting regional value added in the process.

The two processes are integrated by an emerging curriculum in both the visible and invisible colleges. A curriculum mediates between skills required by the technology-driven enterprises and the skills developed by students. Regions with technology-oriented universities that are able to anticipate the requisite skills for emerging technologies with widespread application have an advantage in establishing a leadership position in the new generic applications. Anticipating the skills is about developing an educational delivery system. This includes motivating students to participate from the middle schools to the graduate level. Unless students are attracted to the emerging technologies in the form of career choices, the skills gap will choke the growth process.

Regional technology-oriented universities are potentially powerful in shaping a region's economic destiny, particularly in the era of knowledge-intensive industries. The specific technological skills possessed by the younger members of a region's labor force are the fuel that drives rapidly growing firms in corresponding technologies. In this the curriculum decisions made by these universities are powerful shapers of investment patterns and even technology choices of enterprises.

The formal education of scientists and engineers captures the critical role of advanced skills in production capability and technology transitions that is required in rapid growth experiences. But the education investment challenge does not stop here. Complementary skill formation at the intermediate and lower skill levels is equally important.

Claudia Goldin (1998) dates the American 'high school movement' in the period between the 1890s and 1920s. The male high school graduation rate, which stood at 10–15 percent of the cohort born in 1890 rose to nearly 50 percent for those born after World War I. This spectacular transition accompanied the rise of mass production industries in America and the manufacturing productivity revolution of the 1920s. Relying upon empirical research by John Kendrick (1961), David and Wright (1999) point to an annual leap in manufacturing output per manhour from 1.5 percent in the first decade and a half of the twentieth century to 5.5 percent in the 1920s.

The upgrading of skills across the labor force made it possible to diffuse the new production system and technological capabilities associated with the electrical revolution across much of the manufacturing sector. All three elements of the Productivity Triad were reintegrated at a more advanced level of production capabilities. The 1920s witnessed the transition to the multidivisional model of business organization as captured by Chandler's history of the business enterprise (1961, 1977). The new business model created a managerial hierarchy with the organizational capability to extend the principle of flow to new product applications. The development of mass production capabilities depended upon the invention of distributed electric power which made it possible to conceive of the manufacturing challenge as one of equalizing cycle times (see Chapter 2). Goldin and Katz (1998) identify the origins of a 'technology–skill complementarity' as occurring in the same period. The technology–skill complementary refers to the tendency for new technologies to disproportionately favor more highly educated labor.

The government financing of the high school movement was a powerful, indirect industrial policy. It not only advanced skills of those who worked in manufacturing and managed the new managerial enterprises. It also created a huge pool of students which made it possible to expand engineering and science education at the college level. The growth in this category was equally striking and, as noted in Chapter 4, was the mirror image of the scientific and educational innovations that occurred during the inter-war period.

The formal education of scientists and engineers captures the critical role of advanced skills in production capability and technology transitions. But the education investment challenge does not stop here.

At times of technological transition, the skill formation process involves complementary curriculum changes all along the educational spectrum. The linkage is illustrated in current times in the transition from electronic, circuit-switched networks to optical, packet-switched technology. In the words of Edward March, a Lucent Technologies executive:

Success in the Optical Networking marketplace is dependent upon rapid introduction of new technology. Reduction of the interval from research through commercial product is an imperative. If our workforce is not equipped with the necessary skill level to manufacture advanced products, production capability will not adequately support the volume levels needed to meet customer demand. If this occurs, profitable gain from our research investment will be lost. (Lazonick 2000: 4)

In the production of optical networking equipment, it is estimated that a single graduate engineer can support five or six associate engineers. Combined with a *kaizen* or HPWS capability in operations, the spectrum of skills can compress the times for new product introduction and production processes. But the lack of skills at any level impedes the whole process.

Successful technological followers have developed industrial policies to advance production capabilities and foster entrepreneurial firms. But while the business model varied, careful examination reveals that each program had a skill formation component. Policymakers in Japan sponsored technology transfer programs and R&D projects by lead firms that introduced incremental innovation into work organization. The Electronics Research and Service Organization (ERSO) in Taiwan has fostered the emergence of technology-based enterprises which, in turn, have stimulated cluster dynamics in which technology-oriented educational institutions were closely involved.[27] In Singapore, the Economic Development Board has invested heavily in skill formation including scientists and engineers and in an infrastructure which give incentives for MNCs to transfer product design capabilities to Singapore (Magaziner and Patinkin 1989; SISIR 1992; Dolven 1998).

In each of these cases of rapid growth, technology development and diffusion and skill formation have worked hand in glove. The technology diffusion process depends upon the level of skill formation at the operational as well as advanced engineering levels. The pace of growth is enhanced by a shared supplier base of small and medium-sized firms that can achieve world-class performance standards in cost, quality, and time. This involves making the transition to PS 3 (see Table 2.1) which, at the regional level means the spread of a variant of the *kaizen*

[27] ERSO, a public agency founded in 1974, 'stands between the domestic electronics firms and the rest of the world for the purposes of facilitating the transfer and assimilation of advanced technologies' (Wade 1990: 107). See Wade for a description of ERSO as a catalyst for the development of Taiwan's information technology industries, including the proliferation of design houses (103–8). For a contrast between Taiwan and Singapore industrial policies and industrial organization see Dolven (1998).

or continuous improvement model of work organization across a critical mass of SME supplier firms.

Looked at from a national or regional perspective, advancing shopfloor skills raises the issue of the size, quality, and specialized abilities of the teacher pool. The number of teachers and the appropriateness of the curriculum place limits on the pace of skill formation. Successful programs have a common feature: teacher training is designed into the program.

The Japanese Union of Scientists and Engineers (JUSE) provides an example.[28] It administers the Deming Prize upon which the Baldrige Award in the United States and the European Quality Award have been modeled. JUSE is a nonprofit, mission-driven agency established in 1947 to promulgate total quality management. JUSE fostered a continuous improvement (*kaizen*) capability throughout Japanese industry. JUSE developed an inter-firm teach-the-teachers methodology that diffused the new management philosophy across industry and had a cascading effect. Workers not only teach one another as part of the flexibility required for multi-product flow production, but the plan-do-check-act methodology became embedded in an inter-firm education system which produced not only workers educated in the new system but teachers. Successful trainees gain certificates which make them eligible to teach to the new generation of workers, often in other companies.

Another outstanding model is the Training Within Industry (TWI) program. TWI was developed in America but thoroughly refined in Japan. Some have argued that the most important export from America to Japan was the Training Within Industry program.[29] It deserves special attention, as it illustrates both a successful shopfloor skill-formation diffusion program and successful institutional transfer.

The effectiveness of the TWI program was demonstrated during World War II, when the United States dramatically increased its production while at the same time deploying millions directly in the war effort. It did so by developing a training program for a new labor pool composed largely of women and recruits from non-manufacturing sectors.

[28] JUSE was established in 1947 to promulgate quality control, statistical process control and total quality management, administers two journals, and publishes numerous books. PDCA, for example, has been introduced into numerous enterprises. Kaoru Ishikawa, who invented the fishbone as a problem-solving technique, was a long-term president of JUSE. The JUSE as much as any other single organization has provided Japanese enterprises with a continuous improvement approach to production and a participatory approach to industrial engineering (Ishikawa 1985; Best 1990).

[29] This section draws heavily from A. Robinson and Schroeder (1993).

Undertaken by the Department of War and based on analysis of the most successful industrial training efforts around the nation, TWI broke down the training system to generic skills that cut across enterprises and skills that were enterprise-specific. It specialized on the former. A key to the program was the cascading effect in which individuals were trained both in skills and how to teach the skills.[30]

Skill formation programs can be linked to inter-sectoral transitions toward activities and products demanding more production-complex and knowledge-intensive capabilities. Success can be measured by movement toward the PS 3, 4 and PS 5 poles of Figure 2.1. This means developing and diffusing skills embodied in new product development and systems integration capabilities associated with PS 4 and PS 5 (Table 2.1).

A region that can institute skill formation processes in anticipation of technology transitions has a competitive advantage over regions that lack such a capability.[31] Regions that fail to integrate skill formation and technology change will risk undermining the skill base required to sustain production of once successful industries.

Investment in mid-level skills is important for income distribution purposes, as well. The link between income distribution and technological change has been examined for decades. The research represents a 'venerable and fruitful tradition extending back to Paul Douglas (1926) and Jan Tinbergen (1975) of viewing the evolution of the wage structure . . . as depending on a race between technological developments and educational advance' (L. Katz 1999: 1). When technological change is low-skill labor-saving, it means that the only way that technology-driven growth in productivity can be shared is through advances in education at the lower levels.

Regional governments have both a responsibility and a unique opportunity to play an aggressive role in skill formation. Skills and schools are local, immobile resources. Graduates from regional colleges and technical schools around the world tend to remain in the region. The industrial development role of the regional college or university is

[30] Policymakers in post-war Japan understood its value; particularly the Ministry of Labor who hired United States trainers laid off by the US Government. The Ministry continues to license a range of groups to teach the progam in companies. Toyota has their system; they call it TTWI (Toyota Training Within Industry). In Canon, every single trainer is certified in TWI.

[31] Richard Lipsey points out that skill formation can be turned into a basis for comparative advantage by public policy. He gives the example of Bismarck's education reforms and states: 'Many observers credit the German trade schools, that educate the majority of German youths who do not go on to higher academic education with providing the German comparative advantage in high quality standard consumer goods' (1993: 24–5).

responsive collaboration with industry and government in skill formation targeted to the region's competitive advantage and specific technological capabilities. The investment in skills takes time and strong relationships that cut across educational institutions and business enterprises. The unique technological features of a region's business enterprises can be fostered most successfully by long-term, proximity relationships amongst policymakers, education institutions, and entrepreneurial firms.

CONCLUSION

In this book I have outlined an alternative perspective that starts with a theory of production anchored in organizational principles. The principles are not determined a priori but from close observation of enterprises that have established industrial leadership positions from the early days of industrialization. By thinking of economies in terms of processes involving capability development, or lack thereof, powerful forces driving industrial growth and change come into view. The entrepreneurial firm, for example, is central to understanding capability development. But links between governmental policies and capability development are also brought into focus.

Policymaking for capability development calls for an economics of production to accompany an economics of exchange. The impact on growth of technology management, for example, can be reinforced or undermined by free trade policies. Unfortunately, the potential benefits of free trade are often considered within a policy debate in which production issues are ignored. The resulting policy options are posed in terms of either free trade or protectionism. The question should be 'what are the effects, in particular regional settings, of tariff and exchange rate policies on entrepreneurial firm development or on a region's enterprises seeking to move up the production capabilities spectrum?' The plea here is to examine both trade and protectionism in terms of their impact on capabilities and innovation and to use trade policy as an instrument for fostering productivity-led growth.

This does not make policymaking simple. History suggests that free trade can be a powerful lever to foster local capability development; but it can have entirely the opposite effects. Enterprises that are at the beginning levels in production capabilities need time to develop. But at the same time and with notable exceptions, including early US industrialization, protected industry has a poor track record. This is to be expected from the capabilities and innovation perspective: the entrepreneurial firm shapes a region's productive and technological capabilities in a dynamic process involving market opportunities. Markets are not fixed or static and the idea that production can satisfy a market is to foster production units, often of a rent-seeking character, but not entrepreneurial firms. Protectionism has a second drawback: it cuts firms off from the world's pool of technology. The rapid growth cases of East Asia have been about developing production capabilities to tap this pool.

An important policy implication is that trade policy must be coordinated with production policies. In this chapter a range of production-related policy areas are examined. The primary purpose of industrial policy must be to foster capability development in each of these areas.

CHAPTER

9

The Sustainable Growth Challenge

BEYOND THE GROWTH OR ENVIRONMENT TRADEOFF

Not surprisingly, nearly everyone is for economic growth. Growth is desirable for many reasons. A growing economy is the most powerful employment program any government can enlist. Growth of the American economy in the 1990s has pulled economically and educationally disadvantaged groups into employment as never before in peacetime.[1]

Nevertheless, looming in the background are the fears that growth is not sustainable because it is eroding the natural support systems upon which life depends. Why have we been so slow to embrace the concept of sustainable growth? Part of the reason is the way environmental issues are framed in public debate. The terms of the debate are loaded with an implicit assumption: the pursuit of environmental goals comes at the cost of growth and jobs.

The term 'sustainable growth' is widely used, but its meaning is diffuse. For some, the term is an oxymoron; growth is inherently destructive of the environment. For others, it is about choosing the optimal amount of pollution *given the growth/environment tradeoff*. For them the challenge for government is to first identify the optimal level of pollution and second to 'internalize the externalities' by devising a set

[1] Katharine Bradbury (2000: 6) finds that the gap between black and white male unemployment rates in the United States narrowed by 3.9 percentage points in the 1992 to 1999 years of expansion. The jobless rate for black men declined from 13.6% to 6.9% and for white men from 5.6% to 2.8%.

of taxes and subsidies that would force correspondence between the market outcome and the optimal level.[2]

The growth/environment tradeoff has validity under certain conditions. But conditions have been altered by the refinement in technology management capabilities and the decentralization and diffusion of design in modern production systems. The capabilities and innovation perspective denies the growth/environment tradeoff.[3] The principle of design for sustainability opens up a whole range of opportunities to pursue growth that is simultaneously consistent with preserving the integrity of the environment.

DESIGN FOR SUSTAINABILITY

Design is a means of improving resource productivity. The central idea of design for sustainability is that the way to get more from less is to redesign the process. The concept of sustainable growth is the idea that products, processes, technologies, and organizations can be designed and redesigned according to criteria that account for both competitive advantage and environmental sustainability. The ultimate goal is to design products, materials, and processes according to the criteria of waste free production. Waste is loss from both the revenue stream and environmental ledger. The goal is for all outputs to also be inputs. The concept of production becomes inclusive of environmental waste.

The engineering challenge of design for sustainability is for all products to ultimately be constituted by molecules that are either compostable or recyclable.[4] In this way the earth's waste absorption capacity and its stock of natural resources would not be reduced. Economic

[2] The beneficiaries of the services of power plants do not recompense the payers of the 'external' costs of pollution. The concept of internalizing the externalities implies that policymakers devise a tax and subsidy system that brings such external costs and benefits into the market calculations. The problem has been that the government has no easy way of either measuring externalities (many of which may impact far away places and future generations) or of implementing environmental tax and subsidy measures. This is in part because many externalities are part of highly complex processes that are dimly understood and the effects of which may be unknown, long-term, and interactive (Best and Connolly 1975).

[3] The environment and growth tradeoff is analogous to the unemployment and inflation tradeoff dictated by 'the natural rate of unemployment', a concept that once guided money supply management in America and Great Britain. Both are based upon a model of the economy in which price is the only adjustment mechanism. The capabilities and innovation perspective focuses on the role design can play as an adjustment mechanism.

[4] The analogous ideal in neoclassical economics is to devise a tax and subsidy program that 'internalizes the externalities' and thereby fosters optimal allocation of resources.

growth and environmental sustainability would be mutually achievable goals. They would be features of a single process.

The idea of design for waste reduction is not new to production. Canon, for example, defines its 'fundamental improvement system' in terms of the elimination of nine types of waste (Japan Management Association 1987: 17).[5] Waste is broadly defined as any factor in operations that does not add value. But the definition of waste has been slow to include the costs of depleting the earth's capacity for absorbing pollutants. Fortunately, advances in production and organizational capabilities have created new opportunities for public policy to address the challenge of sustainable growth.

For example, advances in production capabilities have converted the concept of technology management into an ongoing process. Technology management as public policy can become a powerful tool for targeting R&D to achieve advances in environmental sustainability. The examination of technology trajectories in previous chapters highlights the importance of public policy in shaping technology and product possibilities. It is a powerful lever for an economics of sustainable growth.

TECHNOLOGY DESIGN

The cumulative character of technological development in firms, regions, and nations suggests that many technological futures are possible. Government policies, including R&D funding, have been critically important in shaping technology choices (T. Hughes 1989, 1998). Corporate power has played important roles in shaping transportation and energy systems in particular (Snell 1974; Commoner 1979).

The success of Sematech in promoting technological change to revitalize an industry suggests the role that policymaking could play to anticipate and foster technology transitions for the purpose of environmentally sustainable growth. Sponsoring innovation in raw materials for the plastics industry is an example.

[5] Canon's nine types of waste are: waste caused by work-in-progress, waste caused by defects, waste in equipment, waste in expenses, waste in indirect labor, waste in planning, waste in human resources, waste in operations, and waste in start-up (Japan Management Association 1987: 17–18). Eight forms of waste identified by Toyota and Henry Ford are included in the throughput efficiency analysis of Appendix 2.1 above.

Biodegradable Polymers

The first plastics were made from agricultural materials. But petrochemical feedstocks offered improved material properties at lower private costs. However, the durability of petrochemical-based plastics has since become a liability as costs for landfill sites mount. Whereas biodegradable plastics can be broken down in a compost heap, petrochemical-based plastics create a waste problem that in some cases may persist for thousands of years. Consequently, adding the previously displaced or 'external' costs of clean-up to the private costs has created an incentive to return to biodegradable materials.

Following the logic of the quality movement, the idea is that it is cheaper in the long run to design products that are environmentally friendly rather than clean up after pollution has occurred. The critical feature of biodegradable polymers is that they are digestible by microorganisms after use. This fits the sustainability rule: the outputs of one process are the inputs to another.

The companies and regions that lead in the development of the new technologies will gain an immediate competitive advantage with considerable growth potential given the penetration of plastics into virtually every branch of industry. Seeing the opportunity, many of America's leading materials companies have been collaborating in the development of biodegradable plastics at the National Science Foundation Biodegradable Polymer Center at the University of Massachusetts Lowell. Participants are shown in the left of Figure 9.1.

Out of a $0.5 million annual budget, the government contributes only $50,000. The Center illustrates the theme of systems integration in research. The principle researchers combine the disciplines of chemistry, biology, chemical engineering, and soil science. Using University labs, new materials are synthesized in conjunction with research both on manufacturability in terms of a range of plastics processing technologies and on a range of experiments assessing the degradation characteristics.

Research universities are a critical resource in anticipating technology transitions. Companies like 3M and BASF with R&D research budgets exceeding $1 billion collaborate on R&D in the Center to get in on the ground floor of research in a new material or technology. Company representatives make up an Industrial Advisory Board that meets twice annually to review completed research and shape faculty and student proposals for future research projects. The University holds

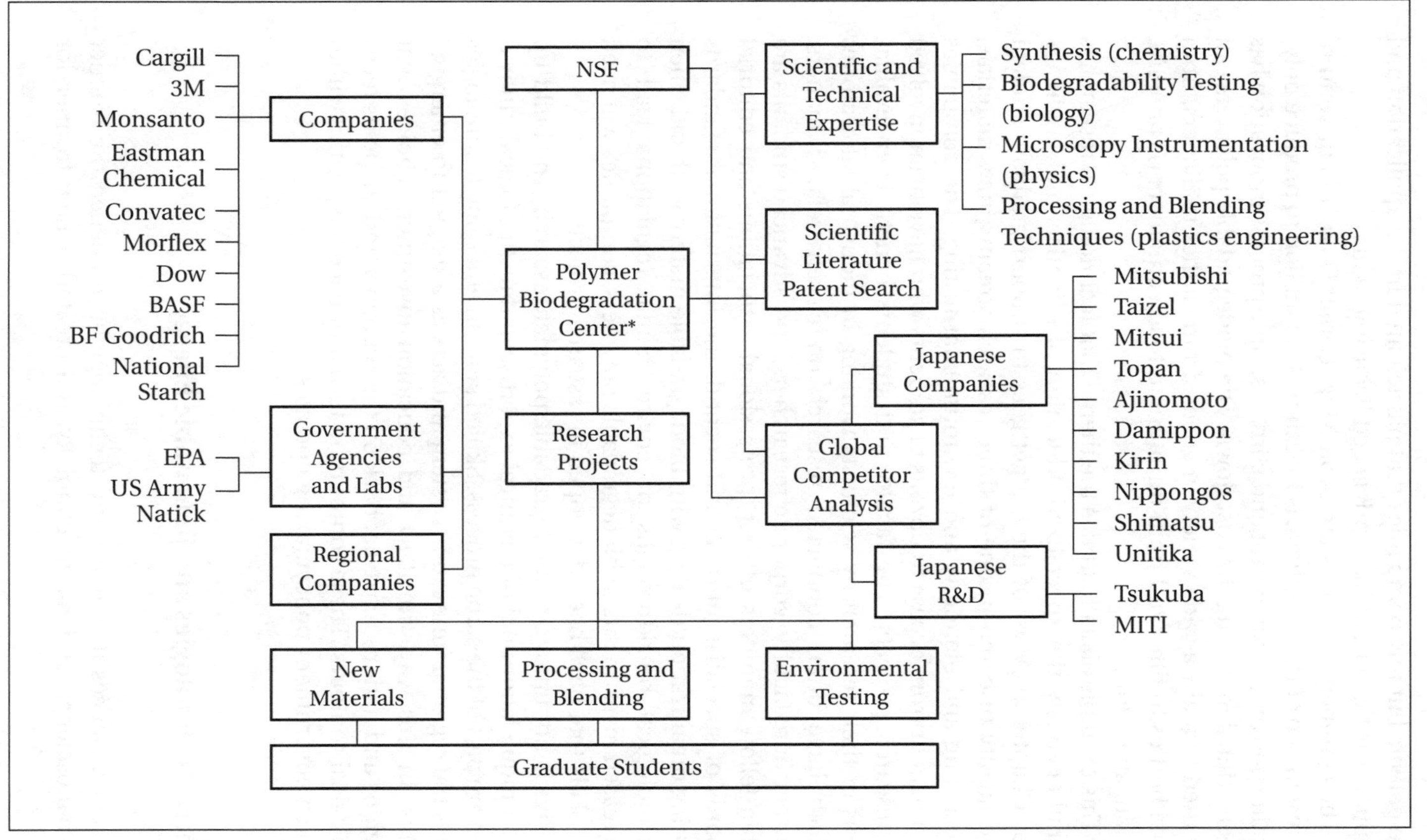

Fig. 9.1. Biodegradable Polymer Research Center

* A National Science Foundation Industry/University Cooperative Research Center at the University of Massachusetts Lowell

the patents but any companies that participated in the application and support for the patent have privileged licensing rights.

The commercial results are promising. Cargill Dow, a joint venture between two of the members, is investing $300 million to produce polylactide polymers from wheat and corn. A simple process innovation has been critical to driving the cost down. The biodegradable polymers can be used to make a wide variety of goods, from clothes to diapers, from soda bottles to film, and from furniture to food containers (*Economist*, 15 Jan. 2000: 101).

This example also illustrates the theme that technological research is simultaneously the specialized education of scientists and engineers (see Chapter 4). Most of the budget goes to support graduate student and faculty research in one of three research streams: new materials, processing and blending, and environmental testing. The companies also benefit from access to dozens of students who have been involved in research projects. The faculty and students benefit from evaluations of their research by scientists working in industrial laboratories which have often conducted research on closely related matters. Furthermore faculty, corporate researchers, and advanced students are often fellow members of first, professional associations and editorial boards of specialist journals and second, the international standards setting organization dealing with biodegradable materials. If and when technological breakthroughs or environmental regulations lead to increased investments in biodegradable polymers, companies will need the skills that have been developed in research projects.

This is not unique to biodegradable polymer research. The build-up of a unique labor pool of technical expertise and technological innovation are part of the same process. Skilled labor in emerging technologies fuels the regional innovation system and acts as a magnet to emerging firms. In this way, the R&D and education investment choices that regions and nations make act back on the economy and shape its technological contours. These contours, in turn influence the politics within which government policymaking operates.

Micro Technologies and Renewable Energy

Recent advances in science and technology have opened the frontier of nanoscience and nanotechnology and created a new frontier for advanced material research and design. The transition from micro to nano size dimensions is to move to billionths of a meter or to the size dimension at which nature constructs. This creates opportunities to mimic biological design principles using biodegradable materials.

A particular area in which scientific and technological advances are moving fast is renewable energy. This is in part because of the technological overlap of telecommunications and the electric power industry. Historically, telecommunications sent electrons down lines for the purpose of delivering messages; electric power generators sent electrons down lines to run electrical devices. Both industries are in the throes of technology platform shifts linked to the transition to nanoscopic materials and optoelectronics or photonics. While the Internet and optoelectronics have engendered a rapid decentralization of the telecommunications industry, scientific and technological advances in micro turbines, fuel cells, and photovoltaics are promising a corresponding new age of decentralized power production.

For both industries a technological roadmap analogous to that provided by Moore's Law in the semiconductor and personal computer industries is emerging (see Figure 5.2). No one can know which specific technologies and product applications will become the standards, but the trajectory is toward ever-smaller light generating/conducting and power generating systems.

Benefiting from advances in light emitting polymers, conversion efficiencies in converting rays from the sun into energy by photovoltaic materials are being improved. The application of the continuous flow production methods to produce multi-layered rolls of plastic photovoltaic sheets could drive down the costs for generating electricity much as mass production has done in other industries.

Similar technological advances are occurring across a range of micro-energy generating technologies including micro-turbines and fuel cells. All of these offer design for sustainability opportunities. The breakthrough innovations may be distributed around many different regions. But only those regions that integrate R&D with production will be able to establish cluster dynamics in rapidly growing product areas with ongoing spin-off applications.

MANUFACTURING DESIGN FOR ENERGY EFFICIENCY

The idea of designing quality into the process was a prelude to a broader concept of design for manufacturability (see Table 2.1 and Box 2.2). The idea is simple and powerful. It states that product designers must simultaneously account for manufacturability and seek to minimize waste and simplify production activities and processes for a given product.[6] It is a tool for designing quality into the process of production. It integrates engineering design, production operations, and quality improvement activities.

The logic of the concept of design for manufacturability led to the integration of previously separate activities into a single process both inside and outside the firm. Success within a company demanded that design for manufacturability be extended along the supplier chain. Nevertheless the production pipeline did not extend beyond the supply chain or into the cellular structure of materials. Thus, while design for manufacturability was not designed to address environmental principles such as recyclability, it offers a methodology for doing so.

An area in which design for manufacturability can be applied that enhances both competitiveness and sustainability is energy usage. Too often, manufacturers and industrial policymakers see energy simply as a cost of production and driver of inflation; the alternative is to see improvements in energy efficiency as a means of advancing manufacturing capabilities and product performance.[7] The question becomes, how can product, technology, process and production methods be redefined to improve energy efficiency? Examples of each follow.

Product Innovation

The Japanese use the term 'mechatronics' to capture the fusion between mechanical and electronic technologies and have used it to great effect

[6] NCR corporation, for example, used design for manufacturability teams to redesign their 2760 electronic cash register. They advertise that an engineer can put it together blindfolded because they reduced the number of parts by 85%, the number of suppliers by 65, and the time to assemble by 25%. The cash register consists of only fifteen vendor-produced components (Heizer and Render 1996: 216).

[7] Industrialists that realized the indirect, organizational advancing effects of unit electric drives gained far more than reduced costs of energy from the new power source. See the example of Ford in Ch. 2, above.

in improving manufacturing competitiveness across a range of industries (see Kodama 1986). Stalk and Hout's (1990: 110–14) description of the takeover of the 3-horsepower heat pump market by the Mitsubishi Electric Company illustrates how moving from mechanical manufacturing processes to mechatronics can promote both product innovation and efficiency in electric energy usage. In nearly every year between 1976 and 1988, the Mitsubishi Electric Company introduced a process and/or product innovation that enabled them dramatically to improve competitiveness and the energy efficiency ratio (EER). The EER increased from 7.4 BTU/Whr in 1976 to a range of 8–14 BTU/Whr (depending on the features) by 1988.

The list of innovations required to drive the improvement in the EER is extensive and illustrates the technology/market dynamic of the entrepreneurial firm: in 1980 Mitsubishi introduced integrated circuits to control the heat pump cycle; in 1981 microprocessors were added along with 'quick-connect' freon lines; in 1982 a high-efficiency, rotary compressor replaced the reciprocating compressor; in 1983 sensors and more computing power were added to enhance the electronic controls; in 1984 an inverter was introduced which enabled a dramatic increase in energy efficiency of electric appliances by allowing 'almost infinite control' over the speed of the electric motor; in 1985 shape metal alloys were added to control the air louvres; in 1986 optic sensors were introduced; in 1987 a remote personal controller was developed; in 1988 learning circuitry was added which enables the heat pump to adapt to the unique environment of each customer; and in 1989 electronic air purifier options were added. Not surprisingly, by 1990 Mitsubishi's 3-HP heat pump had taken over the American market and the former market leading American company had shifted from production of its own product to distribution of Mitsubishi heat pumps (Stalk and Hout 1990: 114).

The example of the heat pump illustrates how a manufacturer can turn the challenge of high energy cost or the requirement for environmental improvement into an opportunity. It was made possible, however, because the company had developed the organizational capabilities of rapid new product development and short production cycle times. These organizational innovations were, in part, a response to a scarcity of resources, both material and energy.[8]

[8] Engineering capabilities are crucial to redesigning material transformation processes; at the same time, innovations in one application can be adapted by technically alert companies because of the limited number of technologically distinct processes. In fact, the number of ways

Technology Substitution

Steel making is a paradigm case in technology innovations that reduce energy intensity. The use of scrap in electric arc furnace processes in the United States has reduced energy consumption by 50 percent compared to traditional basic oxygen furnace processes. Continuous casting, by reducing cooling and reheat cycles, was another seminal innovation in improving energy productivity. But recently the development of thin-slab casting has opened steel's largest market—the sheets used in cars and containers—to the minimills. The energy cost is cut in half at casting/rolling stage between a minisheet plant and a highly efficient integrated plant (Schorsch 1996: 47).

Steel is an example of how shifting technologies can yield dramatic improvements in energy efficiency. Cost-effective energy savings of 20–40 percent are identified for five major energy-intensive sectors by moving to state-of-the-art technologies, in a World Energy Council study titled *Energy Efficiency Improvement Utilizing High Technology* (1995).

While these examples apply to energy-intensive sectors, the potential for similar savings exist for virtually any northern industry by moving to combined heat and power (CHP) technologies. CHP commonly achieve dramatic advances in energy productivity. This is because centralized power plants suffer two-thirds energy loss in the electricity conversion process to heat.[9] For this reason, centralized electricity generation is a major contributor to global warming.

Process Innovation

Why are the Japanese leaders in the introduction of state-of-the-art technologies in energy efficiency? Part of the answer is that high energy

by which electricity transforms materials is three: electromotive, electrothermal, and electrolytic. The electric motor, an *electromotive* phenomenon, accounts for roughly 75% of the electricity consumed in industry. Bulk processing industries (e.g. chemical, paper, primary metal, petroleum) involve *electrothermal* phenomena to produce heat which, in turn, facilitate a physical or chemical change. Chemical changes at the atomic level such as the production of chemical compounds like chlorine use *electrolysis* (examples from Gellings 1994). Developing a regional capability for rapid diffusion of innovations and adaptations across a range of manufacturing enterprises is a feature of rapidly growing regions.

[9] A Department of Energy electricity flow diagram illustrating the 'efficiency' of energy conversion for the United States is reproduced in Best (1997*b*: 92).

costs fostered innovation (Porter and van der Linde 1995). But price differences are only part of the story.

While the Japanese have always focused more on minimizing energy use than have American manufacturers, because of higher costs of energy, their unique approach to manufacturing management, and thereby energy reduction, has been an organizational emphasis on process or system (Deming 1982). Improved energy efficiency ratios have been a by-product of the management philosophy that defines an organization in terms of processes rather than functional departments. Process-oriented organizations set performance standards in terms of advancing flow across specialist activities; functionally departmentalized organizations evaluate performance in terms of department targets.

The distinguishing feature of the quality movement was to design quality into the process, not inspect it in afterwards; the drive to minimize waste was associated with cellular manufacturing which is itself an application of process or flow analysis. The consequence was a holistic business organization that dealt simultaneously with productivity *via* improved flow, quality improvement and energy efficiency. The management innovations that emerged in such organizations included total quality management and continuous improvement that, in turn, fostered a dynamic between process improvement and technical innovation. The example of Mitsubishi and the heat pump is about the application of mechatronics, but it occurred within an organization that focused on process integration, a hallmark of the capabilities and innovation perspective.

This has important implications for a program to improve energy efficiency. If the driver of such a program is cost reduction, it is not likely to be successful. Much of manufacturing industry has electricity costs of no more than 2 or 3 percent of total costs. Eliminating such costs entirely may not improve competitiveness significantly. Furthermore, in many cases, companies that are not organized or seeking to organize in terms of process as distinct from functional departments and local optimization will not have the organizational capability to address the single greatest source of energy efficiency improvement. But it also means that concern over energy efficiency can be a vehicle for addressing and advancing manufacturing competitiveness.

Just as the case of the quality movement, which focused on the elimination of waste, the goal of improved energy efficiency *via* the process of energy reduction simultaneously contributes to productivity advance and cost reduction, but by greater amounts than simply subtracting the defects or diminished energy charges. Building the goals of improved quality and energy efficiency into the day to day activities of everyone in the organization contributed to improved productivity by improving flow and creating targets for innovation.

The focus on process represents a breakthrough in thinking about energy efficiency in industry, just as designing quality into the process was central to the quality movement. In addition, process analysis is about applying the principle of flow, the fundamental principle of production that lies behind both Ford's single-product flow at the Highland Park plant and Toyota's multi-product flow or just-in-time system of production. Deming's (1982) 'theory of the system' is an application of process analysis to quality which revolutionized management thinking and practice. It provided a problem-solving management paradigm based on involvement of the workforce in improving flow via the elimination of defects.

The idea of process energy reduction is an application and extension of process waste reduction. Each represents a different form of waste: defects and energy. In the new management paradigm, increased competitiveness comes from achieving more comprehensive performance standards: increased productivity (measured in flow corollaries such as cycle time for production, new product development, design to manufacture, and technology diffusion rates), improved quality, and product performance. Tackling energy efficiency is part of the same production management system.

In sum, best practice manufacturing enterprises have developed the organizational capabilities to pursue a competitive strategy of rapid new product development, a management system informed by process flow analysis and driven by continuous improvement. This enables them to drive down the cycle time of the new product design to manufacture process. This capability, in turn, has revolutionized technology management in manufacturing: each time that a new product is introduced is also an opportunity to introduce new technologies.

CONCLUSION: SUSTAINABILITY AND THE RED QUEEN EFFECT

The potential for technology, process, and product design to address the environmental challenge has been outside the debate within economics. This is understandable because technology and production have not been central to the resource allocation concerns of neoclassical economics. The slow pace of technological change in many industries did not focus attention on the subject. Furthermore, technological innovation has historically been conducted either by independent inventors or within corporation and governmental funded laboratories. It was not endogenous to the 'economy' in the sense of an ongoing activity built into the primary economic institutions.

But advances in production capabilities have integrated processes of technology management into production systems across much of the economy. Regional innovation systems have replaced centralized laboratories, separated from production. With the advance in production capabilities, the pace of technological change has quickened.

To think about technological change and growth from an environmentally sustainable perspective suggests we become something like the Red Queen in Lewis Carroll's *Through the Looking-Glass* who had to keep running to stay in the same place. A new 'Red Queen' theory of biology holds that evolution is not about progress but about change in order to survive (Ridley 1993). The theme is that humans are in a perpetual struggle against parasites within our bodies and that success depends upon continuously altering our molecular structure. We do this through sex which enables us collectively to recombine our genetic makeup every generation. Sex, then, is a weapon against disease that enables us to change not by progressing ahead but by not falling behind.

If the ecological threats are as serious as many hold, economic institutions could be hard pressed to sustain performance. The economics of sustainability will likely demand instituting processes that can drive a rapid pace of technological change to compensate for environmental imperatives. The challenge will be to deliver the same amount of services to an ever-higher proportion of the planet's inhabitants but from an ever-smaller amount of natural resource inputs. This will involve a rapid pace of technological and organizational change. It will be like running hard to stay in the same place.

The challenges facing technologically rich and poor countries are different but interrelated. Technology-following countries must institute processes that foster growth at the local level. Technology-leading regions are better positioned to shape future technology trajectories. These regions have the research capability and the responsibility of technology leadership to institute processes that foster environmentally sustainable growth even as products become universally accessible. The fundamental challenge of environmentally sustainable energy and production systems has yet to be confronted.

This need not be so. Because of technological and scientific advances the opportunities have never been greater for addressing the environmental challenge. Furthermore, technologies developed in the technology-leading regions become opportunities for establishing new growth dynamics in low productivity regions as well. For example, advances in 'micro-power', clean energy technologies can foster enterprise development with an array of production applications in regions without existing centralized power systems.[10]

My claim is not that the capabilities and innovation perspective is, as yet, an economics of sustainable growth. But by elucidating growth processes from a production perspective, it has established a conceptual framework for engaging the issues in fruitful ways. Critics will point out that the arguments are sketchy and at an early stage of development. They will be right. But this does not obviate the urgency of the need for an economics of sustainable growth. I can only hope that others will see merit in the approach and join in an effort to address a challenge that has been ignored too long.

[10] Micro-power technologies include photovoltaic systems, fuel cells, wind farms, and small-scale turbines. Henry Ford redesigned production to exploit the opportunity offered by distributed power *consumption* within production (see Ch. 2). The opportunities to redesign products and processes to capture the benefits of distributed power *generation* are equally significant in terms of growth potential.

GLOSSARY

Adam Smith's fundamental principle of increasing specialization A process of increasing specialization and division of labor creates wealth, for Smith. Specialization involves the decomposition of the commodity into an ever-greater number of constituent activities; each activity, in turn, is targeted for a refinement in skills and technique. Every increase in the extent of the market increases the number of activities that are subject to 'new improvements of art'.

batch production high inventory systems A multi-product plant without flexible production methods. High changeover costs leads to long runs or large batch sizes and high work in process inventories. Often confused with mass production which has batch sizes of a single unit and virtually zero work in process inventories (see 'economic order quantity', Best 1990: 151).

benchmark analysis The identification of performance gaps between the practices and processes of a plant or business and best practice. Involves studying best-practice or world-class standards.

Big Business A series of organizational innovations associated with the substitution of the visible hand of managerial hierarchy for the invisible hand of market coordination of economic activities (see Chandler 1977; Best 1990: 47–51).

bottom-up entrepreneurial activities Self-directed work teams can communicate directly with the customer and thereby decentralize the production capability and market opportunity dynamic.

Canon production system Used as an example of the extension of the principle of flow from driving down production cycle times to driving down new product development plus production cycle times (PS 4 in Table 2.1).

capabilities and innovation perspective (CIP) In contrast to the efficient resource allocation perspective, CIP focuses on resource creation defined in terms of production and organizational capabilities. This creates a framework for integrating technology and innovation into growth processes.

cellular manufacturing methods Involves co-locating the full range of machining activities required to make a part in a U-shaped configuration. It is a plant layout designed for multi-product, low inventory production. It complements self-directed work teams and requires multi-skilled workers.

cluster growth dynamics Combines the idea of cluster as networked group of firms and support institutions with growth dynamics internal to the firm as shown in Figure 3.1.

CNC machine tools Stands for computer numerically controlled machine tools. Computer controls, rather than the traditional skills of the machinist, guide the machining.

concurrent engineering The product and the production process are designed together.

design/manufacturing cycle time The time it takes to convert a new product design into a scaled-up plant capable of producing at competitive cost and quality standards.

design modularization The design of sub-systems is independent of the system but, at the same time, enhances the flexibility of the overall system. An independently designed machine, for example, in a multi-machine production line that can communicate in the same instruction language as the other machines in the line.

dip-down innovation As opposed to the science-push model of innovation, the idea is that companies seek to 'dip-down' for basic research needs. They seek partnerships with research laboratories to address technological challenges that arise as they advance their core technological capabilities.

disruptive innovation In contrast to incremental innovation, a disruptive innovation changes the technology and the product architecture.

dynamic dialectic A term used by Andrew Grove of Intel to describe a business model organized to combine recurrent phases of bottom-up experimentation and top-down direction.

entrepreneurial firm The growth driver in the capabilities and innovation perspective. The idea of the entrepreneurial firm as an extension of the entrepreneurial function from an individual attribute to a collective or organizational capability is developed in Best 1990.

externally integrated enterprises Productive units coordinated with 'closed system' inter-regional networks or value chains directed by global enterprises.

fractionated electric power With the invention of electricity, it became possible to decentralize the source of power within a plant. This meant that machines could be independently powered; power was said to be distributed or 'fractionated'.

functionally departmentalized organization A business or plant organizational design in which all like activities are grouped by function and separated from other functional groups. Batch production methods tend to be organized by machining function, such as milling, turning, grinding, etc.

group technology Plant organization in which machines are laid out in separate cells, each organized for a 'family' of parts or products involving similarity of sequential machining patterns.

high-performance work systems (HPWSs) These involve work settings in which workers experience greater autonomy over their job tasks and production methods, greater opportunity to upgrade their skills, participate in integrating design and manufacturing, and enjoy incentive pay schemes linked to system performance.

horizontal integration or value networks As distinguished from vertical integration or market coordination across companies, value networks involve partnering for complementary capabilities.

industrial district model Alfred Marshall noticed that firms in a similar industry tended to concentrate geographically (e.g. cutlery in Sheffield).

industrial 'speciation' The emergence of new industry sub-sectors accompanying technological specialization and diversification. Data storage systems, for example, have emerged as a new industrial sector following technological advances in the computer industry.

initial public offering (IPO) A company's shares are offered, for the first time, on a stock market.

interchangeability The production of complete machines or products with methods by which the corresponding parts are so nearly alike that they fit any of the machines or products. It involves breaking down parts into their simplest activities and designing specialist machines for each activity. Distinguished from craft methods in which a craftsman makes each part and hand-fits it into the product (see Best 1990: ch. 2).

kaisha Japanese variant of the entrepreneurial firm which decentralizes design and builds continuous change into the operating units. This business model fostered the principle of multi-product flow and achieved cheaper, better, faster performance standards that established the New Competition for high-volume production. See PS 2–4 in Table 2.1.

kaizen Continuous improvement work system.

kaizen tiean A system for eliciting commitment from every worker to contribute to ongoing improvement.

kanban The visual coordination of work activities within companies and along supply chains.

keiretsu Closed system, long-term, inter-firm relations based on shared network norms.

law of diminishing size The long-term tendency for technological advance to reduce the critical size dimension in manufacturing. Also referred to as the tendency to increasing precision. See Figure 5.2.

liquidity trap No amount of increase in the money supply can stimulate demand and growth without a simultaneous improvement in expectations of future growth.

Massachusetts' Route 128/495 A high-tech region of the United States, America's first high-tech industrial district. Route 128 is a circular road around Boston; 495 is a circular road further removed from Boston.

Moore's Law Computer power doubles every 18 months along with the number of transistors on a single microprocessor chip. Size diminishes inversely.

multi-product flow The production of multiple products on the same production line or manufacturing cell without building inventory. This requires quick changeovers from product to product.

nanotechnology Nano- refers to size dimensions of a billionth of a meter, nanotechnology to building things on that scale.

open systems networking Firms focus on core capabilities and use networks for complementary capabilities. This involves horizontal or multi-enterprise integration as distinct from vertical integration.

plan-do-check-act (PDCA) A methodology developed in Japan to diffuse total quality management.

price-led competition Firms do not organize themselves to introduce new products systematically. Instead, they compete by lower costs for a given product.

principle of flow Organizing production activities to achieve throughput efficiency. It means equalizing the cycle times for all parts required to assemble a product. Otherwise, bottlenecks will occur for longer cycle time products and the longest cycle time activity will determine the pace of production for the whole plant.

process integration A corollary to the principle of flow. Popularly referred to as lean production and re-engineering, it involves sequencing production activities according to the logic of the product not the machining function.

production capabilities See production capabilities spectrum (Table 2.2). Examples:

- *precision machining* based on the principle of interchangeability
- *mass production* based on the principle of flow (synchronization)
- *JIT or lean production* based on the principle of multi-product flow and cellular manufacturing
- *new product development* based on an extension of the principle of flow from production to integration of design and production
- *technology fusion* based on the principle of systems integration
- *incremental innovation* (a.k.a. continuous improvement, *kaizen*, TQM)

production system Regional economic success depends, in part, on the production system that has been developed in the region. See Table 2.1 and Figure 5.3.

productivity growth Economic growth can be broken down into productivity growth and labor supply growth. The second is growth generated by increases in the number of people in work. Productivity growth is the result of advances in production capabilities and is manifest in increases in output per hour worked. Productivity growth may or may not involve increases in capital equipment; it will virtually always involve capability development and complementary technological advance.

Productivity Triad Captures the systemic character of breakthrough advances in productivity at enterprise and regional levels. The three domains of production system, business model, and skill formation are not separable and additive components but interconnected sub-systems. The overlapping domains of the Productivity Triad as shown in Figure 1.1 visually expresses their interconnectedness.

product-led competition Production is organized to be able to produce multiple products without declines in cost and quality standards and to be able to introduce new product designs without disrupting production.

regional growth dynamics model A circular flow diagram encompassing the processes of techno-specialization, techno-diversification, techno-integration, techno-standardization, and industrial speciation (see Figure 3.1).

regional production system capability Extends the continuity of technology capability from the firm to the region. Examples: precision machining, mass production, flexible mass production, design-led industrial districts (flexible specialization), complex product systems. Anchored in specialized and unique application of one or more principles of production and organization.

scientific management Work design based on presumption of a single best method that can be discovered by engineers and for which incentives can be devised to maximize work effort. Productivity is seen as dependent upon work time rather than material flow time. It fosters local optimization (see Best 1990: 55–8).

self-directed work team (SDWT) As opposed to supervisor-centered work team, the SDWT internalizes otherwise managerial functions and thereby economizes on 'indirect' labor costs.

six sigma quality system A quality management methodology developed at Motorola and based on the goal of reducing defects to less than 34 per million chances. It has since been taken up by many leading US companies.

speciation A metaphor borrowed from botany to refer to innovation that emanates from new combinations of technologies that lead to new product applications and industrial classification categories. Furniture, for example, becomes interior design and furnishing.

systems integration The third fundamental principle of production and organization. Operates at the technical and organizational levels. It means the organizational capability to redesign production to exploit design changes in sub-systems in ways that take advantage of interactive effects.

Taylorist *see* **scientific management**

technology The processes by which enterprises transform resources and purchased inputs into outputs. Technologies have both physical and organizational dimensions. All firms have technologies.

technology domain Examples: mechanical, electrical, electronic, photonic, genome, nanotechology. Anchored in scientific disciplines.

technology (engineering) methodology Technology domains, trajectories, and capabilities are converted to regional growth by complementary education processes that scale up the requisite skill base. The engineering curriculum is developed and diffused in partnership with technology/market dynamics of firms.

technology management capability The capability to develop and introduce new technologies, machines, materials, techniques, and methods into production to improve performance. Technology management is not about *optimizing* technological change but about *synchronizing* the three elements of the Productivity Triad around more advanced production principles to institute a process of sustained technological change. See the five models of production systems and technology management in Table 2.1.

technology/market dynamic An abbreviated version of Penrose's productive capability/market opportunity dynamic.

technology (specific) capability Continuity and change of specific technologies. Examples: turbine technology from waterpower to jet engine to power generation.

technology trajectory The never completed aspect of technology. Example: 'Moore's Law' (*v.s.)* predicts doubling in transistors per chip every 18 months.

Special case of the tendency of increasing precision (see also **law of diminishing size**).

'third Italy' Refers to the north central region of Italy that enjoys high per capita income but few large firms. The region enjoys competitive advantage in design-led and fashion industries.

total quality management (TQM) A management philosophy that involves everyone in the design as well as in the execution of work. Quality is designed into the work process rather than being inspected in after the defects have occurred.

unit-drive electricity Each machine has its own source of power.

upas tree effect 'The upas tree of Java (Antiaris Toxicaria), entering European legend through Erasmus Darwin, was believed to have the power to destroy other growths for a radius of fifteen miles. Here it is taken as a symbol of the heavy industries that so long dominated the economy and society of Glasgow' (Checkland 1981: p. i).

vertical integration Involves the internalization of production activities within a single company and coordination by the managerial hierarchy rather than by the market or by networks.

REFERENCES

Abbate, J. (1999). *Inventing the Internet.* Cambridge, Mass.: MIT Press.

Abegglen, J., and Stalk, G. (1985). *Kaisha: The Japanese Corporation.* New York: Basic Books.

Abramovitz, M. (1956). 'Resource and Output Trends in the United States Since 1870'. *American Economic Review,* 46/2 (May).

—— (1993). 'The Search for Sources of Growth: Areas of Ignorance, Old and New'. *Journal of Economic History,* 53 (June).

Adams, D. (1989). *The More Than Complete Hitchhiker's Guide.* New York: Wings Books.

Akamatsu, K. (1962). 'Historical Pattern of Economic Growth in Developing Countries'. *The Developing Economies,* Institute of Asian Economic Affairs, 1/1: 3–25.

Almeida, B. (1999). 'Jet Engine Manufacturing in New England: Regional Roots and Recent Restructuring'. Working Paper, Center for Industrial Competitiveness, University of Massachusetts Lowell.

Appelbaum, E., Bailey, T., Berg, P., and Kalleberg, A. (2000). *Manufacturing Advantage: Why High Performance Work Systems Pay Off.* Ithaca, NY: Cornell University Press.

Arthur, W. (1986). *Increasing Returns and Path Dependence in the Economy.* Ann Arbor: University of Michigan Press.

Balasubramanyam, V. N., and Balasubramanyam, A. (2000). 'The Software Cluster in Bangalore', in J. Dunning (ed.), *Regions, Globalization and the Knowledge Based Economy.* Oxford: Oxford University Press.

Bardon, J., and Burnett, D. (1996). *Belfast: A Pocket History.* Belfast: Blackstaff Press.

Beatty, E. (1997). 'Some Examples of Best Practice in University-Industry Collaboration'. Belfast: Queen's University.

Becattini, G. (1978). 'The Development of Light Industry in Tuscany: An Interpretation'. *Economic Notes,* 2–3: 107–23.

Bell, M., and Hobday, M., with inputs from Singh, P., Abdullah, S. H., and Ariffin, N. (1995). 'Aiming for 2020: A Demand-Driven Perspective on Industrial Technology Policy in Malaysia', in *Technology Development for*

Innovation: Towards Malaysia's Vision 2020. World Bank/UNDP Report. Kuala Lumpur.

Best, M. (1982). 'The Political Economy of Socially Irrational Products'. *Cambridge Journal of Economics*, 6/1: 53–64.

—— (1990). *The New Competition*. Cambridge, Mass.: Harvard University Press.

—— (1992). 'Restructuring the Wood Processing Industry of Honduras'. Vienna: United Nations Industrial Development Organization.

—— (1993). 'A Report on Konles: A Consortium of Slovenian Wood Processing Firms'. Working Paper, Center for Industrial Competitiveness, University of Massachusetts Lowell.

—— (1994). 'Plastics in Massachusetts with Special Emphasis on the Merrimack Valley'. Report to the Merrimack Valley Manufacturing Partnership, Lowell, Mass. and Working Paper, Center for Industrial Competitiveness, University of Massachusetts Lowell.

—— (1995). *Competitive Dynamics and Industrial Modernisation Programmes: Lessons from Japan and America*. Annual Sir Charles Carter Lecture. Belfast: Northern Ireland Economic Council.

—— (1997*a*). 'Electronics Expansion in Malaysia: The Challenge of a Stalled Industrial Expansion'. *IKMAS Working Papers*, Institute of Malaysian and International Studies, Universiti Kebangsaan Malaysia, No. 11.

—— (1997*b*). *Power to Compete: A Study of the Electric Power Industry and Industrial Competitiveness in America and New England*. Lowell: Center for Industrial Competitiveness, University of Massachusetts Lowell.

—— (1998). 'Production Principles, Organizational Capabilities and Technology Management', in J. Michie and J. Grieve Smith (eds.), *Globalization, Growth, and Governance*. Oxford: Oxford University Press.

—— (1999). 'Regional Growth Dynamics: A Capabilities Perspective'. *Contributions to Political Economy*, 18: 125–40.

—— and Connolly, W. (1975). 'Market Images and Corporate Power: Beyond the "Economics of Environmental Management"', in K. Dolbeare (ed.), *Public Policy Evaluation*, Vol. II of *The Yearbook in Politics and Public Policy*: 41–74.

—— —— (1976, 1st edn.; 1982, 2nd edn.). *The Politicized Economy*. Lexington, Mass.: D. C. Heath.

—— and Forrant, R. (1994). 'Production in Jamaica: Transforming Industrial Enterprises', in P. Lewis (ed.), *Preparing for the Twenty-First Century: Jamaica 30th Anniversary Symposium*. Kingston, Jamaica: Ian Randle Publishers.

—— —— (1996*a*).'Community-Based Careers and Economic Virtue: Arming, Disarming, and Rearming the Springfield Armory', in M. Arthur and D. Rousseau (eds.), *The Boundaryless Career*. Oxford: Oxford University Press.

—— —— (1996*b*). 'Creating Industrial Capacity: Pentagon-Led Versus Production-Led Industrial Policies', in J. Michie and J. Grieve Smith (eds.), *Restoring Full Employment*. Oxford: Oxford University Press.

—— —— (2000). 'Regional Industrial Policies: Two Cases from Massachusetts'. *European Planning Studies*, 8/2.

Best, M., and Forrant, R. (*cont.*) and Martucci, D. (1995). 'Defense Conversion Progress: An Industry Survey'. Report to the Office of Defense Adjustment Strategy and the Massachusetts Office of Business Development, Center for Industrial Competitiveness, University of Massachusetts Lowell.

—— and Garnsey, E. (1999). 'Edith Penrose, 1914–1996'. *Economic Journal,* 109 (Feb.).

—— and Humphries, J. (1986). 'The "City" and Industrial Decline', in B. Elbaum and W. Lazonick (eds.), *The Decline of the British Economy.* Oxford: Oxford University Press.

—— and Rasiah, R. (forthcoming). *Industrial Transition in the Malaysian Electronics Industry.* Vienna: United Nations Industrial Development Organization.

Billington, D. (1983). *The Tower and the Bridge: The New Art of Structural Engineering.* Princeton: Princeton University Press.

Bizjak, F., and Petrin, T. (1996). *Uspešno vodenje podjetja* (*Successful Enterprise Management*). Ljubljana: Gospodarski vestnik.

Bradbury, K., (2000). 'How Much Do Expansions Reduce the Black–White Unemployment Gap?' *Regional Review of the Federal Reserve Bank of Boston,* 10/3: 5–7.

Bradley, J., and Hamilton, D. (1999). 'Making Policy in Northern Ireland'. *Administration,* 47/3 (Aug.): 32–50.

Bray, H. (1999). 'Hub's High-Tech Allure Drawing Israeli Firms'. *Boston Globe,* 7 Apr.

Brown, C. (1999). *Carriage Wheels to Cadillacs: Henry Leland and the Quest for Precision.* Windsor, Vt.: American Precision Museum.

Browne, L., and Sass, S. (2000). 'The Transition from a Mill-Based to a Knowledge-Based Economy: New England, 1940–2000', in P. Temin (ed.), *Engines of Enterprise: An Economic History of New England.* Cambridge, Mass.: Harvard University Press, 201–49.

Brusco, S. (1982). 'The Emilian Model'. *Cambridge Journal of Economics,* 6: 167–84.

Burbidge, J. (1968). *The Principles of Production Control* (2nd edn.). London: MacDonald and Evans.

Cartin, E. (1996). 'The Queen's University Experience on the Development of New Enterprises'. Belfast: QUBIS Ltd.

—— (1998). 'Corporate Venturing at the Queen's University of Belfast', Belfast: QUBIS Ltd.

CBI (Confederation of British Industry) (1998*a*). *CBI Innovation Trends Survey.* London: CBI.

—— (1998*b*). *Technology and Innovation Brief,* June. London: CBI.

Chamberlin, E. (1933). *The Theory of Monopolistic Competition.* Cambridge, Mass.: Harvard University Press.

Chandler, A. (1961). *Strategy and Structure: Chapters in the History of the Industrial Enterprise.* New York: Doubleday & Co.

—— (1977). *The Visible Hand.* Cambridge, Mass.: Harvard University Press.

—— (1992). 'Organizational Capabilities and the Economic History of the Industrial Enterprise'. *Journal of Economic Perspectives,* 6/3: 79–100.

CHECKLAND, S. G. (1981). *The Upas Tree: Glasgow 1875–1975.* Glasgow: Glasgow University Press.

CHIA SIOW YUE (2000). 'Singapore: Destination for Multinationals', in J. Dunning (ed.), *Regions, Globalization and the Knowledge Based Economy.* Oxford: Oxford University Press.

CHRISTENSEN, C. (1997). *The Innovator's Dilemma: When New Technologies Cause Great Firms to Fail.* Boston: Harvard Business School Press.

COMMONER, B. (1979). *The Politics of Energy.* New York: Alfred Knopf.

CONNOLLY, W. (1974). *The Terms of Political Discourse.* Lexington, Mass.: D. C. Heath.

COOKE, P. (1998). 'Enterprise Support Policies in Dynamic European Regions: Policy Implications for Ireland', in *Sustaining Competitive Advantage.* Dublin: National Economic and Social Council.

CRINGELY, R. (1992). *Accidental Empires.* New York: Addison-Wesley.

CUSUMANO, M. (1985). *The Japanese Automobile Industry: Technology and Management at Nissan and Toyota,* Cambridge, Mass.: Harvard University Press.

DAHLMAN, C. (1993). 'Electronics Development Strategy: The Role of Government', in B. Wellenius, A. Miller, and C. J. Dahlman (eds.), *Developing the Electronics Industry.* Washington, DC: World Bank.

DAHMEN, D. (1993). 'Semiconductors', in B. Wellenius, A. Miller, and C. Dahlman (eds.), *Developing the Electronics Industry.* Washington, DC: World Bank.

DAVID, P. (1990). 'The Dynamo and the Computer: An Historical Perspective on the Productivity Paradox'. *American Economic Review,* 80/2 (May).

—— and WRIGHT, G. (1999). 'Early Twentieth Century Growth Dynamics: An Inquiry into the Economic History of "Our Ignorance"'. SIEPR Discussion Paper No. 98-3, Stanford University.

DCT (1998). *Personal Computer Material Chain, Figures 1–6.* Penang: DCT Consultancy Services.

DED (Department of Economic Development) (1999). *Strategy 2010.* Report by the Economic Development Strategy Review Steering Group on Northern Ireland. Belfast: DED.

DEGMAN, C. (1998). 'EMC Breaks a Billion'. *Mass High Tech,* 9–15 Nov.

DEMING, W. (1982). *Quality, Productivity and Competitive Position.* Cambridge, Mass.: Center for Advanced Engineering Study, MIT.

DENISON, E. (1979). *Accounting for Slower Productivity Growth.* Washington, DC: Brookings.

DERTOUZAS, M., LESTER, R., and SOLOW, R. (1989) (eds.). *Made in America.* Cambridge, Mass.: MIT Press.

DEVINE, W. (1983). 'From Shafts to Wires: Historical Perspective on Electrification'. *Journal of Economic History,* 43/2 (June): 347–72.

DOLVEN, B. (1998). 'Taiwan's Trump'. *Far Eastern Economic Review,* 6 Aug.: 12–16.

DTI (Department of Trade and Industry) (1998). *Our Competitive Future: Building the Knowledge Driven Economy.* White Paper and Analytical Report (otherwise known as the *Competitiveness White Paper*). London: HMSO.

The Economist (1994). 'Uncle Sam's Helping Hand'. 2 Apr.

—— (1995). Survey. 16 Sept.

—— (1996). 23 Mar.

—— (1997). 'Silicon Valley: The Valley of Money's Delight'. 29 Mar.

—— (1999). 'Innovation in Industry'. 20 Feb.

—— (2000). 15 Jan.

EDWARDS, P. (1996). 'The World in a Machine: Origins and Impacts of Early Computerized Global Systems Models'. Paper presented at the 'Spread of the Systems Approach' conference held at the Dibner Institute, MIT, Cambridge, Mass., May.

Electronics Sector Working Group (1998). *Sector Working Group on Electronics Final Report,* Strategy 2010. Belfast: Northern Ireland Department of Economic Development.

ENRIGHT, M., SCOTT, E., and DODWELL, D. (1997). *The Hong Kong Advantage.* Hong Kong: Oxford University Press.

EPU (Economic Planning Unit) (1996). *Seventh Malaysian Plan 1996–2000.* Economic Planning Unit, Prime Minister's Department, Kuala Lumpur.

—— (1998). *The Malaysian Economy in Figures 1998.* Economic Planning Unit, Prime Minister's Department, Kuala Lumpur.

ERNST, D. (2000). 'Inter-Organizational Knowledge Outsourcing: What Permits Small Taiwanese Firms to Compete in the Computer Industry?' *Asia Pacific Journal of Management,* special issue on 'Knowledge Management in Asia', Aug.

FABRICANT, S. (1954). *Economic Progress and Economic Change.* 34th Annual Report of the National Bureau of Economic Research. New York: NBER.

FAS (Forfas Aiseanna Saothair) (1998). *Manpower, Education & Training Study of the Irish Software Sector.* Dublin: Training and Employment Authority.

—— (1999). *Technology Foresight Ireland—an ICSTI Overview.* Dublin: ICSTI Secretariat.

FLYNN, P., GITTELL, R., and SEDGLEY, N. (1999). 'New England as the Twenty-First Century Approaches: No Time for Complacency'. *New England Economic Review,* Federal Reserve Bank of Boston (Nov./Dec.): 41–53.

FORD, H. (1926). *Today and Tomorrow.* New York: Doubleday Page and Company. Reprinted (1988), Cambridge, Mass.: Productivity Press.

FORRANT, R. (1994). 'Skill Was Never Enough: American Bosch, Local 206, and the Decline of Metalworking in Springfield, Massachusetts 1900–1970', Ph.D. diss., University of Massachusetts, Amherst.

—— (1997). 'The Cutting Edge Dulled: The Post–World War II Decline of the United States Machine Tool Industry'. *International Contributions to Labor Studies,* 7: 37–58.

—— (1998). *Restructuring for Flexibility and Survival: A Comparison of Two Metal Engineering Plants in Massachusetts.* Geneva: International Labour Organization.

—— and FLYNN, E. (1998). 'Seizing Agglomeration's Potential: The Greater Springfield Massachusetts Metalworking Sector in Transition, 1986–1996'. *Regional Studies,* 32/3: 209–22.

FREEMAN, C. (1982). *The Economics of Industrial Innovation.* London: Penguin.

—— (1991). 'Networks of Innovators: A Synthesis of Research Issues'. *Research Policy,* 20: 499–514.

—— (1998). 'The Economics of Technical Change', in D. Archibugi and J. Michie (eds.), *Trade, Growth and Technical Change.* Cambridge: Cambridge University Press.

FRIEDMAN, M. (1962). *Capitalism and Freedom.* Chicago: University of Chicago Press.

GARNSEY, E. (1998). 'A Theory of the Early Growth of the Firm'. *Industrial and Corporate Change,* 7/3: 523–56.

GARUD, R., and KUMARASWAMY, A. (1993). 'Changing Competitive Dynamics in Network Industries: An Exploration of Sun Microsystems' Open Systems Strategy'. *Strategic Management Journal,* 14: 351–69.

GELLINGS, C. (1994). *Utility Marketing Strategies.* Englewood Cliffs, NJ: Prentice Hall.

GIDDENS, A. (1976). *New Rules of Sociological Method.* London: Hutchinson.

GLEICK, J. (1993). *Genius: The Life and Science of Richard Feynman.* New York: Vintage.

GOLDIN, C. (1998). 'America's Graduation from High School'. *Journal of Economic History,* 58 (June): 345–74.

—— and KATZ, L. (1998). 'The Origins of Technology–Skill Complementarity'. *Quarterly Journal of Economics,* 113 (Aug.): 693–732.

GOLDRATT, E., and COX, J. (1984). *The Goal.* Croton-on-Hudson, NY: North River Press.

GOMORY, R. (1992). 'The Technology–Product Relationship: Early and Late Stages', in N. Rosenberg, R. Landau, and D. Mowery (eds.), *Technology and the Wealth of Nations.* Stanford, Calif.: Stanford University Press.

GORECKI, P. (1997). 'Industrial Policy in Northern Ireland: The Case for Radical Reform'. Paper presented at the Manchester Statistical Society.

GOULD, S. (1996). *Full House: The Spread of Excellence from Plato to Darwin.* New York: Random House.

GROVE, A. (1996). *Only the Paranoid Survive.* New York: Doubleday.

HARMON, R., and PETERSON, L., (1990). *Reinventing the Factory.* New York: Free Press.

HAYES, R., and WHEELWRIGHT, S. (1984). *Restoring Our Competitive Edge.* New York: John Wiley.

HEIZER, J., and RENDER, R. (1996). *Production & Operations Management* (4th edn.). Upper Saddle River, NJ: Prentice Hall.

HEKMAN, J. (1980). 'New England's High Technology Industry Is Here to Stay'. New England Economic Indicators, Federal Reserve Bank of Boston, Mar.

HENDRY, M. (1973). *Cadillac, Standard of the World.* New York: Bonanza Books. Reprinted 1979.

HEWITT-DUNDAS, N. (1997). *Corporate Flexibility: A Comparative Analysis of Small Firms in Northern Ireland and Massachusetts.* Aldershot: Avebury.

HICKS, J. (1939). *Value and Capital.* Oxford: Clarendon Press.

HIRSCH, F. (1977). *The Social Limits to Growth.* London: Routledge & Kegan Paul.

HITCHENS, D. M. W. N., WAGNER, K., and BIRNIE, J. E. (1991). 'Northern Ireland's Productivity Failure: A Matched Plant Comparison with West Germany'. *Regional Studies,* 25/2: 111–21.

HOBDAY, M. (1995*a*). 'East Asian Latecomer Firms: Learning the Technology of Electronics'. *World Development,* 23/7: 1171–93.

—— (1995*b*). *Innovation in East Asia: The Challenge to Japan.* London: Edward Elgar.

HORN, C. (1998). 'Building on Ireland's Skill Opportunities'. Expert Group on Future Skills Needs, Dublin.

HOUNSHELL, D. (1984). *From the American System to Mass Production, 1800–1932.* Baltimore: Johns Hopkins University Press.

HUBBARD, G. (1923). 'Development of Machine Tools in New England'. *American Machinist,* 59/1: 1–4.

HUGHES, J. (n.d.). 'Economic Development Strategy: Software Sector'. Jordanstown: University of Ulster, Department of Informatics.

HUGHES, T. (1989). *American Genesis.* New York: Penguin Books.

—— (1998). *Rescuing Prometheus.* New York: Pantheon.

IANSITI, M., and WEST, J. (1997). 'Technology Integration: Turning Great Research into Great Products'. *Harvard Business Review,* May–June: 69–79.

IDB (Industrial Development Board) (1999). Chief Executive's Report, *Annual Report & Accounts 98 99,* Northern Ireland.

IMAI, M. (1986). *Kaizen.* New York: Random House.

Irish Software Association (1998). *To Boldly Go . . . , The Irish Software Industry—A Strategy for Growth.* Dublin: Irish Software Association.

IRTU (Industrial Research and Technology Unit) (n.d.). *Research & Development Capability in Northern Ireland.* Lisburn: IRTU.

ISHIKAWA, K. (1985). *What Is Total Quality Control? The Japanese Way.* Englewood Cliffs, NJ: Prentice Hall.

JAIKUMAR, R. (1986). 'Postindustrial Manufacturing'. *Harvard Business Review,* 64/6: 69–76.

Japanese Human Relations Association (1992). *Kaizen Teian 1.* Portland, Ore.: Productivity Press.

Japan Management Association (1987). *Canon Production System.* English translation by Productivity Press, Portland, Ore. Originally published as *Canon no seisan kakushin,* Tokyo, 1984.

JORGENSON, D. (1996). 'Technology in Growth Theory', in J. Fuhrer and J. Little (eds.), *Technology and Growth: Conference Proceedings*, Conference Series No. 40. Boston: Federal Reserve Bank of Boston.

KATZ, J. (1996). 'To Market, to Market: Strategy in High-Tech Business'. *Regional Review*, Federal Reserve Bank of Boston, 6/4 (Fall): 12–17.

KATZ, L. (1999). 'Technological Change, Computerization, and the Wage Structure'. Paper prepared for conference on 'Understanding the Digital Economy: Data, Tools, and Research', Washington, DC, 25–26 May.

KENDRICK, J. (1956). 'Productivity Trends: Capital and Labor'. *Review of Economic Statistics*, 38 (Aug.): 248–57.

—— (1961). *Productivity Trends in the United States*. Princeton: Princeton University Press.

KENNEY, M., and VON BURG, U. (1999). 'Technology and Path Dependence: The Divergence between Silicon Valley and Route 128'. *Industrial and Corporate Change*, 8/1: 67–103.

KIMMEL, C. (1993). 'Trends in Worldwide Sourcing in the Electronics Industry', in B. Wellenius, A. Miller, and C. Dahlman (eds.), *Developing the Electronics Industry: A World Bank Symposium*. Washington, DC: World Bank.

KLINE, S. (1985). 'Innovation Is Not a Linear Process'. *Research Management*, 28 (July–Aug.): 36–45.

—— (1991). 'Styles of Innovation and their Cultural Basis'. *ChemTech*, 21/8: 472–80.

KLUGE, J., MEFFERT, J., and STEIN, L. (2000). 'The German Road to Innovation'. *McKinsey Quarterly*, 2: 99–105.

KOBAYASHI, I. (1988). *20 Keys to Workplace Improvement*. Portland, Ore.: Productivity Press.

KODAMA, F. (1986). 'Japanese Innovation in Mechatronics Technology'. *Science and Public Policy*, 13/1 (Feb.): 44–51.

KOH TSU KOON (1995). 'The Penang Strategic Development Plan' in Koh Tsu Koon (ed.), *Penang into the 21st Century: Outlook and Strategies of Malaysia's Growth Centre*. Petaling Jaya: Pelanduk Publications.

KOSTOFF, R. N. (1994). 'Successful Innovation: Lessons from the Literature'. *Research–Technology Management*, Mar.–Apr.: 60–1.

KRUGMAN, P. (1991). *Geography and Trade*. Cambridge, Mass.: MIT Press.

—— (1993). 'The Current Case for Industrial Policy', in D. Salvatore (ed.), *Protectionism and World Welfare*. Cambridge: Cambridge University Press.

—— (1994). 'The Myth of Asia's Miracle'. *Foreign Affairs*, 73/6 (Nov./Dec.).

—— and LAWRENCE, R. (1994). 'Trade, Jobs, and Wages'. *Scientific American*, Apr.: 22–7.

KUHN, S. (1982). *Computer Manufacturing in New England*. Cambridge, Mass.: Joint Center for Urban Studies of MIT and Harvard University.

LANDAU, R., and ROSENBERG, N. (1992). 'Successful Commercialization in the Chemical Process Industries', in N. Rosenberg, R. Landau, and D. Mowery (eds.), *Technology and the Wealth of Nations*. Stanford, Calif.: Stanford University Press.

LANDES, D. (1970). *The Unbound Prometheus.* Cambridge: Cambridge University Press.

LAYTON, E. (1971). 'Mirror-Image Twins: The Communities of Science and Technology in Twentieth Century America.' *Technology and Culture,* 12: 562–80.

LAZERSON, M., and LORENZONI, G. (1999). 'Firms that Feed Industrial Districts: A Return to the Italian Source'. *Industrial and Corporate Change,* 8/2: 235–66.

LAZONICK, W. (1991). *Business Organization and the Myth of the Market Economy.* Cambridge: Cambridge University Press.

—— (2000). 'Transforming the Regional Skill Base for Sustainable Prosperity: The Strategic Role of the Technology-Oriented University in the Process of Economic Development.' Working Paper, University of Massachusetts Lowell.

LESLIE, S., and KARGON, R. (1996). 'Selling Silicon Valley: Frederick Terman's Model for Regional Advantage'. *Business History Review,* 70: 435–72.

LIM KAH HOOI (1997). 'Paper on Competitiveness of the Electronics Industry in Malaysia'. ESP Management Consultants, Penang.

LIM, P. (1991). *Intel: From Ashes Rebuilt to Manufacturing Excellence.* Petaling Jaya: Pelanduk Publications.

LIPSEY, R. (1993). *Globalization, Technological Change and Economic Growth.* Annual Sir Charles Carter Lecture. Belfast: Northern Ireland Economic Council.

LITTLE, J. (1993). 'Necessity and Invention: Trade in High-Tech New England'. *Federal Reserve Bank of Boston Regional Review,* 3/1.

LOASBY, B. (1991). *Equilibrium and Evolution: An Exploration of Connecting Principles in Economics.* Manchester: Manchester University Press.

—— (1997). 'Edith Penrose's Place in the Filiation of Economic Ideas'. Photocopy, University of Stirling.

LUCKY, R. (1999). 'Digital Immortal'. *New Republic,* 221/19, 8 Nov.

MAGAZINER, I., and PATINKIN, M. (1989). *The Silent War: Inside the Global Business Battles Shaping America's Future.* New York: Random House.

MANCHESTER, PHILIP (1998). 'Scarcity of IT People with Business Minds', *Financial Times,* 5 Nov., p. xii.

MANSFIELD, E. (1980). 'Basic Research and Productivity in Manufacturing'. *American Economic Review,* 70: 863–73.

MARSHALL, A. (1890, 1st edn.; 1920, 8th edn.). *Principles of Economics.* London and New York: Macmillan.

MARTIN, R. (1999). 'The New "Geographical" Turn in Economics'. *Cambridge Journal of Economics,* 23: 65–91.

MARX, K. (1961; originally 1867). *Capital: A Critical Analysis of Capitalist Production,* Vol. 1. Moscow: Foreign Languages Publishing House.

MATHEWS, J. (1997). 'A Silicon Valley of the East: Creating Taiwan's Semiconductor Industry'. *California Management Review,* 39/4 (Summer): 26–54.

MCGARVEY, A. (1999). 'Managing Change for Regional Development', in Vasil Hudak et al. (eds.), *Regional Policy Goes East: Essays on Trends and Lessons Learned for Regional Development in Central & Eastern Europe.* New York and Prague: East West Institute.

McKenna, G. (1998). *Outline Proposal Submitted to DED: Establishing Science Parks in NI.* Coleraine: University of Ulster.

McLean, M., and Rowland, T. (1985). *The Inmos Saga.* London: Francis Pinter.

Methé, D. (1995). 'Basic Research in Japanese Electronic Companies: An Attempt at Establishing New Organizational Routines', in J. Liker, J. Ettlie, and J. Campbell (eds.), *Engineered in Japan: Japanese Technology Management Practices.* New York and Oxford: Oxford University Press.

MITI (Ministry of International Trade and Industry) (1996). *Second Industrial Master Plan 1996–2005.* Ministry of International Trade and Industry, Kuala Lumpur.

Moore, G. (1996). 'Some Personal Perspectives on Research in the Semiconductor Industry', in R. Rosenbloom and W. Spencer (eds.), *Engines of Innovation.* Boston: Harvard Business School Press.

Morris, C., and Ferguson, C. (1993). 'How Architecture Wins Technology Wars'. *Harvard Business Review,* Mar./Apr.: 86–96.

Mowery, D., and Nelson, R. (1996). 'The U.S. Corporation and Technical Progress', in C. Kaysen (ed.), *The American Corporation Today.* New York and Oxford: Oxford University Press.

—— and Rosenberg, N. (1989). *Technology and the Pursuit of Economic Growth.* New York: Cambridge University Press.

MTC (Massachusetts Technology Collaborative) (1998). *Index of the Massachusetts Innovation Economy.* Westborough, Mass.: MTC.

—— (1999). *Index of the Massachusetts Innovation Economy.* Westborough, Mass.: MTC.

Mulkay, M. (1979). 'Knowledge and Utility: Implications for the Sociology of Knowledge.' *Social Studies of Sciences,* 9: 63–80.

Musgrave, R. (1959). *The Theory of Public Finance.* New York: McGraw-Hill.

Myers, M., and Rosenbloom, R. (1996). 'Rethinking the Role of Industrial Research', in R. Rosenbloom and W. Spencer (eds.), *Engines of Innovation.* Boston: Harvard Business School.

Mytelka, L., and Tesfachew, T. (1999). 'The Role of Policy in Promoting Enterprise Learning During Early Industrialization: Lessons for Africa Countries'. Geneva: United Nations Conference on Trade and Development.

Narayanan, Suresh (1997). 'Technology Absorption and Diffusion among Local Supporting Firms in the Electronics Sector'. *IKMAS Working Papers,* Institute of Malaysian and International Studies, Universiti Kebangsaan Malaysia, No. 9.

National Council for Educational Awards (1995). *Twenty-Second Report, 1995.* Dublin: National Council for Educational Awards.

National Critical Technologies Panel (1991). *Report of the National Critical Technologies Panel.* US Government, Mar.

National Economic and Social Council (1992). *The Irish Economy in a Comparative Institutional Perspective.* Dublin: NESC.

National Science Board (various years). *Science and Engineering Indicators.* Washington, DC: US Government Printing Office.

Nelson, R. (1993) (ed.). *National Innovation Systems.* Oxford: Oxford University Press.

—— (1996). *The Sources of Economic Growth.* Cambridge, Mass.: Harvard University Press.

—— (1998). 'The Agenda for Growth Theory'. *Cambridge Journal of Economics,* 22/4: 497–520.

Ngoh, C. L. (1994). *Motorola Globalization: The Penang Journey.* Kuala Lumpur: Lee and Sons.

Noble, D. (1977). *America by Design: Science, Technology, and the Rise of Corporate Capitalism.* New York: Knopf.

NIEC (Northern Ireland Economic Council) (1993). *R&D Activity in Northern Ireland.* Report 101, May. Belfast: NIEC.

—— (1999). *The Implementation of Northern Ireland's Economic Development Strategy in the 1990s: Lessons for the Future.* Belfast: NIEC.

Northern Ireland Growth Challenge (1995). *Interim Summary of Progress.* Belfast: NIGC.

O'Gorman, C., O'Malley, E., and Mooney, J. (1997). *Clusters in Ireland. The Irish Indigenous Software Industry: An Application of Porter's Cluster Analysis.* Dublin: NESC.

O'Grada, C. (1994). *Ireland: A New Economic History, 1780–1939.* Oxford: Oxford University Press.

O'Sullivan, M. (2000). *Contests for Corporate Control: Corporate Governance and Economic Performance in the United States and Germany.* Oxford: Oxford University Press.

—— (forthcoming). 'The Sustainability of Industrial Growth in Northern Ireland'. *Regional Studies.*

Ohno, T. (1988). *Toyota Production System: Beyond Large-Scale Production.* Cambridge, Mass.: Productivity Press.

Pang, Eng Fong (1995). 'Foreign Direct Investment and Technology Transfer in the Malaysian Electronics Industry', in Nomura Research Institute and Institute of Southeast Asian Studies, *The New Wave of Foreign Direct Investment in Asia.* Singapore: Institute of Southeast Asian Studies.

Pavitt, K. (1980) (ed.), *Technical Innovation and British Economic Performance.* London: Macmillan.

PDC (1994). *Penang Development Corporation: 1969–1994.* Penang.

Penrose, E. (1960). 'The Growth of the Firm—A Case Study: The Hercules Powder Company'. *Business History Review,* 34: 1–23.

—— (1995; originally 1959). *The Theory of the Growth of the Firm.* First edn. (1959), Oxford: Basil Blackwell and New York: John Wiley and Sons. Second edn. (1980), Oxford: Basil Blackwell and New York: St. Martin's Press. Revised edn. (1995). Oxford: Oxford University Press.

PEREZ, C. (1983). 'Structural Change and the Assimilation of New Technologies in the Economic and Social System'. *Futures*, 357–75.

PETRIN, T. (1995). *Industrial Policy Supporting Economic Transition in CEE: Lessons from Slovenia.* Economic Development Institute Working Papers, No. 95–97. Washington, DC: World Bank.

—— VITEZ, R., and MESL, M. (2000). 'Sustainable Regional Development Experience from Slovenia'. Paper presented at the conference 'Approaches to Sustainable Regional Development: The Role of the University in the Globalizing Economy', University of Massachusetts Lowell, 28 Oct.

PIORE, M., and SABEL, C. (1984). *The Second Industrial Divide: Possibilities for Prosperity.* New York: Basic Books.

PORTER, M. (1990). *The Competitive Advantage of Nations.* New York: Macmillan.

—— (1998). 'Clusters and the New Economics of Competition'. *Harvard Business Review*, Nov.–Dec.: 77–90.

—— and VAN DER LINDE, C. (1995). 'Green and Competitive: Ending the Stalemate.' *Harvard Business Review*, Sept.–Oct.: 120–34.

PRENCIPE, A. (1998). 'Modular Design and Complex Product Systems: Facts, Promises, and Questions'. Working Paper, Complex Product Systems Innovation Centre, University of Sussex, May.

PSDC (1998). *Penang Skills Development Centre Update*, June.

RASIAH, R. (1994). 'Flexible Production Systems and Local Machine Tool Subcontracting: Electronics Component Transnationals'. *Cambridge Journal of Economics*, 18/3: 279–98.

—— (1995). *Foreign Capital and Industrialization in Malaysia.* New York: St. Martin's Press.

—— (1998) 'From Backyard Workshop to High Precision Machine Tool Factory: Eng Hardware'. *IKMAS Working Papers*, Institute of Malaysian and International Studies, Universiti Kebangsaan Malaysia.

—— (2000). 'Politics, Institutions and Flexibility: Microelectronics Transnationals and Machine Tool Linkages in Malaysia', in R. Doner and F. Deyo (eds.), *Flexible Specialization in Asia.* Ithaca, NY: Cornell University Press.

REID, P. (1990). *Well Made in America: Lessons from Harley-Davidson on Being the Best.* New York: McGraw-Hill.

RICHARDSON, G. B. (1972). 'The Organization of Industry'. *Economic Journal*, 82 (Sept.).

—— (1975). 'Adam Smith on Competition and Increasing Returns', in A. S. Skinner and T. Wilson (eds.), *Essays on Adam Smith.* Oxford: Oxford University Press.

—— (1999). 'Mrs Penrose and Neoclassical Theory'. *Contributions to Political Economy*, 18.

RIDLEY, M. (1993). *The Red Queen: Sex and the Evolution of Human Nature.* New York: Macmillan.

ROBERTS, E. (1991). *Entrepreneurs in High Technology: Lessons from MIT and Beyond.* New York: Oxford University Press.

Robinson, A., and Schroeder, D. (1993). 'Training, Continuous Improvement, and Human Relations: The U.S. Training within Industries Programs and Japanese Management Style.' *California Management Review*, 35/4.

Robinson, J. (1933). *The Economics of Imperfect Competition.* London: Macmillan.

Roe, J. (1916). *English and American Tool Builders.* New Haven: Yale University Press and London: Humphrey Milford Press.

Romer, P. (1986). 'Increasing Returns and Long-Run Growth'. *Journal of Political Economy*, 94/5: 1002–37.

—— (1994). 'The Origins of Endogenous Growth'. *Journal of Economic Perspectives*, 8/1 (Winter): 3–22.

Roper, S. (1993). *Government Grants and Manufacturing Profitability in Northern Ireland.* Belfast: Northern Ireland Economic Research Centre.

Rosegrant, S., and Lampe, D. (1992). *Route 128: Lessons from Boston's High-Tech Community.* New York: Basic Books.

Rosenberg, N. (1976). *Perspectives on Technology.* Cambridge: Cambridge University Press.

—— (1982). *Inside the Black Box: Technology and Economics.* Cambridge: Cambridge University Press.

—— (1992). 'Science and Technology in the Twentieth Century', in G. Dosi, R. Giannetti, and P. A. Toninelli (eds.), *Technology and Enterprise in a Historical Perspective.* Oxford: Clarendon Press.

—— (1996). *Perspectives on Technology.* Cambridge: Cambridge University Press.

Rosenberg, R. (1999). 'Growing with the Flow: Endless Stream of Data Spawns Computer-Storage Firms'. *Boston Globe*, 14 Apr.

San Gee, and Wen-jeng Kuo (1998). 'Export Success and Technological Capability: Textiles and Electronics in Taiwan', in D. Ernst, T. Ganiatsos, and L. Mytelka (eds.), *Technological Capabilities and Export Success: Lessons from East Asia.* London: Routledge Press.

Sapolsky, H. (1990). *Science and the Navy.* Princeton: Princeton University Press.

Saxenian, A. (1994). *Regional Advantage: Culture and Competition in Silicon Valley and Route 128.* Cambridge, Mass.: Harvard University Press.

Scherer, F. (1982). 'Inter-Industry Technology Flows and Productivity Growth'. *Review of Economics and Statistics*, 64 (Nov.): 627–34.

—— (1999). *New Perspectives on Economic Growth and Technological Innovation.* Washington, DC: Brookings Institution Press.

Schmookler, J. (1952). 'The Changing Efficiency of the American Economy'. *Review of Economic Statistics*, 39 (Aug.): 214–31.

—— (1966). *Invention and Economic Growth.* Cambridge, Mass.: Harvard University Press.

Schonberger, R. (1986). *World Class Manufacturing.* New York: Free Press.

Schorsch, L. (1996). 'Why Minimills Give the US Huge Advantages in Steel'. *McKinsey Quarterly*, No. 2.

Schumpeter, J. (1942). *Capitalism, Socialism and Democracy.* New York: Harper and Brothers.

SEKINE, K. (1990). *One-Piece Flow.* Portland, Ore.: Productivity Press.

SEN, A. (1992). *Inequality Reexamined.* Oxford: Clarendon Press and Cambridge, Mass.: Harvard University Press.

SHAPIRA, P. (1998). 'Manufacturing Extension: Performance, Challenges, and Policy Issues', in L. Branscomb and J. Keller (eds.), *Investing in Innovation.* Cambridge, Mass.: MIT Press.

SHEEHAN, M., with ROPER, S. (1994). *Government Grants and the Investment Decisions of Northern Ireland Manufacturing Companies.* Belfast: Northern Ireland Economic Research Centre.

SHERWIN, C., and ISENSON, R. (1967). 'Project Hindsight'. *Science,* 156: 1571–7.

SHIBA, S., GRAHAM, A., and WALDEN, D. (1993). *A New American TQM: Four Practical Revolutions in Management.* Portland, Ore.: Productivity Press.

SINGH, A. (1995). 'How Did East Asia Grow So Fast?' Geneva: United Nations Conference on Trade and Development, No. 97, Feb.

SIN-MING SHAW (1997). 'Is Singapore's Future in Malaysia?'. *Asia, Inc.,* Mar., 64.

SISIR (Singapore Institute for Standards and Industrial Research) (1992). *Technology Adoption by Small and Medium-Sized Enterprises in Singapore.* Singapore Institute for Standards and Industrial Research, Saskatchewan Research Council, and University of Saskatchewan. Published by Saskatchewan Research Council, Saskatoon.

SMITH, A. (1976; originally 1776). *An Inquiry into the Nature and Causes of the Wealth of Nations,* ed. R. H. Campbell, A. S. Skinner, and W. B. Todd, 2 vols. Oxford: Oxford University Press.

SMITH, G. (1996). 'Forfeiting the Future'. *Audacity,* 4/3: 24–39.

SMITH, M. (1970). *Harpers Ferry and the New Technology.* Ithaca, NY: Cornell University Press.

—— (1995). 'The Military Roots of Mass Production: Firearms and American Industrialization, 1815–1913'. Paper, Program in Science, Technology & Society, MIT.

SNELL, B. (1974). *American Ground Transport: A Proposal for Restructuring the Automobile, Truck, Bus, and Rail Industries.* Presented to the Subcommittee on Antitrust and Monopoly of the Committee of the Judiciary, US Senate. Washington, DC: Government Printing Office.

Software Industry Federation (1998). *IT Skills Action Team: The Way Forward.* Belfast: Software Industry Federation.

SOLOW, R. (1957). 'Technical Change and the Aggregate Production Function'. *Review of Economic Statistics,* 39 (Aug.).

—— (1994). 'Perspectives on Growth Theory'. *Journal of Economic Perspectives,* 8 (Winter).

SORENSEN, C. E. (1957). *Forty Years with Ford.* London: Cape.

STALK, G., and HOUT, T. (1990). *Competing Against Time.* New York: Macmillan.

STIGLER, G. (1951). 'The Division of Labor Is Limited by the Extent of the Market'. *Journal of Political Economy,* 59 (June).

SUZAKI, K. (1987). *The New Manufacturing Challenge.* New York: Free Press.

TANG, H. K. (1996) 'Hollowing-Out or International Division Of Labour? Perspective from the Consumer Electronics Industry and Singapore'. *International Journal of Technology Management*, 12/2: 231–41.

TEH, A. (1989). 'Ancillary Firms Serving the Electronics Industry: The Case of Penang', in S. Narayanan et al. (eds.), *Changing Dimensions of the Electronics Industry in Malaysia: The 1980s and Beyond.* Penang: Malaysian Economic Research Association and the Malaysian Institute of Economic Research.

TERKLA, D. (1998). 'Greater Boston—Hub of the Commonwealth's Economy'. *Massachusetts Benchmarks*, 1/4 (Fall): 9–11.

TILLY, C., and HANDEL, M. (1998). 'The Diagnostic Imaging Industry: What Prognosis for Good Jobs?' Working Paper No. 224. Annandale-on-Hudson, NY: Jerome Levy Economics Institute.

TULL, B. (2000). 'The Springfield Armory as Industrial Policy: Interchangeable Parts and the Precision Corridor'. Ph.D. diss., University of Massachusetts, Amherst.

UNDP (United Nations Development Program) (1995). *Human Development Report 1995.* New York: Oxford University Press.

VON TUNZELMANN, G. N. (1995) *Technology and Industrial Progress: The Foundations of Economic Growth.* Brookfield, Vt.: Edward Elgar.

WADE, R. (1990). *Governing the Market: Economic Theory and the Role of Government in East Asian Industrialization.* Princeton: Princeton University Press.

WATSON, G. (1993). *Strategic Benchmarking.* New York: John Wiley.

WEISBORD, M. (1987). *Productive Workplaces: Organizing and Managing for Dignity, Meaning and Community.* San Francisco: Jossey-Bass.

WICKS, F. (1999). 'Renaissance Tool Man', *Mechanical Engineering*, Nov.: 74–7.

WILLIAMS, K., HASLAM, C., and WILLIAMS, J. (1992). 'What Henry Did, or the Relevance of Highland Park', in K. Cowling and R. Sugden (eds.), *Current Issues in Industrial Economic Strategy.* Manchester: Manchester University Press.

WOMACK, J., JONES, D., and ROOS, D. (1990). *The Machine That Changed the World.* New York: Rawson Associates.

World Bank (1993). *The East Asian Miracle: Economic Growth and Public Policy.* New York: Oxford University Press.

YAMANOUCHI, T. (1995). *A New Study of Technology Management.* Tokyo: Asian Productivity Center, distributed in North America and Western Europe by Quality Resources, New York.

YOUNG, A. (1928). 'Increasing Returns and Economic Progress'. *Economic Journal*, 38 (Dec.).

ZIZZA, R., PELCZAR, S., and EISENMANN, N. (1999). 'Cascade Communications and its Offspring', College of Management, University of Massachusetts Lowell.

INDEX